MW00450622

BUILDING THE GREAT PYRAMID IN ONE YEAR

BUILDING THE GREAT PYRAMID IN ONE YEAR

AN ENGINEER'S REPORT

Gerard C. A. Fonte

Algora Publishing
New York

ISBN-13: 978-0-87586-521-8 (trade paper)
ISBN-13: 978-0-87586-522-5 (hard cover)
ISBN-13: 978-0-87586-523-2 (ebook)

Library of Congress Cataloging-in-Publication Data —

Fonte, Gerard C. A.
  Building the Great Pyramid in a year : an engineer's report / Gerard C. A. Fonte.
    p. cm.
  Includes bibliographical references and index.
    ISBN 978-0-87586-521-8 (trade paper: alk. paper) — ISBN 978-0-87586-522-5 (hard
cover: alk. paper) — ISBN 978-0-87586-523-2 (ebook) 1. Pyramids—Egypt—Design and
construction. 2. Great Pyramid (Egypt) I. Title.

  DT63.F66 2007
  932—dc22
                            2007004713

Front Cover: One man moving a 4200-pound block using technology that was available
to the ancient Egyptians.

Printed in the United States

To Nellie, who enjoys the unconventional and whose support
and encouragement made this book possible.

TABLE OF CONTENTS

Chapter 1. The Egyptian Pyramids

Introduction

This book represents a forensic-engineering exploration of the construction of the Egyptian pyramids. Most archaeologists believe that about 25,000 workers spent about 20 years to build the Great Pyramid (or Khufu's Pyramid) at Giza in Egypt over 4,500 years ago (Lehner, 224). But, by closely examining the clues and relics left behind, and by assuming that the Egyptians were intelligent and creative, it is found (conservatively) that about 10,000 workers could have built the Great Pyramid in about 346 days. However, there is evidence that 4,000 workers were used (Lehner, 225). And by using a relaxed production schedule, a value of four to six calendar years is probably a more reasonable estimate.

These values are based entirely upon archaeological evidence, logic, common sense, and scientific and engineering principles. Every aspect of pyramid building will be examined in detail. This includes quarrying the blocks, moving the blocks, lifting the blocks, fitting the blocks, placing the top-most blocks and finishing the outer casing blocks. It will be shown that each of these challenges can be successfully addressed using the materials and crafts that the Egyptians are known to have possessed. Additionally, tool specifications, wood requirements and machine designs will be appraised. Surprisingly, such an analysis has not been done before.

Not all of the important factors that allowed the pyramids to be built are directly related to these construction procedures. General pyramid geometry, available worker population, the social effects of large works, and scale factors in engineering are critically important as well. Lastly, there is the concept of "Energy Management" or, more simply: work smarter — not harder.

Other Books

There are many, many books and papers about the pyramids. Generally these can be broken into three main classes: picture books, specialized approaches, and archaeological works. Interested readers most often turn to picture books. They provide a general history of the pyramids with many beautiful pictures of Egyptian constructions and antiquities. And without any doubt, Egyptian artifacts can be exquisitely beautiful. Most often these books only briefly discuss the mystery of how the pyramids were built. Typically they provide a few pages of speculations that are based on the generally accepted view that it took 25,000 workers about 20 years. Little original work is found here.

The "specialized approaches" usually examine one aspect of pyramid building, often without regard to the archaeological evidence. These writers often have a specific idea that they believe could be applied for moving blocks, or lifting blocks, etc. These works have a very focused approach, typically with application to a single aspect of pyramid building. Unfortunately, while the work is often very imaginative and original, it doesn't match what has been found in Egypt. Nor are these approaches applicable at the massive engineering scale necessary for the Great Pyramid. Some of these will be examined in more detail later.

The archaeological works are where the important information comes from. But archaeologists are not engineers. They cannot be expected to recognize important engineering functions of various artifacts or specialized tools. Generally, their works are descriptive. They offer drawings and photographs of things found at the pyramid sites. Of course, since their interest is in archaeology, they tend to focus their effort on items that relate to ancient Egyptian society. Tools that have no obvious function are, naturally, only mentioned in passing. One very important archaeological work is J. P. Lepre's *The Egyptian Pyramids* (1990, McFarland & Company). This is an extremely detailed compilation of information from all of the Egyptian pyramids. Lepre is also extremely precise in his descriptions and drawings. For these reasons his book will be referenced with regularity in the following pages. Note that there are many variations in the spelling of Egyptian names and places. Unless otherwise noted, the spelling that Lepre uses will be incorporated here. It is also important to note that Lepre is an archaeologist, not an engineer or mathematician. As such, there are a number of mathematical errors in his book.

Currently there seems to be increasing interest in the building techniques employed for the Great Pyramid. In particular, Dr. Mark Lehner, in association with the NOVA television program, went to Giza and actually built a small pyramid using the "standard methods" of sledges and ramps. This work is documented in his book *The Complete Pyramids* (1997, Thames and Hudson) and of course, the television program, "This Old Pyramid." This experiment provides some useful benchmark information that will be examined closely. Additionally, Dr. Lehner is arguably the foremost archaeological authority on pyramid construction today. For that reason, his book is also an important reference.

Lastly, there is the very recent book by Dr. Craig Smith, *How the Great Pyramid was Built* (2004, Smithsonian Books). Dr. Smith is an engineer with experience as a construction executive for public works projects. His book is written from a program manager's perspective, or "top-down" approach, and is oriented to the high-level planning and construction of the Great Pyramid. He relies heavily on Dr. Lehner's work as well as that of Dr. Zahi Hawass (secretary general of the Supreme Council of Antiquities and the Director of Excavations at Giza and Bahariya Oasis). Dr. Hawass is generally considered to be a leading archaeological authority on the Giza plateau constructions. It is clearly necessary to address the approaches that are presented in Smith's book. This will be done, in detail, in a later chapter and it will be shown that the standard methods are simply not feasible.

For convenience, book references will provide the author and a page number so that the reader will be able to locate the appropriate passage easily. Non-book references will provide an author or internet source and the date. All book and non-book references are fully listed at the end.

The approach taken here is different from these other works. Instead of using the standard methods of dragging blocks with sledges and lifting blocks with ramps, new strategies will be developed that will be based on evidence and creativity. There is no doubt that the Egyptian builders were brilliant. The simple fact that their some of their creations have lasted nearly 5,000 years is a testament to their ingenuity and intellect. If we assume from the start that the Egyptians were intelligent, organized and resourceful, the task becomes one of deciphering the clues that they left behind in order to determine the methods they used. It will be found that critical clues have been overlooked or ignored that offer clear and direct insight into the Egyptian construction techniques.

THE GREAT PYRAMID

The Great Pyramid, or Khufu's pyramid (occasionally called Cheops's pyramid), at Giza is the largest of the Egyptian pyramids (Lepre, 129; Smith, 59; Lehner, 14). It was apparently built during his 23-year-reign from 2789 to 2767 BC, or 4772 to 4795 years ago (Lepre, 61; Smith, 59; Lehner, 108). The term "apparently" is used because it is generally assumed that any pyramid was built during the reign of that particular pharaoh. In the case of the Great Pyramid, there are some who feel that 23 years was not enough time to build such a massive structure. They suggest that the effort took longer and was started before his reign and/or completed afterwards (Lehner, 108). However, there is little supporting evidence for this. And, while this is possible, nearly all scholars accept that the Great Pyramid was really built within the documented 23-year-reign of Khufu.

The pyramid is not unscathed by time and vandalism. Virtually all of the casing stones (the outer layer of exquisitely fitted and polished limestone blocks) are gone. Only 138 out of about 80,000 casing stones remain (Lepre, 71) and most of these are badly damaged. Only seven are reasonably intact. The pyramidion, or capstone, is also missing. There are some who say that it was never placed (Lepre, 67); however, this seems unlikely and implausible given the precision and attention to detail that was applied to the rest of the pyramid and associated structures.

The original height was 485 feet and the base was 763 feet on a side. Until the Eiffel Tower was built in France in 1887, Khufu's pyramid stood as the tallest man-made structure in the world. The base still covers over 13 acres. It was composed of 2,500,000 blocks with an average block weight of 5,000 pounds or 2.5 tons and measuring about 4 feet by 4 feet by 2.5 feet. Its volume was over 94 million cubic feet. There were 210 courses (or layers) of block. Curiously, the base-to-height ratio (763/485) is 1.571, or one-half Pi. There are many who think that this is very significant. Perhaps it is. However, other pyramids have other base-to-height ratios ranging from 1.34 to 2.22 (Lepre, 309). This ratio provides a slope of 51.85 degrees (calculated).

Its size can be described but its scale can't be readily imagined. It is beyond colossal. The only way to appreciate the scale of the Great Pyramid is to compare it to something more contemporary. It seems fitting to relate it to the Houston Astrodome, which was initially called "The Eighth Wonder of the World." Comparing numerical specifications is not a good means for visualizing the two structures. Instead simple scale models were made. They were made to "N" scale, which is 160 to 1, and is a common model-railroad scale. This allows "N" scale models of people, automobiles and railroad cars to be incorporated to provide accurate visualizations. Figures 1-1 to 1-4 show people, automobiles and a railroad car in relation to the Astrodome as the view is pulled back. Note that the people become nearly invisible. Figures 1-5 to 1-8 keep exactly the same camera distance. The camera is only rotated to bring the Great Pyramid into the frame. If one looks closely at Figure 1-8, a model railroad track, cars and (perhaps) people are visible in front of the pyramid. It can now be seen why the Great Pyramid is indeed one of the Wonders of the Ancient World.

Previous page Above: Figure 1-1: Start of zoom-out with N-scale models.
Below: Figure 1-2: Zoom-out showing height of Houston Astrodome.
Above: Figure 1-3: N-scale Astrodome dwarfs rail car.
Below: Figure 1-4: Last zoom-out. Note people are hard to see.

Figure 1-5: Start of pan-left. Same as Figure 1-4.
Figure 1-6: The base of N-scale Great Pyramid becomes visible.

Above: Figure 1-7: The Great Pyramid is twice as tall as the Astrodome.
Below: Figure 1-8: Final pan-left. Compare this to figure 1-5.

Surprisingly, the Great Pyramid and the other structures at Giza, which are generally considered to be the pinnacle of the technology, were built very early in the pyramid building eras. The first small pyramids were built as early as 2887 BC but were only about 50 feet high and contained about 0.1% of the volume of the Great Pyramid. The first large construction that is generally classified as a pyramid is the "step pyramid" of Djoser, built about 2850 BC — or only about 75 years before Khufu. It consists of six equally thick layers of limestone blocks, where each layer is smaller than the one below it. Each layer was built up of many layers of stone about a foot thick. The original height was 204 feet and the volume was about 10 million cubic feet, or about 11% of the Great Pyramid. This is still a considerably large structure. But it was Sneferu, Khufu and Khafre that built the two massive pyramids at Giza and the two huge pyramids at Dahshur (Bent Pyramid and Sneferu's North Pyramid). Sneferu reigned from 2813 to 2790 BC; his son Khufu reigned from 2789 to 2767 BC; Khafre, Sneferu's grandson, ruled from 2758 to 2742 BC. During this period of only 71 years, the four largest Egyptian pyramids were built. These four pyramids alone comprise over 270 million cubic feet of limestone. Many other stone structures were built during this time as well.

For about 1,000 years after this period, nearly all of the pyramids that were built were much smaller than even Djoser's pyramid. The last large pyramid was built by Senusert III, who reigned from 1998 to 1960 BC. It was only 255 feet high and consisted of only 10.4 million cubic feet of bricks (not limestone blocks), or about 11% of the Great Pyramid. The largest pyramid since Khafre was Khui's pyramid; he reigned from 2458 to 2456 BC. His pyramid was estimated to be 250 feet high and contained 14.7 million cubic feet of bricks, or about 16% of the Great Pyramid's volume. The remaining 46 pyramids built since Khafre (that have remains that can be evaluated) average about 2.5% of the Great Pyramid's volume. Appendix 1 summarizes the 100 Egyptian pyramids that Lepre discusses in detail, and provides volume information.

There are two important points to note. The first is that the massive pyramids were all built within 70 years, or about one lifetime. The second point is that virtually all the later pyramids are smaller by at least an order of magnitude. These points will be discussed in more detail in later chapters.

There seems little doubt that the Great Pyramid is the most studied and discussed Egyptian pyramid. Nevertheless, it wasn't until 1940 that it was accidentally discovered that the structure actually has eight sides. A British pilot, P. Groves, flying overhead at precisely the proper moment, noticed that exactly half of one pyramid face was in shadow and he managed to take a now-famous photograph (Figure 1-9). This vertical indentation or hollowing out of the pyramid's sides amounts to 36 inches (over 763 feet). This is completely invisible to the naked eye except under the proper lighting conditions. (Tompkins, 110, claims that Egyptologist W. M. F. Petrie noted this fact in his precise measurements made in the late 1800s. However, that reference could not be obtained. And no other author found has made that reference.)

The important point here is that this variation from a straight line would normally be quite apparent by measurement. It's a variation of about 0.4%, or nearly one-half of a degree of indentation. The reason this relatively large discrepancy went unnoticed for so long is apparently because of the condition of the pyramid. As noted before, it is not pristine. This is especially true near the base, where there are piles of rock fragments and debris. The removal of the fine casing stones has caused further damage to the underlying stones. What this means is that the measurement precision for any physical aspect of the Great Pyramid beyond two to three decimal positions is suspect. We will later examine some authors' claims that special physical relationships exist with a precision of seven decimal places.

Evolution of the Pyramid

There is a clear and well-documented evolution of the pyramid. For about 1,000 years before the first pyramid, Egyptians were burying important people. At first, simple pits were dug, much like today's graves. Later a mound of dirt was placed over the pit as a marker. As time passed this mound was covered with mud-bricks. Still later, this brick-covered mound became a burial tomb. However, the body was still buried beneath the tomb. This required physical access to the burial chamber, so a shaft into the ground with a short corridor to the sarcophagus was needed. This was the beginnings of the mastaba.

A mastaba was a burial tomb of religious significance for royalty. It consisted of an underground burial chamber with a vertical shaft that opened into an above-ground structure. This solid structure was generally rectangular with inward sloping sides. Early mastabas were fairly modest with the above ground structure being about ten feet high and about 30 feet on a side. Later mastabas grew in size and complexity. Thethi Kheneri's mastaba was about 208 feet long and about 30 feet high. It contained five shafts, seven rooms and a number of corridors (all underground).

The step-pyramid can be considered as a mastaba on top of a mastaba, where the upper mastaba is smaller than the lower one. Generally five or six layers were used. The layers are always about the same thickness in height. There are few step pyramids.

Figure 1-9: The sides of the Great Pyramid are indented, but that is normally invisible to the naked eye.

Next came the true pyramid. This is a square-based solid with sloping sides. The slope is most often about 50 degrees, but there is considerable variation as noted above. However, the religious and cultural factors remained the same. The pyramid still contained a burial chamber, associated corridors, additional rooms and shafts. The extent of these features varied with the pharaoh. But most often, the interior designs were quite simple. Additionally, most often there was no interior to the pyramid proper. It was one solid mass. The burial chamber and associated constructs were fabricated underground, much as with the mastabas. The Great Pyramid is an exception. Khufu was entombed high inside the pyramid at the 50th course. (Curiously, this is very close to the center of mass of the pyramid, which is approximately the 44th course.) It should be noted that there is an unfinished chamber under the pyramid.

PYRAMID CONSTRUCTION

Pyramid construction was evolving and experiencing problems just prior to the erection of the Great Pyramid (see Appendix 1). Large step pyramids of 2868 BC and 2849 BC (about 400 feet per side) were quite successful. Then in 2844 BC a modest "layer" pyramid was built (275 feet per side). Unlike all the other pyramids that were built with (nearly) horizontal layers, this pyramid was built outward rather than upward (Lepre, 36). The procedure was to build a small pyramid and enlarge it by adding outside layers. In 2843 BC a very large pyramid (590 feet by 650 feet base) was started but never finished at Zawaiyet-el-Aryan (Lepre, 269). Considerable effort was spent preparing the site and cutting out stairways and other subterranean features but few, if any, stones were used to actually start the pyramid proper.

Then in 2837 BC a large pyramid at Maidum (base 472 feet per side) collapsed. The exact date of the collapse is not known but some believe that it occurred during construction or closely after construction was finished (Lehner, 97). There is additional circumstantial evidence to support this theory, which is presented in Chapter 4. The pyramid was associated with both Pharaoh Huni and Pharaoh Sneferu, according to Lepre (p. 46), and was the first true pyramid with sloping sides (Lehner, 97). However, Lehner suggests that only Sneferu was associated with that pyramid. Sneferu was the father of Khufu.

Sneferu built two large pyramids during his reign that started 2813 BC, the "Red Pyramid" and the "Bent Pyramid." Each was about one half the volume of the Great Pyramid. The Bent Pyramid is generally understood to be flawed. There does not appear to be any scholar who believes that the original design called for the pyramid's slope to change during the middle of construction. There are some who believe that the slope change was made in response to the failure of the Maidum pyramid. This is certainly a possible reason.

The Great Pyramid follows this series of failures and experiments in 2789 BC. Of the five pyramids (with a base length of more than 200 feet) immediately preceding the Great Pyramid, only the Red Pyramid can be considered fully successful. This was certainly an important consideration for the pyramid builders.

THE PYRAMID AT MAIDUM

The partially collapsed pyramid at Maidum offers true insight into the construction of a pyramid. Additionally, some subtle construction changes were first incorporated in that design. Probably most archaeologists feel that the Maidum pyramid was originally a step pyramid that was converted to a true pyramid by filling in the steps (Lehner, 97). The reason for this belief is the fine stonework that remains exposed, which can be easily seen in Figure 1-10. The argument is that this stonework effort would not be wasted by burying it within the pyramid proper. Therefore the original pyramid is what remains after the covering stonework fell away.

Figure 1-10: The basic core of the Maidum Pyramid is all that remains standing. Photograph copyright 2003 by Robin Fingerson, used with permission

However, this does not appear to be the case. First of all, step pyramids were no longer being built. The last one built was three pharaohs earlier. Secondly, the steps of a step pyramid are all about equally high. Clearly this is not the case for the Maidum Pyramid. No other pyramid or mastaba demonstrates such an asymmetry in step heights. Lastly, as can be easily seen in Figure 1-11, there is a stonework band that is clearly of much less precision and quality than the rest of the stonework. This is entirely out of character for the exterior work of the Egyptians. Their work is always meticulous, with exceptional attention to detail.

Therefore it seems appropriate to accept that the Maidum Pyramid is an illustration of the actual internal structure of a pyramid, which can certainly resemble a step pyramid. As such, we see that the structure is quite complex. The hole in the stonework shows internal core packing stones surrounded by an internal casing. Other pyramids display outer casing stones, with additional structures of backing stones behind the casing, core facing stones behind these, and core stones in the middle (Lepre, 19). The idea that a pyramid is a simple pile of stones is not correct. It is a complicated design in which most of the structure is not visible. This is especially true for those pyramids that have survived nearly intact. The internal structure of successful pyramids, such as those at Giza, is not obvious.

There is another subtle but significant construction change that originated after the Maidum Pyramid. This is the incorporation of horizontal layers (Lepre, 49). Before that time, the layers were inclined slightly towards the center. This inward tilting created significant internal forces and pressures directed inward. However, if these forces were unbalanced, the result could be asymmetrical forces that could be detrimental to the stability of the whole. It is not known if the outer layers of the Maidum pyramid that fell away were horizontal or not. Obviously, horizontal layers do not create such internal lateral forces. It seems that this pyramid was a key learning experience for the pyramid builders. After Maidum, all pyramid layers were made horizontal (Lepre 49), which suggests that the collapse occurred at or shortly after the time of construction. It was a major engineering turning point in pyramid construction and will be discussed in more detail in Chapter 4.

The Great Pyramid shows a very slight variation from the perfectly flat courses. As noted before, the pyramid is actually eight-sided. Additionally, the casing and facing stones tilt very slightly towards the center of the face (Lepre, 70). Note that they are not tilting inwards. They are tilting very slightly laterally, towards the center line of the face. This is because the blocks at the edges are very slightly taller than the blocks at the center of the face. This difference is not readily apparent by sight and this angle is much, much smaller than the previously described inward angle of the earlier pyramids. Therefore the lateral forces are much less. However, the Great Pyramid is the only Egyptian pyramid to show this feature (as well as the only pyramid to have eight sides).

GREAT PYRAMID CONSTRUCTION CLUES

There are a number of clues that can be used to determine the most likely construction methods. Some of these clues derive from examining the Giza pyramids themselves. Some come from artifacts left behind by the ancient Egyptians. More clues can be gleaned from the quality of workmanship. There are clues from the geometry of a pyramid as well as from the scale of the Great Pyramid. Some clues can be inferred by examining non-pyramid constructions. The source of the pyramid stone is another important clue. And there are social and political matters which also provide clues to how the Great Pyramid was built.

To begin with, there are two "mysterious" tools that have been found at pyramid sites. The first is the wooden "quarter-circle" or "rocker." These are fabricated from solid cedar and are curved on one side and flat on the other. Cedar is not native to Egypt. Additionally, there must have been a substantial number of these quarter-circles because wood does not typically survive nearly 5,000 years, even in the desert. It is known that Pharaoh Sneferu sent a fleet of 40 ships to Lebanon for cedar (Lepre, 257). It will be shown that these quarter-circles can be instrumental in moving stone blocks weighing over 5,000 pounds each.

There is the "proto-pulley" that Dr. Lehner describes (p. 211). These granite stones are somewhat mushroom-shaped with groves in the head and holes in the stem. Clearly these are important tools because of the effort required to fabricate them. A forensic examination of these objects will uncover compelling evidence for the means by which the Egyptians lifted the blocks.

The quarry for the Great Pyramid is located very close to the pyramid proper. Approximately 97,500,000 cubic feet of stone was removed from this quarry (Lehner, 206). The Great Pyramid contains about 94,000,000 cubic feet of stone. This leaves only about 3.5% as wasted or lost stone. This is a subtle but critical clue. It indicates that the quarrying operations were very efficient in terms of wastage. It will be shown that the Egyptians had the means and technology to perform such quarrying operations. Additionally, the quarry volume eliminates the possibility of using large ramps.

Figure 1-11: The interior of the core is very different from the exterior core. Photograph copyright 2003 by Robin Fingerson, used with permission.

The precision of the casing stones of the Great Pyramid (and the other pyramids at Giza) is beyond peer. The joints between the outer casing stones are nearly invisible. The sides are nearly perfect 90 degrees with an error of only 0.01" over their length. There are no tool marks evident. But other non-casing stones show clear tool marks, so it must be assumed that the Egyptians had techniques for fabricating large numbers of precision-cut stones. There are simple methods of achieving this, if one is willing to accept that the Egyptians were creative and intelligent.

GENERAL PYRAMID GEOMETRY

In order to understand the construction requirements of any pyramid it is important to understand general pyramid geometry. The volume of a pyramid is equal to the base length times the base width times the height, divided by three (volume = LWH/3).

It is useful to note that a pyramid one-half the size of another pyramid contains only one eighth the volume. For example, a pyramid with a square base 100 feet long with a height of 50 feet contains 166,666 cubic feet. A pyramid that has a base of 50 feet on a side and is 25 feet high contains only 20,833 cubic feet or one eighth the volume of the larger pyramid. This is not really surprising. The volume of any solid varies as the cube of the dimensions. Nevertheless it is an important fact: the volume of a pyramid varies with the cube of its height.

The Great Pyramid is not made up of identically sized blocks. Generally, the layers (courses) are thicker at the bottom than at the top. There is considerable variation of the course heights. It appears that the Egyptians would place a series of courses in descending thickness. After about 10 to 15 courses they would repeat the pattern from thick to thinner (Lepre, 69). Lepre identifies 19 such series. Smith (p. 103) provides a graphic chart based on Petrie's examination of the Great Pyramid in 1883. The course height variations are most prominent in the lower half of the pyramid. However, Petrie and Lepre disagree on how many courses make up the Great Pyramid. Petrie says that there are 218 courses while Lepre says that there are only 210 courses.

There are about 2.5 million limestone blocks that make up the Great Pyramid (Lepre, 62). The average block is typically considered to be about 2.5 tons (Lepre, 62) with typical dimensions of 4 feet by 4 feet by 2.5 feet (Evans, 84). The inclination face-angle (center of face to top) is calculated to be 51.85 degrees. The inclination corner-angle (corner of pyramid to top) is calculated to be 42.03 degrees. Most generally, the face-angle is used to define the pyramid's slope. However, Smith (p. 59) incorrectly diagrams corner-angles with face-angle values. (It is interesting to note that the Bent pyramid has a calculated face-angle inclination of 54.5 degrees and a corner-angle inclination of 44.75 degrees at the base.

About a third of the way up, the face-angle changes to 43.3 degrees (Lepre, 59), which is very close to the original corner-angle of 44.75 degrees.)

With this basic information it is possible to create an ideal course-by-course layout of the Great Pyramid using identical-sized blocks of "average" size, which is 4.00 feet by 4.00 feet by 2.31 feet. While tedious, this provides a very useful table and it is presented in Appendix 2. It verifies that about 2.5 million averaged-sized blocks are necessary to build the pyramid.

However, we see that just about 50% of the blocks comprise the first 44 courses. This means that the average block only needs to be lifted to 99.432 feet. This is substantially less than 485 feet of the full height of the pyramid. Additionally, we see that only 11.1% of the blocks need to be raised over 250 feet. Only 1% of the blocks (about 25,140) have to be lifted the last 44 courses or to the top 100 feet.

These values are important construction parameters. They define how much energy is needed to lift an average block. It is seen that the pyramid is very bottom heavy. These facts determine the best approaches for construction. In order to develop appropriate construction procedures, the average block will be used. However, while it is useful to use the average block, it is important to realize that not all blocks are average. In order to be of practical construction use, any means applied to average blocks must also be applicable to blocks that are not average.

CONCLUSION

The Great Pyramid is a fantastic creation, unmatched in longevity and a testament to the brilliance of the ancient Egyptians. It only seems reasonable to examine their spectacular achievement with an open mind. There are mysterious artifacts that must have had functions. How is it possible to suggest how the Great Pyramid was built without first understanding the tools that the Egyptians used? Additionally, by examining the workmanship and quantity of these tools it becomes apparent that these tools were important.

Chapter 2. Pyramid Fallacies

Introduction

There is a lot of popular culture concerning the pyramids that is simply not true. Movies and television shows consistently repeat these fallacies over and over until many people believe them as the truth. Separating fact from fiction is a critical necessity if one is to determine realistic pyramid construction methods. And, while it can be very entertaining and amusing to watch these shows, it is important to remember that Cecil B. DeMille was of course not an archaeologist. Nor is there any evidence that pyramids are the landing pads for interstellar spaceships and, so far as this writing, wormhole gateways have never been found in or near any pyramid.

Slaves

The Great Pyramid was not built with slave labor. This now seems abundantly clear. The idea that thousands of slaves, working under brutal conditions with merciless masters whipping them into action, is not true (Lepre, 251; Lehner, 224; Smith, 130). These people were paid for their efforts with food, grain and other materials. Money had not been invented yet (Lepre, 252). It is generally accepted that these people were conscripts (Lepre, 251; Lehner, 224). This idea is apparently based on the work of archaeologist L. DeCamp, who makes that suggestion in his book *The Ancient Engineers* (1979). He also suggests that farmers were used during the yearly Nile flooding season, when they would be idle.

However, Smith (p. 130), citing Hawass (unreferenced), says that there was a permanent skilled workforce of about 5,000, based on the size of the workers' cemetery. Smith (p. 219) goes on to say that about 50% of the workforce was married, with spouses and children living at the site. This seems to contradict the idea of conscripting farmers. And, when the social effects of large works are examined later in this book, the idea of conscription will be brought into question. An all-volunteer workforce will be shown to be practical as well as socially beneficial. It is also useful to note that the "permanent skilled workforce of about 5,000" fits well with the premise that about 4,000 workers built the Great Pyramid (rather than 25,000).

PYRAMID BLOCKS

There are several misconceptions concerning the blocks that make up the Great Pyramid. The first is that they were brought in from a quarry miles away. This is not the case. The blocks for the core of the Great Pyramid (which comprises about 97% of the volume) come from a quarry near the base of the pyramid. The quarry has roughly the same footprint as the Great Pyramid and is located about 750 feet from its base. This makes the average lateral movement (from the center of the quarry to the center of the pyramid) about 1500 feet or about a quarter of a mile (Lehner, 204) over smooth and reasonably level ground.

The Great Pyramid, with the exception of the internal chambers, is made entirely of limestone, which is a relatively soft stone. This includes the core and casing stones. There are other pyramids that utilize a hard stone casing, such as granite. Granite is very much harder to work. This is especially so considering that the Egyptians did not have hard metals such as iron and steel for general use, although there is evidence that worked iron was known to them (Lepre, 245). However, Menkara's pyramid at Giza does have an outer casing made from granite (Lehner, 134) for the bottom 16 courses. Most of these stones are unfinished or "undressed." This pyramid is over an order of magnitude smaller in volume than the Great Pyramid. So it can be seen where the confusion may have come from. There will be more discussion concerning the hardness of various types of stones, limestone working and the tools available in the later chapter on quarrying.

However, the outer casing stones of the Great Pyramid apparently did not come from the local quarry. They came from Tura and Masara, which were located on the east side of the Nile River near what is now Cairo (Lehner, 202). The Giza plateau is situated on the western side of the Nile and the current suburbs of Cairo come to the foot of the plateau (Lehner, 204). These approximately 80,184 casing stones were apparently shipped about 10 to 15 miles. The very few, but very large, granite blocks (about 200) for the interior chambers were indeed shipped from a considerable distance from Aswan, or about 400 miles away (Lehner, 202). Some of these blocks have been estimated to weigh 80 tons (Lehner, 109).

The core of the pyramid is not made up of finely finished stones. Rather, these stones are used just as they are quarried. They are (relatively) roughly cut and there are spaces of an inch or so between the blocks which are sometimes filled with gypsum mortar (Smith, 90). Of course, the actual core of the Great Pyramid cannot be examined directly because it is not exposed. The outer backing stones are visible. And some stones that line the internal passageways and chambers are visible. But these latter stones would be expected to be special because they are part of the internal design. Other pyramids that have not faired as well show that the core is not made up of dressed stones. And realistically, it makes no sense to dress stones that will never be seen. However, it is seen that the inner core of the pyramid of Maidum does not match the outer stones. Therefore, while it is reasonable to believe that the core blocks are not dressed, it may not be reasonable to assume that they match the exposed backing blocks. This will be discussed in more detail in the chapters on moving blocks.

Passageways and Chambers

It seems that every fictional movie, book and television show has the pyramids riddled with complex passageways. Characters run through large and well lit corridors with horizontal floors, high ceilings and room for several people to pass side by side. They show the interior of the pyramid as being like an office building with lots of rooms and chambers. Nothing could be further from the truth.

The Step Pyramid of Djoser does have a very complex set of tunnels and rooms under the pyramid (Lehner, 88; Lepre, 34). But these are really tunnels and excavations rather than constructions. It is clearly much easier to place a pyramid over such a network than it is to create an intricate maze within the pyramid proper. Supporting open areas within a structure made up of stone blocks is very difficult. The overweight problem is very troublesome to address.

In fact, the Great Pyramid has the most complex internal structure of any Egyptian pyramid (Lepre, 54). Yet, there are only two rooms in the Great Pyramid: the King's chamber and the Queen's chamber. It should be noted that the Queen's chamber is called that because it is smaller than the King's chamber. It was not a burial place for the queen (Lehner, 112). The King's chamber is 19 feet 1 inch high, 17 feet 2 inches wide and 34 feet 4 inches long (Lepre, 92). This is about the size of a three-car garage and is tiny when compared to the pyramid as a whole. Many diagrams show the interior details at an improper scale in order to enable viewers to visualize the details (Lepre, 64; Smith, 92; Tompkins, 246). However this leaves the impression that the internal aspects are much larger than they really are. The diagram by Lehner (p. 16) appears to be scaled properly and, as such, the King's chamber is difficult to identify.

The Queen's chamber is smaller still, being 15 feet high by 17 feet wide by 19 feet long (Lepre, 110). This is about the size of a two-car garage. It is curious that Lepre reports these measurements in exact whole feet. Smith (p. 95) measures the same chamber (in meters) and the dimensions (converted to feet) are a height of 20 feet 5 inches, a width of 17 feet 2 inches and a length of 18 feet 10 inches. The large discrepancy in height may be due to the fact that the ceiling is peaked. (The King's chamber has a flat ceiling.) Smith measured the maximum height of the chamber. Lepre does not specify how his height measurement was taken. The height of the peak appears to be about 5 feet (Lepre, 112). Lehner has the height being about 9 inches shorter and the width being about 3 inches larger and the length 2 inches longer than Smith. It is seen that three different scientists measuring the same room (Queen's chamber) produce three sets of different measurements (see Figure 2-1). This is pointed out to illustrate again that the basic physical measurements of the Great Pyramid are not as precise as many believe.

Smith's measurements of the King's chamber are close to but not in exact agreement with Lepre (p. 92) as well. Smith's measurements (p. 98) (rounded to the nearest inch) have the height and the length one inch greater than Lepre. Both agree on the width. Lehner and Smith agree on the dimensions of the King's chamber (Lehner, 112).

Figure 2-1 Three different scientists measure the Queen's Chamber differently.

Scientist	Length	Width	Height
Lehner (p. 112)	19 feet	17 feet 5 inches	19 feet 8 inches
Lepre (p. 110)	19 feet	17 feet	15 feet*
Smith (p. 95)	18 feet 10 inches	17 feet 2 inches	20 feet 5 inches

* Lepre may have been measuring the wall height instead of the peaked ceiling height.

There is an underground room that is cut out of limestone bedrock and is not finished. Technically this is not part of the pyramid proper. However it is clearly part of the pyramid design. The dimensions of this chamber are 55 feet by 30 feet by 12 feet high (Lepre, 114), or 45 feet by 24 feet by 17 feet high (Lehner,

112). Since the room is very irregular some difference in the measurements is to be expected. However, it seems clear that the differences are substantial.

In total, there are two rooms inside the pyramid and one room below it. The volume of the whole pyramid is over 94 million cubic feet. The volume of the two rooms inside the Great Pyramid total 16,092 cubic feet (using Lepre's measurements). This means that a negligible 0.017% of the Great Pyramid volume is used for rooms. For most practical considerations, the Great Pyramid can be treated as one large solid object.

There are only four basic corridors in the Great Pyramid. Obviously, with three rooms there must be a corridor to each room. These three corridors are straight. The fourth corridor is quite convoluted and joins the corridor just outside of the subterranean chamber to an upper corridor near the middle of the pyramid.

The geometry of the three main corridors is quite simple. From a single entrance a single corridor angles downward at a steep 26 degrees. This "descending passage" corridor is only 47.75 inches high and 42 inches wide and 350 feet long (Lepre, 72, 73). This straight corridor continues downward to just outside the subterranean chamber where it becomes horizontal and enters the subterranean chamber.

About 120 feet from the entrance the descending corridor branches upward. This "ascending passage" rises at an angle of about 26 degrees as well (Lepre, 79). (Curiously, the angle between the ascending and descending passageways is 52 degrees. The slope of the pyramid is also 52 degrees.) This corridor has a maximum height of 53 inches, a maximum width of 42 inches (Lepre, 73), is perhaps 150 feet long (Lehner, 113) and terminates at the "Grand Gallery."

The Grand Gallery is indeed grand and is unique to the Great Pyramid (Lepre, 79) (Lehner, 16). It is 153 feet long, 28 feet high and 7 feet wide at the base, tapering to about 42 inches at the ceiling (Lepre, 79). It maintains the 26 degree inclination and terminates at the King's chamber.

Near the junction of the ascending passage and Grand Gallery there are two branches. The first is a straight horizontal passage to the Queen's chamber. This is 47 inches high and 41.5 inches wide (Lepre, 73) and about 120 feet long (Lehner, 113). This is the only horizontal passage of significant length in the pyramid. The second branch or "Well Shaft" leads downward to the descending passage just outside the subterranean chamber. This branch is not straight. It is made up of six straight segments (Lehner, 113) totaling about 300 feet (Lepre, 116). Two of the segments are vertical (Lepre, 116) and rest are very steep. It is approximately 28 inches square (Lepre, 116).

In summary, it can be seen that the passageways in the Great Pyramid, specifically, and other Egyptian Pyramids in general, are not meant to be used in a conventional manner. The typical height of the passageways is only about four feet. And they are rarely horizontal. It is probably better to think of the passageways as tunnels.

It is also interesting to note that the smallest dimension Khufu's sarcophagus is one-half inch larger than the largest dimension of the ascending passage. This means that the sarcophagus was put in place and the pyramid built around it (Lepre, 94). At the unfinished pyramid of Zawaiyet-el-Aryum (mentioned in chapter 1) a sarcophagus was found (Lepre, 269). Again this suggests that the pyramid was to be built around the sarcophagus. This provides a useful clue to the construction mind-set of the builders of the Great Pyramid.

SECRET PASSAGES

Another popular feature of fictional pyramid entertainment is the presence of many secret passages that open to the proper touch. Sections of wall that in reality would weigh many tons are pushed aside with a nonchalant hand, conveniently ignoring the problems of friction and inertia. Then there are the ingenious traps that are sprung when the hero-explorer inadvertently activates a trigger of some sort. Slowly sliding blocks drop to trap the intruder. Or worse, a ceiling descends to squash the explorer into a gooey mess. Naturally, the creativity of the writers of these stories is not limited by archaeological evidence.

There is however a very small amount of truth to this. There are indeed many secret passages in the pyramids. In reality, every passage is a secret until it is found. And, the Egyptians went to considerable length to hide the passages. But they did this to protect the sacred remains of their rulers and to prevent the tomb from being robbed because many valuable items were buried with the pharaoh (Lepre, 20). There is not the slightest evidence of any trap or deadfall. Nor is it likely that such a mechanism would function properly after nearly 5,000 years. Nevertheless, it is quite clear that the Egyptian pyramid designers considered the problem of grave robbers by including numerous obstacles and barriers.

For example, in the Great Pyramid there are three granite "plug stones" at the lower end of the ascending passageway (Lepre, 76) to prevent access to the King's chamber and the Queen's chamber. The largest of these stones is five feet long and weighs an estimated seven tons (Lepre, 75). These granite stones are much harder than limestone which makes this an effective blockade. These stones are still in place. Explorers passed this point by removing the softer limestone and going around them. It should be noted that these plug stones were hidden by a ceiling stone in the descending passage until it was accidentally removed to expose the plug stones (Lepre, 279).

There were three great two-ton portcullis stones made from granite that blocked the entrance to the King's chamber (Lepre, 86). These have been destroyed but the mechanism for lowering them remains. This lowering mechanism did use counterweights, which remain in place today (Lepre, 87). Therefore, the full weight of the blocks was not required to put them in place. It seems likely that once they were in place, the ropes to the counterweights were severed in order to make access more difficult. It is also interesting to speculate if the number three has special significance.

It has been suggested that there was a flap-door entrance to the Great Pyramid. But there is no remaining evidence that such a door existed (Lepre, 72). There is a well-known illustration by explorer Sir William F. Petrie which is based upon the remnants of a similar door at the Bent Pyramid (Lepre, 293-295). According to the design suggestion by Lepre (which seems reasonable and practical), the door appeared to be an ordinary casing stone, but it had a hidden internal hinge ("ball-and-socket mechanism"). If one pushed on the base of the stone, it would open inward. It is unknown how much force was required. However, stone bearings cannot be considered to be low friction even if the stone was well-balanced. It is also clear that such a hinge would wear quickly. Finally, this entrance was 35 feet above the ground (Lepre, 71). Simply reaching that point is very difficult and that assumes that the proper block can be identified. The smooth sides and the steep angle preclude climbing up the wall. A ladder would be required. Once a person is in place, at the top on a 35 foot long ladder, the pressure required to open the flap-door may be significantly more than one person can apply from that position and angle. It seems certain that this entrance was rarely used.

It makes more sense to consider that door as an exit. If this is true, then the door would be only used once, to allow the people a way out of the pyramid after performing the funeral ceremonies inside the pyramid. As such, the door would be propped open until after the ceremonies, and then closed. It would be hinged in such a way as to make it impossible to open from the outside because of the weight of the stone. This approach is similar to the one used to block the entrance into the main chamber of Bent pyramid (Lepre, 56). In this instance, a five ton portcullis block is held in place on an incline. Once the prop is removed, the stone slides tightly into place.

STILL SECRET PASSAGES

It is a "Mistaken belief that the pyramids have been fully explored" (Lepre, 266). There are many reasons for this, ranging from difficult to access desert locations to government bureaucracy. But the principal reason is because the Egyptians were clever and intelligent. It wasn't until 1920 that the Valley of the Kings was accidentally discovered (Lepre, 266). Lepre (p. 270) suggests that there may be "whole pyramids buried beneath the desert sands." It certainly seems reasonable to believe that more Egyptian constructions will be found in the future. As recently as 1989 new archaeological remains were found at Giza when a suburban sewage system was being installed (Lehner, 204).

In December 1977, Lepre (p. 276) discovered a nearly imperceptible joint in the foundation bedrock at the Great Pyramid. This section would have originally been covered with pavement stones (now removed) so its presence would not have been visible at all. This joint is rectangular being about 4 feet by 10 feet. The clear inference is that the pyramid builders placed this inset stone for a reason. Lepre suggests that this may be a burial chamber for Khufu, since there seems to be some question if Khufu was indeed placed in the sarcophagus in the King's chamber of the Great Pyramid (Lepre, 278).

There may be a second entrance into the King's chamber (Lepre, 270). There is a block at the base corner of the west wall that has relatively poor joints. While the rest of the granite blocks on the chamber are fitted with nearly imperceptible joints, the workmanship of this block is strikingly poor in comparison. The side joint gaps are a quarter of an inch and an eighth of an inch, with the top joint being about one sixteenth of an inch. This corner block is diagonally across from the entrance which is also located at the base corner of the wall. Additionally, the size of the block (38 inches wide by 46 inches high) is close to the size of the entrance (43.5 inches by 41.5 inches) (Lepre, 73). Many of the blocks that make up the walls of the King's chamber are substantially larger (Lepre, 98). Entrances to chambers are usually in the lower corner block of the wall (Lepre, 103).

There are four "air shafts" unique to the Great Pyramid (Lepre, 94), two in the King's chamber and two in the Queen's chamber. There is one shaft on the north wall and one on the south wall of the chambers. These are about 5 inches by 7 inches (Lepre, 99) and extend (with some bends) upward, at about 45 degrees and outward to the outside of the pyramid (Lepre, 97). In 1872, Mr. Wayman Dixon discovered these camouflaged openings and tried to use a simple method to locate where the air shafts exited on the face of the pyramid. He made a fire in the southern air vent of the King's chamber so that his assistants outside the pyramid could see where the smoke exited. The smoke went up the air shaft. But no smoke came out of the pyramid face (Lepre, pg. 274). One explanation for this is that there is another chamber that communicates with the air shaft. It would have to fill up with smoke before additional smoke would be carried outside.

In 1986, a French expedition used a very sensitive gravity meter inside the Great Pyramid to determine if there were variations in rock density (Lepre, 104). The ultra-sensitive meter can actually detect the gravitational force created by the massive amount of stone contained in the Great Pyramid. They detected several apparent hidden cavities. With permission from the Egyptian government, they were able to drill a small hole into one of these cavities, which was found to be filled with sand.

There are additional curious features noted by Lepre in regard to the Great Pyramid as well as other pyramids. It seems that it would be a simple thing to test some of these ideas. In particular, removing the corner block in the King's chamber appears straightforward. However, according to Lepre (pp. 104, 265, 266, 278) the Egyptian government is more interested in restoration and preservation than exploration. This is understandable, but disappointing and frustrating to those who have an ardent interest in ancient history.

THE GREAT PYRAMID AND *PI*

It seems that the Great Pyramid is the focal point for more mystical and mathematical theories than any other structure in the world. The mystical theories will not be discussed. However, some of the mathematical ones, if true or at least reasonable, might provide some insight into the minds of the builders.

The ratio of the length of a side of the pyramid to the height is indeed close to *pi*/2. This is 763 divided by 485 which is 1.57. Multiply that by 2 and the result is 3.14. This certainly appears significant. It becomes clear, upon a little reflection, that any pyramid with an angle of 51.85 degrees (calculated) must have this base-to-height ratio. The question is then: did the builders choose this angle because it incorporated *pi*, or for some other reason?

Note that Khafre's pyramid also at Giza has a base of 707 feet and a height of 471 feet (Lepre, 139), which makes the ratio 1.50 (and a calculated angle of 53.11 degrees). Doubling 1.50 gives a value of 3.00 for an error of about 5% from 3.14. Lepre gives the angle of 52 degrees for this pyramid (Lepre, 139). It is seen that a small angle change of a degree or so creates a fairly large change in the "value" of *pi*.

Additionally, it important to remember that there are more pyramids than the Great Pyramid or the pyramids at Giza. The Red Pyramid built by Sneferu (Khufu's father) has the smallest angle of 43.5 degrees (Lepre, 309). The calculated angle is 41.6 degrees and the base-to-height ratio is 720 to 320, for a value of 2.25. Doubling that makes "*pi*" equal to 4.50. The Bent pyramid, also built by Sneferu, started out at a steep 54.5 degrees (Lepre, 59). Of the large pyramids, the one with the largest angle was built about 900 years after the Great Pyramid, in 1998 BC (Lepre, 212). This is Senusert III's pyramid at Dashur, which had a base of 350 feet and a height of 255 feet (calculated angle of 55.5 degrees) for a ratio of 1.46 and making "*pi*" equal to 2.92.

It can be seen that the pyramid builders used many angles for their pyramids. Additionally, using the face-angle is somewhat arbitrary. As noted near the end of chapter 1, while the face-angle is the current conventional measure of the inclination, the corner-angle can also be used. Measuring a corner-angle is much easier in the field than measuring a face angle. The position of the corner is easy to locate. To measure a face-angle, the precise center of the base must be found. For a base 763 feet long, finding this center point is not without some difficulty. It seems reasonable to suppose that the builders chose to use corner-angles for their convenience. This does not change any base-to-height ratios, of course, but it may provide some insight into why those angles were chosen.

The Red pyramid has a calculated corner-angle of 32 degrees. As noted in chapter 1 this is the only really successful true large pyramid before the Great Pyramid. The angle of repose for dry sand is about 33 degrees. (The "angle of repose" is the maximum stable slope of a pile of particulate material. More simply, it is impossible to pile dry, loose sand at an angle greater than 33 degrees. The angle of repose depends on many factors including the size of the particles of the material, their shape, texture, etc.) Clearly, the Egyptians had considerable experience with sand. And it does not seem unreasonable that such an angle might have significance in both a practical and aesthetic terms.

Going further, the Egyptians would have certainly understood that the face-angle and corner-angle of the Red pyramid were not the same. The face-angle was obviously larger (41.6 degrees versus 32 degrees). Since the pyramid was successful, and engineers (and perhaps pharaohs' sons) always like to improve on success, it is again not unreasonable to consider the engineers would incorporate this knowledge and experience in later pyramids. Since the pyramid was stable with a face-angle of 41.6 degrees, a steeper corner-angle would seem feasible. The natural thought would be to make the new corner-angle equal to the old face-angle of the Red pyramid. The corner-angle of the Great Pyramid is 42 degrees (calculated), very close to the face-angle of the Red pyramid, which is 41.6 degrees (calculated). Concluding, the angle of the Great Pyramid may not have any deep mathematical significance at all.

There is also considerable verbiage about "squaring the circle," which again suggests that the Egyptians knew the value of *pi* (Lepre, 126-127; Tompkins, 197-200). This is an apparently very difficult problem to solve, which relates the height and perimeter of the pyramid to the radius and perimeter of a circle (Tompkins, 197). Given a circle with a perimeter equal to the Great Pyramid's perimeter (3052 feet), the radius of that circle is 485.8 feet (calculated). The height of the Great pyramid is 485.5 feet high (Lepre 127). This appears significant, at least on the surface. However, closer examination brings up some questions. The first is that Lepre later gives the height of the Great Pyramid as precisely 485 feet (p. 129).

It seems clear that this is really just a continuation of the previous relationship between the base and height of the pyramid. Defining the angle of a pyramid (assuming a square base and congruent sides) defines all the relationships between the base and height. Since this relationship is close to *pi*/2, it is not at all unexpected that *pi* would appear in other relationships between the base and height. Again, as noted above, it is an important fact that other pyramids have other angles and relationships.

Squaring the circle depends upon the accurate measurements of the base and height. According to Hopkins (pp. 202-203), in 1925 a precise survey of the base of the Great Pyramid was undertaken by Ludwig Borchardt. He employed J. H. Cole to perform the actual measurements to the best available precision at the time. His measurements were: 230.215 meters (+/- 0.006 meters error) for the south side, 230.454 meters (+/- 0.010 meters error) for the north side, 230.391 meters (+/- 0.030 meters error) for the east side and 230.253 meters (+/-0.030 meters error) for the west side (Tompkins, 202). However, Tompkins shows a diagram on page 203 which conflicts with these measures (see Figure 2-2). The diagram has only the east side agreeing with the measurements. The west side value given on the diagram (230.357 meters) does not match any value in the text (the unmatched text value is 230.215 meters). It is noted that Cole did not discern the concavity of the sides of the pyramid, as mentioned in chapter 1. (For reference, 0.030 meters is about 1.2 inches.)

Figure 2-2: Tompkins has two sets of measurements that do not agree.

	North Side	East Side	South Side	West Side
Illustration (p. 203)	230.253 m	230.391 m	230.454 m	230.357 m
Text (p. 202)	230.454 m	230.391 m	230.215 m	230.253 m

These measurements assume that the four corners of the Great Pyramid can be identified with precision. Although there are cutouts for the corner stones, these stones are missing. There is considerable damage at the base because of removed casing stones. Nevertheless, the measurements will be taken as given. Note that the values with errors greater than 0.010 meters should properly be reported to only two decimal places (230.391 meters should be 230.39 meters). This is current engineering and scientific practice.

Summing the side lengths (using the text values) gives the perimeter of the pyramid, which is 921.313 meters or 3022.828 feet. This is about 30 feet less than the value of 3052 feet used above, or a difference of about 1%. However there is also the problem of determining the precise height of the pyramid because the top-most courses are gone. Lepre puts the height at 485.5 feet. Evans (p. 83) says the original height was "about 481 feet." In fact, most authors (Lehner, Smith) use the value of 146.6 meters, which is 481 feet. Again this is a difference of about 1%. No references could be found of someone who actually measured the height recently. It is again seen that there are discrepancies in the measurements and procedures that preclude any possibility of obtaining precision calculations of more than two or three significant digits. These variations in measurements make the significance of the relationships lose clarity.

NUMEROLOGY

A typical numerological premise is developed by Livio Stecchini and is presented as a lengthy appendix in Tompkins' book *Secrets of the Great Pyramid*, starting on page 287 and ending on page 382. The basic concepts and rationale that he presents will not be discussed. Instead an examination of a typical calculation will be performed. Stecchini states, on page 364, "I interpret Cole's figures to mean that the basic length of the side was 439.5 cubits [or] 230,363.18 millimeters," which is 230.36318 meters. This conversion illustrates the common problem of the incorrect use of significant digits.

Fundamentally, it is impossible to extend the precision (number of significant digits) of the calculations beyond the precision of a simple measurement. (Note: there are special complex statistical procedures that can be used under certain circumstances to achieve this. But this is not such a case.) For example, suppose you have a ruler that measures in whole inches only. You measure the sides of a book with it. One side falls between the 6- and 7-inch marks, but closer to 7. The other side falls between the 10- and 11-inch marks, but closer to 10. You are forced to say that the book is 6 inches by 10 inches, with an error of +/- 0.5 inches. This is the standard scientific and engineering practice.

The diagonal length of the book is calculated to be 12.2065556 inches (using the Pythagorean Theorem). But it is clear the real diagonal length is not known to one ten-billionth of an inch! Therefore the final calculation must be limited to the precision of the original measurement. In this case, it must be rounded to the nearest inch, or 12 inches with an error of +/- 0.5 inches. In reality, all that can be truly stated is that the diagonal length is somewhere between 13.0384048 inches and 11.6619038 inches, guaranteed. But since we can determine that the side lengths are closer to a particular inch, it is possible to reduce the uncertainty from about a range of 1.5 inches (or +/- 0.75 inches) to 1 inch (+/-0.5 inch). Note that the final error is equal to one-half the measurement precision. This is again because it was determined that the length of the book was closer to one mark than it was to another.

With this understanding, it is clear that Stecchini is making two conversions. The first is when he converts Cole's side length measurement of the pyramid into cubits ("I interpret Cole's figures to mean that the basic length of the side was 439.5 cubits"). This is a proper conversion because Cole's accuracy is 5 digits (see above). The second implied conversion, "439.5 cubits [or] 230,363.18 millimeters" (230.36318 meters) is clearly incorrect in the number of significant digits. The best precision obtainable from this conversion is 230.4 meters. Using the exact conversion to millimeters (230,400 millimeters) is also improper because it implies that the measurement resolution is to a single millimeter. In truth, the resolution is 100 millimeters. Suggesting that the length of the side of the Great Pyramid is known to 0.01 millimeter (or 0.007 inches — which is about the thickness of a sheet of paper) when the best actual measurement has about an inch of error is misleading and improper.

THE NOSE OF THE SPHINX

While not precisely a pyramid fallacy, there is a general belief that Napoleon (or one of his men) removed the nose of the Great Sphinx with cannon fire. This belief is partly based on the fact that many old pictures show the sphinx with an intact nose. However, these pictures are more fanciful than faithful. In particular, a 1579 drawing by Helferich (Lehner, 43) shows a distinctly female face complete with nose and a bountiful and bare bosom. This seems to be clearly more fantasy than fact — at that time the Sphinx was buried in sand up to the neck (Lehner, 45). A more precise rendition was made by Norden in 1755, about 40 years before Napoleon went to Egypt. He provides a very accurate representation of the Sphinx which clearly shows a missing nose. While there is still debate about how the nose was lost, it seems that Napoleon had nothing to do with it.

CONCLUSION

It is seen that popular culture is riddled with false ideas and assumptions. Some of these come from the creativity of writers and producers of works of fiction. Other ideas come from physical relationships which are interesting but not well considered. This does not mean that the physical relationships are not special. They could be. However, examining these measurements beyond meaningful precision results in examining "noise." The superfluous digits can be considered random numbers. And if enough random numbers are examined, any desired pattern will eventually be found. This is especially true when the source values can be chosen from values that vary by a few percent.

CHAPTER 3. SCALE FACTORS IN CONSTRUCTION AND ENGINEERING

INTRODUCTION

Size matters. The Great Pyramid is built with such mammoth proportions as to be nearly unimaginable. However, there is much more to making an object larger other than just increasing the dimensions. The same is true for construction projects. Simply adding workers is not always the most efficient method for speeding up production. These problems are neither trivial nor obvious. Their solutions require careful consideration and imagination. The Great Pyramid still stands today as mute testimony to the Egyptians' ability to master the intricacies of the problems of scale.

In order to examine this topic it will be necessary to review some basic engineering terms and concepts. It is important that these concepts be understood so that a critical evaluation of the proposed techniques, as well as other people's techniques, can be performed. Without such an introduction, arguments may appear sound, but in reality, be seriously flawed.

ORDER OF MAGNITUDE

An engineering rule of thumb holds that every time there is a change in size by an order of magnitude (a factor of ten), there is a corresponding change in the fundamental design of the object.

Let's look at a bridge, as an example. In the first instance a gap of one foot needs to be bridged. The simplest solution is to put a bare piece of plywood across the gap. This is perfectly acceptable. People walk on "bridges" of plywood every day. Plywood floors span joists that are typically spaced 16 inches apart. However, if the span in increased to ten feet, it is clear that this simple, bare plywood approach will not work. To span ten feet the plywood will have to be supported by dimensional lumber underneath (typically 2" by 10" lumber). Again, ordinary floors in houses often span ten feet without a problem by using joists to support the plywood. However, this approach cannot span 100 feet. Wood can be used to cross 100 feet but a complicated design is required. And it is not practical to build a bridge of 1,000 feet with wood.

This rule manifests itself in many areas. For example, if a single item is to be produced, it is probably easiest to do it by hand. If ten identical items are required, templates and fabrication aids are used. If 100 items are needed, special tools may be built to simplify and speed up the assembly. And so forth and so on. In this case, an infrastructure is developed to accommodate the increased number of units to be produced. This infrastructure can be very large if many units are to be produced. But overall this initial investment in infrastructure saves labor.

This order of magnitude rule is an important concept. Engineering failures or inefficiencies occur when designs or procedures are applied that do not match the magnitude of the task. For example, it makes little sense to use a suspension bridge design for a simple highway overpass. Nor is it likely that a highway overpass bridge will succeed in bridging a river that is 1,000 feet wide. While not as obvious, task management is similar. A project that requires 100 people is managed very differently from a task that requires 10 people or 1,000 people.

The Egyptian Pyramids span more than three orders of magnitude. There are a number of very small pyramids that are only about 30 feet high and 50 feet on a side for a volume of about 25,000 cubic feet (see Appendix 1). Compare these to the Great Pyramid that has a volume of over 94,000,000 cubic feet. The Great Pyramid has 3760 times more volume than one of these small pyramids. Therefore it seems clear that the methods used to build these small pyramids were not likely to be the same as those used to build the large pyramids.

It is initially surprising that the pyramid design itself seems to ignore the order of magnitude problem without apparent contradiction. However, upon closer inspection it is seen that the order of magnitude rule does not really apply to the "design" of the pyramid. This is because the physical design is basically nothing more than a mound of stone. As long as the angle of the pyramid is reasonable, the physical design will be stable. A pyramid can be thought of as a man-made mountain. And mountains can rise miles into the air. There is no real structural strength requirement for a pyramid (as there is for a bridge). All that is necessary is that the stone be able to support the weight above it. Again, like a mound, this is easy to accomplish and does not follow the order of magnitude rule. Rock piles can be large or small.

SIZE VERSUS STRENGTH

It has long been known that simply increasing the scale of a working model does not guarantee that the larger model will work. This is the fundamental engineering problem of size versus strength. As things get bigger, their mass increases by the cube of their size while the strength increases by the square of the size. A simple experiment can illustrate the problem well.

An ordinary wire coat-hanger is typically made of soft iron or steel and is about 0.075 inches in diameter. If the coat-hanger is straightened into a single piece of wire, it will be about 3.5 feet long with a weight of about 1 ounce. It is an easy matter to hold this wire horizontally from one end. There will be some noticeable sag at the far end of the wire but the wire is clearly self-supporting.

It is useful to determine the supporting strength of this wire. Since the weight is evenly distributed, the center of mass is halfway between the ends of the wire. And since half of the weight is between the center and the end being held, it can be stated that half the length of the wire supports itself and an equal amount of weight. This is a somewhat convoluted way of showing that 1.75 feet of 0.075-inch diameter wire can horizontally support at least 0.5 ounces (in addition to itself). This configuration of holding one end and leaving the other end unsupported is called "cantilevering." The bending force, or torque, is related to the length of the cantilever and its weight and is usually measured in foot-pounds. In this case, the torque is 1/32 of a pound times 1.75, feet or 0.0547 foot-pounds. This is a very small number.

What happens if the wire is enlarged? Consider the effects when every dimension of the wire is increased by two orders of magnitude (or 100 times). The diameter becomes 7.5 inches and the length becomes 350 feet. The total weight of the "wire" becomes a staggering 52,326 pounds. This corresponds to a 7.5-inch diameter cantilever that is 175 feet long and supporting 26,163 pounds. The torque is found to be an incredible 4,578,487 foot-pounds. This is a very big number. This large cantilever is not self-supporting. It requires a physical strength that is well beyond steel or any other material known to man (or likely to be ever known by man).

This shows that a scale factor increase by 100 causes the forces to increase by over 1,000,000. Upon reflection, this makes sense. The mass (or weight) of an object is related to its volume. Doubling the sides of a cube from one inch to two inches causes an eightfold increase in the volume or mass (1 cubic inch versus 8 cubic inches). Increasing every dimension of an object by 100 times increases its volume (and weight) by 1,000,000 times (100 x 100 x 100).

However, the strength of an object is related to its cross section area. In this case, the diameter of the wire defines how strong it is. The area of a wire increases with the square of the diameter. Doubling the diameter increases the area by a factor of four. Increasing the diameter 100 times increases the strength by 10,000 times (100 x 100).

Note that the increase in strength is less than the increase in weight. This is the fundamental problem with simply scaling upwards. The forces applied to the model depend upon its weight, which increases faster than the strength of the material. In the example of the wire, the relative strength of the large version is only 1% of the actual size version. This concept applies to every object.

Children regularly crash toy cars together with at speeds that would annihilate full-sized autos. A small toy automobile can be dropped onto the lawn from the top of a house with impunity. Obviously a real car would be destroyed by the same fall. Both may be made from the same metal, but if the larger car is 10 times bigger, the forces acting on it are 1,000 greater (10 x 10 x 10). The pattern of size versus strength is constantly visible, if it is looked for.

As noted above the size, and thus these forces, is not directly a concern for the general pyramid design. A pile of stones can be of any volume. The consideration of size is necessary for the stability of large structures. A pyramid that is unbalanced will not stand. The larger the pyramid, the more important it is that the forces on it be balanced because they rapidly become so huge that only a slight asymmetry can be sufficient for it to fail. The pyramid at Maidum that was discussed in the first chapter is an example of this. The forces multiply at an incredible rate as the structure gets bigger.

Another concern is in the blocks that make up the pyramid. As they get larger the tools needed to move and support them must be stronger as well. Techniques that may work for small blocks can become impractical for larger blocks. For example, consider the concept of using small wooden rollers. These are certainly a practical consideration. Modern roller conveyers, which use small metal rollers, are used in manufacturing applications throughout the world. They allow the easy transportation of all sorts of objects up to several hundred pounds or more.

However, using small wooden rollers for pyramid blocks is not simple. Assuming that the rollers could be properly made and kept parallel, there is the problem of scale. Wooden rollers require a hard, flat surface to roll on. The block is obviously hard, as well. All of the 5,000-pound weight of the block would rest on two points: the top and bottom of the roller. This squashes the roller, slightly. As it does this, the fibers of the wood break and eventually the roller will split.

The larger the roller, the longer it will last. But doubling the diameter requires four times the volume of expensive, imported wood. And doubling the relative size may not be sufficient for large, heavy blocks. A fourfold increase in diameter, or more, may be required. Suddenly the scaling up of a "simple" idea becomes not so simple. This is the insidious problem of scale.

FORCES

Three general types of forces can be applied to a building material or a machine part. These are: tension, compression and shear. In concept they are quite simple. In practice they can be quite complicated because they do not always act in isolation.

Tension is a pulling force. The most typical example of this is illustrated with a piece of rope. Pulling on the ends creates the force of tension. Rock generally has very poor tensile strength. It is relatively easy to pull stone apart. This is seen in cracks in stonework and basement walls and as large splits in rock faces. A cliff will often have large crevices near the edge as it pulls away from the body of the bedrock. Steel and many other manufactured materials have good tensile properties. Even wood is better than most rock. The exception to this rule is that crystalline minerals like quartz and diamond and other similar materials have fairly good tensile strength.

Compression is exactly the opposite of tension. This is when a force presses inward from opposite ends of a material. Pliers and vises compress materials between their jaws. Rocks have excellent compression strength. Some mountains are miles high; the compressive force at the base of a mountain is immense. Hardness, as measured by the Mohs scale, can be loosely considered a measure of compressive strength. The act of scratching a material applies a compressive force to its surface until the surface fails. (Actually scratching an object is a complicated interplay of all the forces.)

Shear is when an unbalanced force is applied to one side of a material. Shear is a sliding force. For example, pulling out a book that is tightly held between two others is accomplished by applying a shear force. Twisting off a bottle cap requires a shear force. This is a bit different from compression and tension. But it is not something that is foreign in everyday life.

Long horizontal clear spans (unsupported by vertical posts) are difficult to achieve with stone because of its poor tensile strength characteristics. Consider a horizontal, round member of stone about ten feet long and one foot in diameter supported only at the ends. By examining the situation at the unsupported center it is seen that there is a tendency for the beam to sag because its weight.

This sag, or bend, causes two forces to appear. The first is a compressive force at the top of the beam in the concave part of the bend. In this area the rock is being forced into a smaller volume. Since rock has a good compression factor, not much happens. However, on the bottom there is a second or tensile force that is generated. This is the convex side of the bend that stretches the rock. Since stone has poor tensile strength, the tendency is for the rock to pull apart or split in this position. Typically, practical clear spans of solid rock are limited to about twenty or thirty feet (with shorter spans being much more common). Quite simply, stone doesn't work well in this application.

This is one reason why both the King and Queen Chambers in the Great Pyramid are only about 17 feet wide. They require massive granite beams, each weighing about 50 tons, to achieve this (Lepre, 92) clear span. Even at this relatively short length they are only capable of supporting themselves. There is a complicated and intricate configuration of additional massive blocks above them that deflects the weight of stone above away from the chambers (Lepre, 93). At the top of this complex design are sets of beams placed in an inverted V configuration. These have the effect of changing the overburden force (from blocks above the chamber) into a mostly compressive force. This is a very complicated engineering solution to a very difficult problem.

There are two very important points to ponder. The first is fairly straightforward. Large chambers in a pyramid are not possible (regardless of what is seen on TV and at the movies). The forces are too big for the physical characteristics of the materials available. The second is both far more subtle and far more revealing. The Egyptians fully understood the nature of compressive and tensile forces. They may not have been able to numerically measure them or have the proper mathematical formulas to calculate their precise values. But it is clear that they recognized that they existed and were able to design complicated structures that were successful in managing them. Their ability to master these forces on such a grand scale is just as impressive as the grand scale of the Great Pyramid itself. The builders of the Great Pyramid were truly experienced and gifted people in many disciplines.

Related to the concept of force is the concept of energy. Energy creates forces. It takes energy to close a vise, stretch a rope or twist off a cap. When energy is used to move an object, that energy is defined as work. Most typically, work energy is used to counteract forces in order to move things from place to place. For example, pulling a sledge is actually applying a shearing force to overcome the friction between the ground and the sledge runners. It is not so important to understand the interplay of forces as it is to realize that work is the specific application of forces in a directed manner. This means that as the structures get large, the work forces (or energy) necessary to build the structure increase at a great rate. It is seen that it is necessary to control this energy properly in order to manage the building of very large structures.

ENERGY MANAGEMENT

In any physical construction, two factors determine the cost of building the structure. The first is the cost of the materials. The second is the energy required to assemble those materials. Sometimes these factors are simply called materials and labor. However, labor is not really a precise term. It generally only applies to the workforce. Energy is a more generic term that can be applied to the system as a whole.

Energy Management is the top-down design of system with efficiency being the most important factor (Fonte, 2005). For similar construction projects the amount of materials is usually closely fixed. Two different plans for a railroad bridge spanning 200 feet will require about the same amount of steel and concrete. However, one plan may allow the use of pre-fabricated sections to reduce the overall cost significantly. That is, the energy of assembly is managed better. Note that the designs could be identical. Different people and businesses will have different methods of assembly. Not all of these methods are equally efficient.

Most ordinary efficiency improvements are applied in a piecemeal manner as they are discovered or identified. This is certainly useful but it is not optimal. Energy Management begins at the preliminary stages of a project to plot out the best use of tools, methods and ideas. Every single part of the project is closely examined to determine the optimal efficiency of the whole project. This means that some parts may be handled in a way that is "less efficient" if this results in an overall increase in efficiency of the system. Energy Management often requires a significant investment in infrastructure.

Energy Management is much more important for large projects than for small ones. This is because the costs become greater the larger the project is. For example, it is more energy efficient to use a hand-cart to unload 50-pound boxes of nails all day from a truck. However, to unload one box it is simpler to just carry it. The loss of efficiency for such a small action becomes insignificant to the overall costs of the action. What is seen is another instance of the order of magnitude rule. The need for Energy Management is greater as the size of the project grows.

The idea of Energy Management is not new. Probably the best known application of Energy Management is Henry Ford's assembly line. He designed a whole factory with the goal of producing automobiles in the most efficient manner. In this way he was able to produce his cars at a fraction of the cost of other methods, which allowed him to sell cars for a lower price than his competitors and increased his sales volume and his profits.

Another example is the Liberty Ships of World War II. Over 2750 Liberty ships were built in the years spanning 1941 to 1945. Normally it takes a year or two to build a cargo ship. And even the first few of these Liberty Ships took about 230 days. However, the rate quickly dropped to an average of just 42 days per ship. The Robert E. Peary was launched in an astounding 4 days and 16 hours. The technique used was to pre-fabricate sections of the ships off-site in an assembly-line fashion and then assemble the pieces in dry-dock.

The last example is the Lake Pontchartrain Bridge in Louisiana. The first span of nearly 24 miles was built in 1956 and a second span was added in 1969 at a cost of $26 million ($133 million in 2004 dollars). The bridge is so long that land cannot be seen from the middle of the bridge. (The lake is very shallow and there are many supports going into the bottom of the lake. This is not a bridge with a 24 mile clear span!) It used Energy Management ideas (although they were not called that). This should be compared to the Seven-Mile Bridge (actually 6.79 miles) in the Florida Keys. The second span of this was built in 1979 at a cost of $45 million ($117 in 2004 dollars) (Fernandes 2005). Both bridges are very similar in appearance and design and use about the same amount of materials per mile. However, the Lake Pontchartrain Bridge cost only about $5.5 million per mile while the Seven Mile Bridge cost about $17 million per mile. This is a difference of more than a factor of three and is due solely to better management of energy costs.

ENERGY MANAGEMENT COST

Energy Management does not come without cost. Fundamentally it is an upfront expense in order to save more as the project progresses. Most typically this is seen as a fabrication of a relatively complex infrastructure. Quite often this infrastructure, in isolation, may not appear to have a direct relationship to the endeavor. This can be confusing.

For example, in automobile assembly lines there are what appear to be railroad tracks in the middle of the factory. They do not attach to existing rail lines, and start and end with no apparent railroad logic. If one considers these rails as actual parts of a railroad they simply have no rational meaning. It makes no sense to have either a locomotive or a rail car operate over a short distance in the center of a manufacturing facility.

However, upon the realization that this is an assembly line, the rails make perfect sense. The car body is moved down these rails and assembled piece by piece until it is complete and rolls away at the end of the line. The rails are part of the infrastructure that is necessary for the assembly line to function efficiently. Obviously it takes substantial effort in cost and time to build this infrastructure, but overall there is a considerable savings in labor, or energy. This reduces overall costs. Henry Ford was able to undersell all of his competitors with this approach.

The Lake Pontchartrain Bridge cost a third of the Florida Keys Bridge (on a per mile basis) because it was pre-fabricated on land. There were special forms for casting the flat concrete parts and special machines to fabricate the round supports. These were partially pre-assembled and towed to the necessary location. There they were connected in place. The Lake Pontchartrain Bridge has been likened to a large Erector Set where parts were simply added together. This is very different from the more typical in-site bridge construction practice which requires pouring concrete in the middle of the lake and assembling every piece in place. Additionally, the special tools used to pre-form the Lake Pontchartrain components would not be found at a conventional bridge-building site. And if the procedure for building the bridge was not known, these machines could certainly be very puzzling.

It becomes clear that the acceptable expense of Energy Management depends upon the size of the project. It makes little sense to build an assembly line to manufacture a single car. But as the scale of the task increases the need to manage the energy also increases. There comes a point where Energy Management (in some form) is the only feasible method to accomplish a given mission. Building nearly 3000 Liberty-type transport ships in only four years is a conspicuous example of this. It is simply impractical to accomplish this by employing the standard methods of construction.

SCALE FACTORS AND THE PYRAMIDS

Different pyramids are very different in size. This means that the methods used to build them were probably different as well. This idea is something that archaeologists tend to overlook because they are not engineers and do not appreciate the significance of scale as it applies to construction. Often they will have in mind an idea that would work satisfactorily with a small pyramid but not for a large one.

The volume of a pyramid varies by the cube of its height (given a fixed inclination angle). A pyramid twice as tall as another has eight times the volume.

This is nearly an order of magnitude difference. This is a significant consideration. Conversely, a pyramid one half as tall contains only one eighth the volume. And while the pyramid shape may not be concerned with the engineering rule of thumb stated at the start of this chapter, the amount of labor required to build it will be. The order of magnitude rule does apply to management.

The scale factor of a pyramid block is also something to consider. The "typical" pyramid block is considered to be 4 feet by 4 feet by 2.5 feet. Defined as such, it contains 40 cubic feet of stone. Increasing each of the dimensions by only 1 foot (5 feet x 5 feet x 3.5 feet) more than doubles the volume to 87.5 cubic feet. This large variation block volume due to a relatively small change in dimensions will be shown in later chapters to have significant implications.

The Great Pyramid is built on such a huge size that it is impossible not to consider scale factors in its construction. Efficient methods for moving, lifting, placing and finishing the vast quantity of stones must be considered as necessary factors for success. Like the Liberty Ships, it does not appear that the standard methods of construction (large ramps and sledges) will provide the efficiency that is essential. For that reason new methods must be examined and/or developed which will allow such a massive structure to be built.

ENERGY MANAGEMENT AND THE PYRAMIDS

It seems apparent that the proper management of energy is a critical factor in building the Great Pyramid. It also seems apparent that the ancient Egyptians were smart enough to realize and address this concern. Pyramids were not something new to them. They were clearly familiar with the appropriate scale factors in both the physical construction as well as the management of labor and energy.

There are two basic forces that they would be concerned with. These are the forces of friction and that of gravity. Friction impedes the movement of the blocks from place to place. Friction is very high for dragging a sledge loaded with a 5,000 pound block. It wastes a lot of energy. The second force, gravity, makes lifting the blocks difficult. And while the average block is only lifted about 100 feet, the vast quantity of these blocks is certainly something to ponder. If they could develop efficient methods to manage these forces than they would be able to build the Great Pyramid with much less energy and in much less time than usually accepted.

Therefore, the examination of the techniques employed by the ancient Egyptians will include the possibility that they used Energy Management concepts. To that end, the investigation will search for odd or mysterious tools and/or artifacts found at the pyramid sites that do not have any clear and direct application to the standard methods of pyramid building. These special devices will then be analyzed to determine if they are part of an Energy Management infrastructure. If an infrastructure can be established, then it may be possible to develop reasonable estimates of the energy requirements and the time needed to build the Great Pyramid. Such an approach apparently has not been attempted before.

CONCLUSION

As projects change in size different techniques and considerations apply. Most typically, an order of magnitude change in a construction project requires a different style of design. The design for a 100 foot bridge is different from a 1,000-foot or 10-foot bridge. The management of tasks follows a similar rule. There are different management concerns for projects that require 10 or 100 or 1,000 workers. The scale of the Great Pyramid is such that different management and construction techniques are likely to be employed than those employed for smaller pyramids. Energy Management and an associated infrastructure would be expected to be used in some manner by the ancient Egyptians. Therefore it seems likely that remains of this infrastructure may be found at the various pyramid sites if it is looked for. The Egyptians were very smart engineers and builders. It is logical that they would search for efficient tools and methods to reduce the energy required for moving and lifting the 2.5 million, 2.5 ton blocks that comprise the Great Pyramid.

Chapter 4. Moving Blocks

Introduction

One of the great mysteries of the pyramids is determining the method by which the Egyptians moved huge blocks of stone that could weigh up to 80 tons (Lehner, 109). And while it is possible to imagine ways to move one huge block, it becomes much more difficult to consider moving millions of blocks weighing an average of 2.5 tons apiece. The scale of such an effort cannot be overstated. There are over 2,500,000 blocks, each averaging four feet square, that comprise the Great Pyramid. If these blocks were placed end-to-end they would stretch nearly 1900 miles or from New York City to San Antonio, Texas. It seems clear that the Egyptians would expend considerable thought to this problem. Nor would they undertake such a project as the Great Pyramid unless they had addressed this significant issue.

Sledges

Sledges are wooden platforms attached to wooden runners (very much like a child's sled). The load is placed on the platform and pulled to its destination. Sledges were certainly used in ancient Egypt (Lepre, 238; Lehner, 209; Smith, 84). They have been unearthed and various illustrations have been discovered (Lepre, 243; Lehner, 203; Smith, 186). However, no records or illustrations or paintings about how the pyramids were actually built have ever been found (Smith, 153). Because of their utility, it seems certain that sledges were probably used in some manner. However, is not known if they played a significant role in moving pyramid blocks. Pulling large, heavy blocks on a sledge is not the most efficient means imaginable. Nevertheless it is generally accepted that the Egyptians used this procedure for moving blocks (Lehner, 203, Lepre, 242; Smith, 89). Is it possible that they used a different method?

Wheels

It seems certain that ancient Egyptians did not use wheels (Smith, 48). No evidence has been found to show that they did. However, that does not mean that we can assume that they did not understand wheels. They did understand and use rollers of various types (Smith, 48; Lepre, 235). They also had hand-driven potter's wheels for making vases and other containers. A potter's wheel requires a hub and axle, which are the hallmarks of the modern wheel; it is simply vertical in orientation and not used for transportation. The question is: if the Egyptians understood the wheel, why didn't they use it for transportation?

It must be realized that Egypt was fundamentally a desert with the Nile River running through it. Quite literally, the waters of the Nile gave life to Egypt. There was virtually no rainfall (Lepre, 251). People lived near the river banks because it was easier to survive there. And at that time, survival was not something to be compromised. Water was (and is) necessary for human life, and for livestock and crops. Moving away from the Nile meant moving away from easy access to water, which made living harder to maintain. Additionally, the only fertile land was created by the annual flooding of the Nile. All in all, there was a clear driving force for people to live as close to the Nile as practical.

Settling near fresh water supplies is a natural human behavior. It is repeated over and over in history. In this sense the Nile region is not unique. However, it is not common for a river to run through a desert. This creates a stronger than usual pressure for the people to settle extremely close to the river. Living only a mile away from the Nile would present considerable difficulties. And again, unlike non-desert locales, only the ground adjacent to the river is fertile, because it is the annual flooding which deposits rich soil in an area that otherwise is sandy.

In order for wheels to be used for transportation, there must be hard-surfaced roads (at least hard enough to support continuous use). This requires a significant infrastructure. The pharaoh had the ability and power to create roads; but was there a need to do so? River traffic was easy and commonplace. There was no need to create roads along the river; "The main artery for transportation was the Nile River [itself]" (Smith, 84). And as seen above, the population was compressed very close to the river, so there was no real need to push roads away from the river.

And where would a road be laid? Whether it ran right along the river or farther away, the costs seem to outweigh the possible benefits. If a road were run close to the Nile, that would have consumed valuable farm land which was a precious and life-giving commodity of very limited supply. The second problem was that the annual flooding of the Nile would drown the road every year. This could certainly destroy it and at the least would require significant annual maintenance. And, of course, during the flood season the road would be impassible.

Siting a road away from the Nile would mean running it close to or through the desert. There were fewer people there anyway, so the road would not be as useful. It would be difficult to build or use a road on sand; and then, blowing and drifting sand would make the road difficult or impossible to passage. Only a few inches of sand are needed to make the use of wheels awkward. Keeping the roads clear of sand would take considerable effort.

It now becomes clear that the physical world in which the ancient Egyptian society functioned was not conducive for the use of wheels as a means of transportation.

Finally, there was little suitable wood in the area (Smith, 49; Lepre, 257), and it is difficult to consider any other common material that could be substituted for wood to make wheels. Nor is fabricating a wheel a trivial endeavor. Making it round and strong enough to be useful requires skill and effort. The axle and wheel bearings are also non-trivial components. Lubrication of some sort is required. This in itself is not a concern since the Egyptians understood the function of lubricants (Lepre, 238). However, any lubricant used will also attract dirt and worse, sand. Any significant amount of sand in the bearings will wear the wooden components to sawdust quickly.

With these considerations in mind, we can conclude that the wheel may not have offered much utility as a transportation device in ancient Egypt. That the Egyptians failed to use the wheel does not mean that they were ignorant and didn't understand the wheel. It may only indicate that they realized that the wheel was not an effective tool for their particular situation. With the clear mastery of geometry that is evident in their incredible constructions, it seems reasonable to accept that the Egyptians were aware of the theory of the wheel, but chose not to implement it.

WHY THINGS ROLL

Understanding the theory of the wheel and understanding why things roll are two different things. It is easy to see that round things roll readily and square things don't. It is not as clear why. This knowledge can be gleaned by studying the geometry and physical relationships of rotating objects. On the surface this seems very complicated and beyond the mathematical capability of the ancient Egyptians. However, upon closer examination, and assuming that ancient Egyptians had the same intellectual potential as anyone today, it can be seen that they could solve this riddle. High level mathematical concepts are not necessary. All that is required is creativity, close observation of physical processes and rational thought. Unquestionably, these qualities were possessed by the designers of the pyramids.

The first step is to examine what happens when a circle is rolled and a square is rotated. This is shown in Figures 4-1 and 4-2. The center of a circle moves horizontally when the circle rolls. The center of a square moves upward, until the square is exactly on edge and then moves downward. It will be assumed that the circles and squares are made of a homogeneous material, such as stone or wood, so the center of rotation is also the center of mass. This makes the analysis simple and straightforward. The center of mass of a square-shaped object moves up and down as it rotates while the center of mass of a circular-shaped object doesn't.

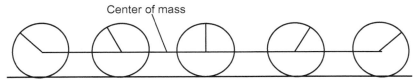

Figure 4-1: A rolling circle's center of mass does not move up or down as it rotates. Therefore, no lifting energy is needed or wasted.

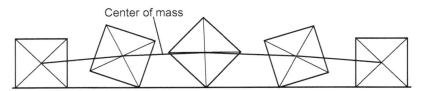

Figure 4-2: Rolling a square requires the center of mass to be lifted about 20% of the side-length of the square. This energy is released during the downward movement but it is not in a useable form and is wasted.

It is also easy to see that the amount of vertical movement, or amplitude, of the square's center of mass is related to the diagonal length and is constant for any square. Specifically, the amplitude is one-half the difference between the side and diagonal lengths. In this case, the amplitude is 0.20711 times the length of a side. (A unit-square has sides of 1 and a diagonal of 1.41421. One half the difference of these values is 0.41421 / 2.)

With this relationship it is possible to measure the effort of rolling a square as a means of lateral movement. A ninety degree rotation of the square will generate a horizontal movement of 1 (using a unit-square). To achieve that lateral movement, the center of mass must be lifted 20.711% of the side length. Fundamentally, energy equal 20.711% of the square's weight must be consumed to move the square the length of its side. This length to height ratio corresponds to pushing it up an 11.7 degree incline — ignoring friction. It is true that this energy is released as the center of mass drops during the second half of the rotation. However, this energy cannot be used and is lost. It is this loss of energy that causes the square to be a poor roller. A circle's center of mass does not move up or down so there is no "lifting energy" loss at all.

It is useful to compare the energy requirements of rolling a block and that of a sledge. Given a block that weighs 5,000 pounds, the average force required to move it by rotation is about 1036 pounds. (This was calculated using the "equivalent incline" as noted above.) The force required to rotate a square is greatest at the start and diminishes as the job progresses. Smith (p. 172) suggests that about 14 men are needed to haul a 5,000 pound block with a sledge (based on Lehner's work). If each man weighs about 150 pounds and can pull with about 50% of his weight, they will produce about 1050 pounds of force. It is somewhat surprising that these values are so close to each other. (Note: Lehner [p. 203] shows 20 men pulling a two-ton block on a sledge for the NOVA experiment. He uses the term "easily" but the photograph shows the men exhibiting considerable effort. This corresponds to 25 men for a 5,000 pound block, or about twice Smith's estimate.)

While the falling energy of the block cannot be recovered, the energy does not have to be wasted. The efficiency of rolling a square can be improved markedly by preventing the square's center of mass from falling to the lowest point. This is shown in Figure 4-3. Here a fulcrum is placed halfway. When the square starts to fall the fulcrum prevents it from falling to the minimum. This saves substantial energy. The precise amount of energy saved depends upon the height of the fulcrum and will not be calculated except to note that 50%–75% energy savings can be realized without difficulty. This reduces the calculated force required from 1036 pounds to about 500 pounds or less.

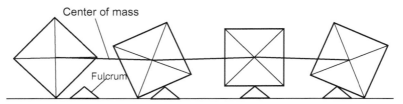

Figure 4-3: Using a fulcrum to prevent the center of mass of the block from falling completely to the ground significantly reduces the amplitude variation and the energy loss.

The important point is that rolling a block with a fulcrum takes significantly less effort than using a sledge. This is not an advanced concept. Nor is a mathematical approach necessary to understand it. (As children, my brother and I used the fulcrum approach to move large pieces of slate when playing at the nearby creek.) This procedure is clearly within the grasp of the Egyptians and it seems unlikely that they wouldn't be aware of it, given the vast experience they had with moving large stones. They may not have had the mathematical tools to precisely calculate the savings in energy, but they plainly had the intelligence to recognize that one approach was better than the other. Simple tests would have proved that.

QUARTER CIRCLES

Some very peculiar objects have been found at a number of pyramid sites, variously called a "rocker" or "quarter circle" (Lepre, 248). They are made of cedar, a wood that is not native to Egypt but would have been imported from Lebanon (Lepre 257). They are flat on one side and rounded on the other, approximating 90 degrees of arc (hence the term quarter circle). The flat side is approximately length of an average pyramid block. The fact that they have been found at pyramid sites suggests that they played a role in the construction of the pyramids. That they have been found at all suggests that there were many of them.

This is because wooden artifacts survive poorly over thousands of years. Insects, moisture, mold, fungi, bacteria, sunlight and other agents naturally break down wood and recycle it like any other organic material. It is extremely unlikely that any individual quarter circle could possibly endure thousands of years. Additionally, it is important to note this wood has a very high intrinsic value. It is very unlikely that any "unaccounted for" pieces of cedar would go unclaimed in one manner or another. Valuable property left unguarded was in those days, as it still is, at risk. (This fundamental aspect of human nature is why the pyramid entrances were hidden and blocked.) Therefore, in order to offset the incredibly small probability of survival, it is reasonable to postulate that there were many, many quarter circles, with only the very few exceptional cases being discovered relatively recently.

Egyptologists generally believe that these wooden tools were used to lift blocks (Lepre, 247). The procedure was to place the block on the flat side and rock the stone back and forth while placing thin shims under the rocker. In this manner, the block could be gradually lifted. This approach does not appear to be feasible or practical or efficient. Even Lepre (p. 247) does not think that this is the purpose of the quarter circles. (And it will be shown in a later chapter that there are better ways of lifting blocks.)

One very creative idea was to attach quarter circles to a square block with the rounded sides outward. This turned the block into a large wheel (Bush 1978). In December of 1981, Mr. John Bush and six other men used this method to roll a 2.5 ton concrete block up a steep loading ramp (Lepre, 247).

However, there are significant problems with this approach. The first is that Bush used ropes to hold the quarter circles and block together. This required holes in the wood. Unfortunately, the quarter circles found do not have holes (Lepre, 247). Nor can any other reasonable means be deduced that the Egyptians could have used. Adhesives and strong fasteners were simply not available at that time. Theoretically, a rope could be passed around the circumference of the assembly to hold the pieces together. However, that would place the rope between the wood and the ground. Such an arrangement would crush the rope quickly. Then there is the practical problem of knotting the rope. This would cause a significant bump every revolution.

Another problem, alluded to above, is that this approach has the effect of turning a block into a massive wheel. Wheels require roads. More significant is the problem of weight. A 2.5-ton wheel has all its weight concentrated at the point where it rests on the ground. Unless the roadway is solid rock, the wheel will sink into the ground to some degree. This makes the wheel much harder to rotate, which lowers its efficiency and effectiveness. Secondly, this sinking ruins the roadway. It churns the surface. This makes rolling the assembly that much more difficult, which means that continuous roadway maintenance is needed.

The idea of wrapping circular parts around a large object to make it roll has been tried before in ancient times. Lepre (p. 246) relates that the Roman engineer Chersiphron assembled wooden wheels around large stone columns so that they could be rolled rather than dragged. This approach is certainly applicable on occasion. However, applying it to 2.5 million blocks seems doubtful for the reasons noted above. Plus there is the problem of scale that was noted in Chapter 3.

Attaching and removing eight wooden pieces to each and every stone would take considerable effort. It is not clear that this procedure would actually save time.

QUARTER CIRCLE TRACK

Instead of making wheels with the quarter circles, suppose they were turned upside down with the flat side on the ground and used as rolling fulcrums, as described above. It seems possible that a properly designed quarter circle could be built that would exactly offset the center of mass amplitude variation as the square rotates over it. This is shown in Figure 4-4. This concept is wholly feasible. An inverted quarter circle completely and exactly compensates for the center of mass variation as the square rotates. By abutting quarter circles end-to-end a track is formed (Figure 4-5) which permits square blocks to be rolled end-over-end with no energy loss at all (excluding friction). It is assumed that two parallel tracks were used for stability (like railroad tracks). Examining this concept shows a host of important construction advantages.

Center of mass

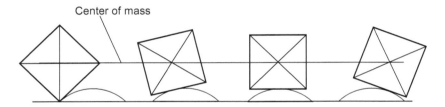

Figure 4-4: A quarter circle exactly compensates for the center of mass amplitude variation. The result is that a square rolls like a circle without any lifting energy and the associated loss.

Figure 4-5: By abutting the quarter circles a track is formed that allows the blocks to roll over them. Probably two parallel tracks were used (like railroad tracks) for stability.

The first and most important advantage is the obvious energy savings. If the only energy loss is from rolling friction, which can be extremely low, a single person should be able to roll a block at a reasonable speed (of about a slow walk). Overcoming the static friction, which is higher than the rolling friction, would be the hard part. Once the block is rolling the inertia would help to keep it moving, thus maintaining the speed would be considerably easier. (Note that this is not at all like pushing an automobile. Relatively, a car has extremely high rolling resistance because of the flattening of the tires. A better comparison would be to moving a boat on water. Massive boats can be moved by hand quite easily. This point will be discussed in more detail in the next chapter.)

Additionally, while not immediately apparent, there is a two-fold mechanical advantage to this approach. This can be seen by using the example of lifting a board. Lifting one end of a board while the other end is on the ground is easier than lifting the whole board. This is because the board acts like a lever with the ground as the fulcrum and the center of mass halfway along the board. Lifting one end of the board two feet lifts the center of mass one foot. (Naturally, the foot-pound product remains unchanged.) Whether it's lifting a board or moving a block over quarter circles, the geometry is the same. The center of mass is halfway between the edge and the fulcrum on the ground. Lifting a corner gives a two-to-one mechanical advantage. This, in effect, gives the block the rolling friction of a block weighing about 2,500 pounds rather than 5,000 pounds.

It is useful to compare this approach to a sledge. Smith (p. 172) suggests that an average block can be moved at a rate of about 10 feet per minute with 14 men. The quarter-circle method should allow a single worker to move a block at about 2 feet per second. This is an improvement in efficiency by a factor of 168. (Or by a factor of about 300, if Lehner's manpower estimate [p. 209] is used). There are a host of other advantages as well.

For example, the flat bottoms of the quarter circles distribute the great weight of the rolling blocks instead of concentrating it. This reduces road-wear considerably. There may still be some embedding of the quarter circles into the roadway as the heavy blocks roll over them. But this is actually beneficial because it stabilizes the tracks and keeps them from moving.

Placing the flat side down allows the quarter circle to act as a ramp for small rises in the roadbed and a bridge for small indentations. This simplifies road construction and reduces the difficulty of moving a block over uneven ground. (Note that a wheel requires significant energy when moving over even a small obstacle. Consider rolling a dinner plate over a pencil. Basically the plate's center of mass must be lifted over the pencil. Wheel chocks for airplanes are very small in relation to the size of the wheel.)

As blocks are rolled over the quarter-circle track, they will tend to auto-align themselves. As a block rolls over a corner, it will tend to fall into the "V" made by abutting quarter circles. If a block is a little too big or small, this will help to keep the block synchronized properly to the track. If the block twists slightly and starts to wander off the track, falling into the "V" will re-register the block parallel to the track.

The quarter circles act like pallets and keep the block off the ground. This makes looping ropes around the block, for lifting, extremely easy. This is a very important and useful feature that simplifies many operations.

The final position of the block is precisely defined, simply by where the track ends. This may seem obvious. However, it is less obvious that if the final set of quarter circles is removed after that block is placed, the next block will be positioned precisely as well. This positioning is not exact but it will never be more than +/- 0.5 block-lengths out of position. This final block positioning, and the track positioning patterns that could be used to greatly simplify block placement, will be discussed in further detail in the next chapter.

The track approach can be used in conjunction with ramps as well as on the pyramid proper. The steepness of the ramp is an important issue; it would hardly do to have blocks rolling backwards, out of control. However, gentle inclines are certainly addressable. (Ramps will be discussed in much more detail in the chapter on lifting blocks.) Moving blocks on the pyramid proper is an important aspect that is generally ignored. The quarter circle track is suitable for this. The not-so-perfect layers of rock support the track with ease and the imperfections are compensated for by the flat side of the quarter circle. The track is easy to put down and move as required. It is hard to imagine any other approach that is so energy efficient.

Crossed quarter circles permit easy 90-degree rotation (see Figure 4-6). The operation is straightforward. The block is rolled up to the top of the tool and stopped. For safety, chocks can be placed at the corners to prevent the block from falling. The chocks should be just slightly lower than the peak of the crossed quarter circles. Then the block is rotated ninety degrees, the appropriate chocks removed, and the block is rolled off the tool in the proper direction. (If the block is a cube, the rotation is not necessary.) The energy requirement to rotate the block is very small because it rests on a relatively small area and is well-balanced.

It is seen that these "mysterious" tools are an integral and vital engineering component in the infrastructure of the pyramid design. Their utility is astounding. Their simplicity is startling. Their efficiency is awesome. The Egyptians' concept of using quarter circles as a transportation mechanism is truly a work of genius.

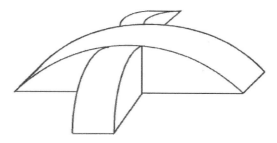

Figure 4-6: Crossed quarter circles permit easy 90 degree rotation for a block on a quarter circle track. Roll the block up to the top, rotate it and then roll it down in the appropriate direction. Chocks can be used for safety.

BLOCK SIZE

It is clear that in order to use the quarter circle track effectively, all the blocks must have the same square cross section. Blocks too big or too small by more than a few inches simply won't roll properly. This is a clear and necessary requirement. However, it is also clear that the exposed blocks of the Great Pyramid are not all the same size. Is there an explanation for this that makes sense? Yes, but a forensic examination of the Maidum pyramid as well as the Great Pyramid's sister pyramid, Khafre's pyramid, is needed to develop this.

As noted in Chapter 1, the Maidum pyramid was built about 50 years before Khufu's reign. Sneferu, Khufu's father, was associated with this pyramid as was pharaoh Huni. The outer portions of the pyramid fell away, leaving the core exposed (see Figures 1-9 and 1-10). It was also noted that previous to that pyramid, the normal construction method was to tilt the layers inward whereas in later pyramids the layers were horizontal (Lepre, 49). Additional information can be extrapolated from these facts.

The Egyptian engineers seem to have followed the wisdom that is summarized in today's engineering adage, "If it works, don't fix it." When something worked well, like corbelled ceilings, they maintained the design. They would not have changed the basic design without a good and significant reason. Yet there was a significant change in the way pyramids were constructed after the Maidum pyramid, when builders shifted from using inward leaning layers to horizontal layers. The inward leaning design had been successfully used for mastabas and step pyramids for hundreds of years. However, the failure of a major pyramid is certainly a sufficient reason to re-examine a design approach. All of this strongly suggests that the Maidum pyramid failed during construction or closely thereafter, before the next major pyramid was to be built.

Obviously, the Egyptian engineers and their Pharaoh would want to understand why the structure failed. This is simply human nature. It is certainly within their capacity to understand that inward leaning walls create forces that must be precisely balanced. If not, twisting or "shear" forces are developed. With such a large structure, once these forces exceed the friction holding the blocks in place, the structure will fail. (The blocks were not held together by mortar.)

Shear forces can be removed by making the layers horizontal. This completely eliminates the weight of the blocks pressing inward.

The friction consideration is more subtle. It could scarcely escape observation that the core of the Maidum pyramid remained virtually intact. This is very significant. It demonstrates that the core was inordinately stable. During the collapse of the outer layers significant stresses were certainly placed upon the core. Nevertheless, the core survived well.

Examining the core it is seen that the outer core is very smooth with the interior core packing stones of fairly uniform size (Figure 1-10). (It is again noted that the interior packing stones are very different from the exterior stones.) This smoothness of the exterior core allowed the outer stones to slide down the sides with virtually no damage. This would provide the Egyptians with two pieces of important information. The first is that the core of a pyramid can be made smooth and regular and it will be stable. The second is that the outside of the pyramid is more susceptible to shear forces. This can be viewed as a lever with the fulcrum at the center of the pyramid. The farther away from the fulcrum, the greater the forces can be. Therefore, the outer stones should interlock as much as possible to increase the friction and reduce the effects of shear forces.

This is not to suggest that the Egyptians performed detailed and complex mathematical calculations to determine the exact amounts of friction and shear forces. Instead, it illustrates that the concepts of force and friction were within the Egyptians' understanding. It seems abundantly clear that anyone who builds huge monuments must have an understanding of these basic principles. Intelligent engineers, studying the failure of their creation, certainly would have had some grasp of these ideas.

Therefore it is not unreasonable to consider that the core of the Great Pyramid is built of square blocks of equal cross section to allow the use of a quarter circle track. The height of the blocks can vary, as long as one cross section is square and the same. The core would incorporate the great majority of the blocks. This approach is similar to the Maidum pyramid and there is no reason that they would abandon this successful core design. Additionally many earlier and later pyramids and mastabas used bricks instead of stone blocks (see Appendix 1). Bricks are molded and generally are of uniform size. So the use of equally-sized blocks is a well-known construction technique that has been repeated many times. Unfortunately every large pyramid built by Sneferu, Khufu and Khafre still stands and is reasonably intact. Their cores remain invisible, so we do not know what their cores are really like.

The outer layers would then consist of various sized blocks that would interlock better and increase friction to offer greater resistance to shear forces. With equal-sized blocks, a force will push a row in a linear fashion. With varied sized blocks, the force will cause the smaller blocks to twist; this passes the force to lateral blocks. This distributes the force among more blocks, reducing the overall effect of the force.

This is precisely what is seen in Khafre's pyramid (Figure 4-7). Here more stones have been removed to expose deeper layers of the pyramid. "Just beneath the lowest surviving course of casing stones, a band of regular stepped core stone is visible. The rest of the surface down to the base...consists of very rough, irregular, loose stones." (Lehner, 122). Close examination of Figure 4-7 shows that there is a maximum size for the blocks that is quite uniform. This would be expected if a quarter-circle track was used. The properly sized blocks would be rolled to the site, where they would be broken down as needed for the various sizes of exterior backing stones.

Many non-pyramid structures use stones of wildly different sizes. Khafre's Valley Temple at Giza is a good example. Only the top is level. There are no actual layers to the walls and the blocks are entirely random in size and shape. This strongly suggests that the techniques used for building the pyramid are different from building a relatively small temple. This is not unexpected, but it is noteworthy.

The use of horizontal layers makes the quarter-circle track much easier to use on the pyramid proper. Inclined layers require energy to control the block going downward and energy to push the block upwards. Additionally, trying to roll a block obliquely across an angle can create significant problems.

Finally, there is human nature. No one likes to fail. And failing in such a public and profound manner is especially humiliating. After the Maidum pyramid came the Bent pyramid, which cannot be considered an engineering success, and the Red pyramid which had a very shallow and timid angle of only 43.5 degrees.

There is an interesting piece of circumstantial evidence that the Egyptians took to heart the failure of Maidum with the next big pyramid after those mentioned above, which was the Great Pyramid. The angle that they used was a bold and spectacular 51.85 degrees (calculated). The angle of the Maidum pyramid was 51.9 degrees (calculated). This does not seem to be a coincidence. Building a structure bigger and taller and four times as massive as the failed Maidum pyramid, while incorporating the same dangerous angle, was a profound proclamation. The Egyptians were declaring to the world that they were the masters of the craft. They were and still are.

Figure 4-7: Khafre's pyramid at Giza shows where additional blocks have been removed which exposes inner blocks that are much more regular in size and shape. The outer stones that lie just behind the casing stones are seen in the lower half of the picture. The top shows the pyramid more or less intact. Combining this observation with the observations of the core of the Maidum pyramid suggest that the core of this pyramid and that of the Great Pyramid may be composed of very regular blocks that were moved with quarter circles. Photograph copyright 2006 by Len Schwer and used with permission.

After examining the evidence it becomes reasonable to suggest that the Egyptians did use the quarter circle track for moving the blocks even though the outer blocks are not the same size. Most importantly, quarter circles have actually been found at pyramid sites. They have been shown to be extremely powerful tools with many important and useful features. There is evidence that the core of a pyramid is not at all the same as the outside. The internal core of the pyramid at Maidum is composed of similar-sized stones. Khafre's pyramid shows that deeper blocks have greater regularity. It has been realized that the use of variable sized blocks on the outside of the pyramid improves stability by distributing shear forces, which explains why they are not uniform in size. The horizontal layers of the Great Pyramid match the requirements of the quarter-circle track. Upon review of all the available information, it seems difficult to come to any other conclusion. The Great Pyramid design is based on experience and intelligence and the quarter-circle track is an integral part of this design.

Quarter Circle Shape

Two specifications of the quarter circle are easy to define. The curved side must equal the side of the square; because the square side rotates over the curved side, they must be equal. If not, it is easy to see that problems will occur. This is very much like two gears working together. It is essential that they match.

The second specification that is easy to define is the maximum height of the quarter circle. As described above, this is one-half of the difference between the diagonal length and the side length or 0.20711 of the side length. This is the maximum amplitude change of the center of the square as it rotates. This is also readily apparent.

However, while these two specifications do provide significant limitations to the shape, they do not specify the shape of the curved side. And, while it seems clear that the shape must be symmetrical and smooth, as long as the shape of the curve is not defined, the length of the flat side cannot be defined either. It turns out that the shape of the quarter circle is a puzzle.

The optimum shape for the quarter circle is not actually circular. It is very close to a section of a circle, but it is definitely not part of a circle. Considerable effort was expended during this research to determine what the optimum shape actually was. Step-wise calculations were performed incorporating the rotation of a square and the appropriate lateral movement to identify individual positions of the center of the square as it moved. (Note that simply rotating a square on an edge creates a circular section and does not consider the proper lateral motion.) These calculations were used to create a point-by-point shape of the optimal quarter circle. A number of common functions were compared to this shape to determine if there was a match. Neither a circle, an ellipse, parabola, hyperbola, sine wave or any other standard curve fit. All could be made to match the calculated crescent to within a few percentage points, but none was exact.

It turns out that the correct shape would be a catenary (Wagon 1970). An animation produced by Djun M. Kim, posted by the University of British Columbia at "An Amusing Property of the Catenary" (http://www.sunsite.ubc.ca/LivingMathematics/V001N01/UBCExamples/Animation/catenary.html), shows a square rolling over abutting catenaries. This is the required curve in that the center of the square has zero amplitude change. Therefore, the proper shape for the quarter-circle curve is conclusively a catenary. It is somewhat surprising that this relationship between the rolling square and catenary was not determined until 1960 in a paper by Robison (Robison 1960).

EGYPTIAN QUARTER CIRCLES VERSUS CATENARIES

There are a number of issues that arise in regards to the Egyptian quarter circles that have been found at the pyramid sites. The first question is whether the quarter circles are actually catenaries. Unfortunately, this question may never be answered definitively because of the great age of the quarter circles found. Since they are made of wood, it would not be surprising if their dimensions have changed slightly over such a long period. Warping causes wood to change shape and a change in moisture content can cause the wood to change its size. Thus the curve now may not be precisely what it was 4500 years ago. As noted above, there are many curves that will match to within a few percentage points.

Because no published dimensions of a quarter circle have been found in the literature, it seems that the best possible approach is to compare the size relationship between a quarter circle and catenary for a particular pyramid block. If there is a close correspondence between them, then it can be reasoned that the quarter circles were indeed used for transportation and that they were shaped as catenaries. Lepre is very precise in his drawings, with great attention to detail, so it is interesting to compare his drawing that relates the size of a quarter circle to a pyramid block (Lepre, 248) and compare that to a catenary and a properly-sized square. The quarter circle and block relationship is shown in Figure 4-8. (Note that the quarter circle is shown improperly as being used as a rocker.) Figure 4-9 shows a properly-scaled square and catenary in the same relationship. The comparison between the two is striking.

The Egyptians could have created the catenary tool by several different methods. They could have developed the shape directly from the concept of eliminating the amplitude variation as a square rotates. This approach (which was this author's technique) directly compensates for the center of mass variation and is a theoretical method. It requires the understanding of Pythagorean Theorem and the ability to perform square roots. This certainly seems beyond the mathematical capabilities of the time. However, there is some evidence that they did understand the Pythagorean Theorem in some manner because certain important features in the King's chamber of the Great Pyramid have relationships that are three to four to five, which create a right triangle (Lepre, 101). However, this

theoretical approach is probably not the most likely method of creating the catenary shape.

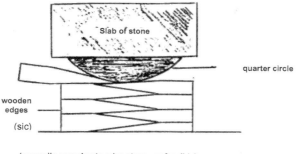

Figure 4-8: Lepre (p. 248) shows a quarter circle (improperly) being used as a rocker
with wooden wedges. The important point is the size and shape of the quarter
circle and its relationship to the block. (Note: Lepre has "wooden edges" and it
should be "wooden wedges.") From The Egyptian Pyramids: A Comprehensive,
Illustrated Reference © 1990 J P Lepre by permission of McFarland & Company, Inc., Box 611, Jefferson NC 28640.

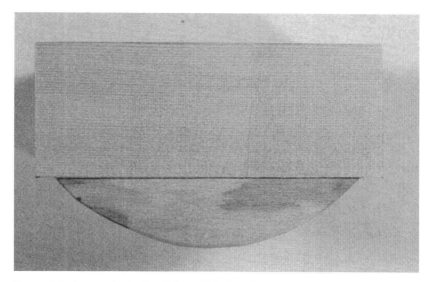

Figure 4-9: A properly sized and shaped block and catenary/quarter circle are placed
in the same relationship as in figure 4-8. The similarities are striking.

Another method, which is based on a conceptual approach, is to actually
measure the center of mass change as a square rotates (including the proper lat-

eral motion) and then use these measurements to create the proper shape. The idea is again to create the shape directly from the theory. This was certainly within the capabilities of the Egyptians of that time. They plainly could have built models and made the necessary measurements. The only tool that is needed is a ruler and we know that they possessed the equivalent of that (Lepre, 239; Smith, 74). While possible, this procedure also does not seem likely.

It seems that the most likely method of creating the catenary shape comes from experimentation. They recognized that the primitive fulcrum approach noted above and shown in Figure 4-3 saved considerable work, and from there it would not require any real theoretical or mathematical aptitude to consider using a curved shape for better efficiency. Also, as noted previously, the height and length of the curved side are easy to determine, logically. Probably a circular shape would initially be considered. This would work well because the catenary varies only a few percent from a circular curve. The circular shape provides a very good first estimate. However, they could certainly realize and measure that the amplitude was not perfectly eliminated. These measures would provide the appropriate correction factors to change the circular shape into the catenary shape. This is a very simple and direct approach which matches the Egyptians' demonstrated abilities. (The circular shape might still have been incorporated, because the error is small and the shape is easier to define.)

TIME ESTIMATE

It is now possible to create a time estimate for moving the blocks from the quarry to the proper location on pyramid. This does not include lifting the blocks, which will be addressed in a later chapter. In Chapter 2 it was determined that the average lateral distance that an average block had to be moved was about 1500 feet. It was shown that with the use of a catenary track a single person should be capable of moving a block at about two feet per second. This means that a single man could theoretically move a block 1500 feet in about 750 seconds, or about 12.5 minutes.

However there is a great difference between theory and practice. It is unrealistic that perfect efficiency can ever be achieved or maintained. Additionally, what can be performed once fairly easily often cannot be performed all day, every day, for years. For these reasons a conservative estimate will be employed. The conservative estimate is that three workers will require twenty minutes to roll one block 1500 feet. This corresponds to one man-hour of time to move an average block the average distance or about five times the theoretical possible.

Even this conservative estimate surpasses the estimated sledge speed by a huge factor. Smith's estimate of 14 men at 10 feet per minute requires 2.5 hours to travel 1500 feet. This is 35 man-hours or 35 times the catenary track method. (And recall that Lehner's estimates are nearly twice as large as Smith's.) A close examination of Smith's estimates and methods will be conducted in a later chapter.

CONCLUSION

By examining the strange quarter-circle objects from an engineering point of view is it found that these relics have a clear and useful purpose. They can be used to reduce the energy needed to move blocks by over a hundredfold. (However, to be conservative only a factor of 35 will be used.) Investigation of the Maidum pyramid as well as Khafre's Pyramid shows that the internal core of these pyramids is not the same as the exterior. This suggests that the internal core of the Great Pyramid may be reasonably considered to be built from blocks different to those on the exterior, specifically blocks that have an equal and square cross section making them suitable for transport via catenary track. It has also been recognized that the outer blocks are of different sizes for the specific reason of better stress relief.

Most fundamentally, however, it is realized that these tools cannot have been created by chance. Once the form and function of these curious artifacts are determined it is clearly seen that the Egyptians were brilliant and astute virtuosos of geometry. They were beyond peer in their understanding of why things roll, and this can been seen in their use of the deceptively simple and elegant form of a catenary.

Chapter 5. Rolling Block Experiment

Introduction

In the previous chapter it was stated that a single person should be able to roll a pyramid block over a catenary track. This statement was based on experience with moving heavy objects and the observation that heavy objects are often moved manually in industry. However, significant criticism has been made of that statement. In fact, there are some who believe that "The idea that three men can roll a block as easily as pushing a bicycle is simply not credible." For that reason an experiment was designed and publicly performed on December 5, 2003, to determine two basic questions: 1) Is a catenary track a practical method for moving blocks and 2) does the efficiency of such a system match the previously stated expectations?

Manually Moving Heavy Objects

It will be useful to briefly examine moving heavy objects manually. Unfortunately, it is true that few people have experience with moving objects weighing over a ton except for an automobile. And pushing a recalcitrant motor vehicle does seem to be an ordeal that has touched a very large number of people. The problem is that pushing a car does not properly represent rolling friction very well. This is because cars have relatively high rolling resistance that is related to the flattening of the rubber tires. The tires actually perform several functions. They obviously roll, which allows the vehicle to move. They also act as part of the shock absorbing system by deforming when going over a bump. (This is much more evident on a bicycle, as anyone who has ridden one with a flat tire will attest.) Lastly they provide traction and distribute the weight of the car over a fairly substantial area by flattening out on the bottom somewhat.

There is a trade-off with the footprint of a tire. The larger the contact area, the greater the traction for starting and stopping and the less weight there is applied to the roadway (in pounds per square inch). Traction is another word for friction. And clearly it is very important for a car to stick to the road well. Starting, stopping and turning the automobile rely on the friction between the tire contact area and the road to maintain control. From that standpoint, increasing the contact area by a large amount would be a good thing. However, this increases friction, which increases rolling resistance and also increases the flexing of the tires, which increases tire heat. These are bad things for tires and gas mileage.

Reducing the tire footprint, via higher tire pressure, reduces the rolling resistance (which is well known) but increases the weight concentration on the highway. If the tires did not deform at all, then all of the weight of the vehicle would be concentrated onto a very small area. As noted in Chapter 4, such a situation can churn the roadway surface and ruin it quickly. And the ability to handle the car would be greatly compromised. Therefore car designers must balance a number of factors to achieve optimal performance at highway speeds. Since a powerful engine normally moves the car, designers do not generally consider the problems of pushing a car manually. That is why pushing a car does not give us a good sense of what wheels can really do.

In industry, moving heavy objects manually is a common occurrence. The key to doing so is to reduce the wheel contact area as much as possible. The problems of traction and high speed operation are not important because they don't really apply to manual operations. By using hard metal wheels on metal tracks or concrete, which are much less susceptible to churning, the footprint can be minimized. This reduces rolling resistance by up to a factor of ten when compared to rubber tires. The metal-to-metal approach is seen repeated over and over; it is fundamentally a large roller-bearing or a ball-bearing. Mine carts that have metal wheels can hold a ton or two of ore and are often pushed on metal tracks by one or two workers. Manual pallet movers that have three-ton capacities are common. (And it should be noted that there are actually two sources of friction in all of these examples. The first is the stated wheel-rolling resistance. The second is the friction of the axle bearings. When rolling a block over catenaries, there is no axle bearing friction because there is no axle.)

There are more examples of low-friction movement in which wheels are not used. One example is the movement of floating objects. A row-boat with six adults weighs about 1,000 pounds can be pushed away from the dock with a casual one-handed shove. Another example is with suspended objects. Huge, multi-ton metal girders held at the proper height are manually oriented and adjusted for precise placement in the skyscraper skeleton.

The point of this discussion is to show that the manual movement of heavy objects is not as rare or difficult as it may seem, as long as the friction is kept very low. It is important to dispel inaccurate perceptions and prejudicial opinions in order to fully appreciate the brilliance of the Egyptian builders. If friction is sufficiently small, very heavy objects can be moved, by hand, easily.

Step 1: Hypothesis

The fundamental hypothesis of the experiment was to determine if the quarter circle/catenary track is a practical method for moving pyramid blocks. An additional goal was to measure the efficiency of such a transportation system. This baseline data would then provide a verification or refutation for the man-hour estimate made at the end of Chapter 4.

Step 2: Apparatus

The fundamental approach was to fabricate a number of quarter circles and a concrete block of the approximate size of a pyramid block. There were some practical differences from the precise materials that the Egyptians used. The quarter circles would be made from available wood, rather than cedar. The pyramid block would be formed from concrete instead of limestone. It was assumed that these variations were insignificant and that the experiment would not succeed or fail because of these differences.

CREATING THE CURVE

The first step was to generate the proper shape for the quarter circle. (At that time, the quarter circle shape had not yet been identified as a catenary.) One quarter circle will service 90 degrees of rotation. Since there are four sides to a square, four quarter circles are needed for a full 360 degree rotation of the block. The shape was created by calculating the center of mass amplitude change with the proper lateral motion in a step-wise fashion for every five degrees of rotation of the square up to 45 degrees. Forty-five degrees would provide the upward curve and because the block was to be square, the downward curve would be a mirror of that. It was assumed that these 19 points would define the shape sufficiently so that the difference from a proper curve would be small. These step-wise calculations created a series of lateral and vertical displacements for a unit-square and could be applied to any square by multiplying them by the side length of the desired square. It should be noted that the lateral steps are not the same distance even though the steps are all five degrees. These steps are shown in Figure 5-1. (Figure 5-1 also includes the values for a square block that is 45.75 inches on a side. This was the size of the block to be built and is discussed below.)

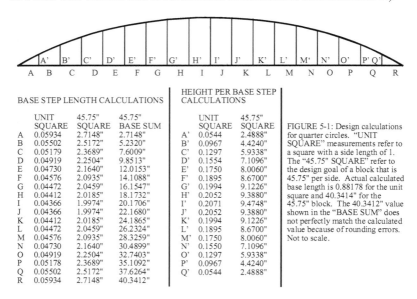

BASE STEP LENGTH CALCULATIONS

HEIGHT PER BASE STEP CALCULATIONS

	UNIT SQUARE	45.75" SQUARE	45.75" BASE SUM		UNIT SQUARE	45.75" SQUARE	
A	0.05934	2.7148"	2.7148"	A'	0.0544	2.4888"	FIGURE 5-1: Design calculations
B	0.05502	2.5172"	5.2320"	B'	0.0967	4.4240"	for quarter circles. "UNIT
C	0.05179	2.3689"	7.6009"	C'	0.1297	5.9338"	SQUARE" measurements refer to
D	0.04919	2.2504"	9.8513"	D'	0.1554	7.1096"	a square with a side length of 1.
E	0.04730	2.1640"	12.0153"	E'	0.1750	8.0060"	The "45.75 SQUARE" refer to
F	0.04576	2.0935"	14.1088"	F'	0.1895	8.6700"	the design goal of a block that is
G	0.04472	2.0459"	16.1547"	G'	0.1994	9.1226"	45.75" per side. Actual calculated
H	0.04412	2.0185"	18.1732"	H'	0.2052	9.3880"	base length is 0.88178 for the unit
I	0.04366	1.9974"	20.1706"	I'	0.2071	9.4748"	square and 40.3414" for the
J	0.04366	1.9974"	22.1680"	J'	0.2052	9.3880"	45.75" block. The 40.3412" value
K	0.04412	2.0185"	24.1865"	K'	0.1994	9.1226"	shown in the "BASE SUM" does
L	0.04472	2.0459"	26.2324"	L'	0.1895	8.6700"	not perfectly match the calculated
M	0.04576	2.0935"	28.3259"	M'	0.1750	8.0060"	value because of rounding errors.
N	0.04730	2.1640"	30.4899"	N'	0.1550	7.1096"	Not to scale.
O	0.04919	2.2504"	32.7403"	O'	0.1297	5.9338"	
P	0.05178	2.3689"	35.1092"	P'	0.0967	4.4240"	
Q	0.05502	2.5172"	37.6264"	Q'	0.0544	2.4888"	
R	0.05934	2.7148"	40.3412"				

Preliminary Quarter-Circle Evaluation

The dimensions specified in Figure 1 were transferred manually to plain paper and cut out to form a template. This was used to manually fabricate a single curve out of 5/8" thick particle board with a band saw. This material was chosen because it has no grain and is dimensionally stable (for wood). A 45.75 inch square was manually cut from ½-inch-thick rigid foam insulating material with a razor-knife. In the center of the insulation an ordinary pen was pressed through so that just the tip protruded from the other side. Before the quarter circle was fixed in place and the square was set to roll over it, paper was positioned in such a manner that the pen tip would leave a mark on the paper. The square was manually rotated over the quarter circle and the mark left on the paper was extremely close to a perfectly straight line. The deviation from a straight line was approximately +/- 1/16 of an inch. This error was certainly well within the expected error of the test (manual rotation, center of the square error, error in fabricating the quarter circle, etc.) Therefore, it was concluded that the quarter circle calculations were correct.

FABRICATING A BLOCK

It is critical that the quarter circle and block match precisely. Because working with concrete is more difficult than working with wood, it was decided to define the block first and then build quarter circles to match the block (in case the as-built dimensions of the block varied from the desired size).

The block was to approximate the size of an average pyramid block, or about 48 inches by 48 inches by 30 inches, and was to weigh about 5,000 pounds. Plywood was selected for the concrete form. The procedure chosen to fabricate the square, with bracing, did not allow the full size of the plywood (48 inches) to be employed, reducing the square's internal size to 45.75 inches. (This size was anticipated in the preliminary test above.) The thickness of the block was chosen to be about 24 inches, also for the sake of convenience. This would reduce the block's weight somewhat, to something over 4000 pounds — still heavy enough to provide adequate experimental results.

One significant concern with using concrete is that the weight of the wet cement can exert considerable pressure at the base of the mold. This pressure could easily deform the straight sides of the square or push out the bottom. This would result in curved sides and sides that were not perpendicular with the top and bottom. Obviously, this had to be avoided. (This was not a problem for the Egyptians because they were cutting blocks out of solid rock, not pouring cement.)

The technique employed to eliminate this problem was to use pre-cast concrete blocks for a significant part of the block. In this way extremely little wet cement came in contact with the wooden form. The blocks have the strength to keep the proper shape and are about 10 inches deep by 16 inches wide by 8 inches tall with large vertical holes. These blocks are commonly available and are typically used for concrete walls in buildings and sometimes used for basement walls in houses. These blocks were placed in a layer on the bottom a few inches apart with the holes oriented vertically. Cement was poured up to the top of the blocks and into their holes. Another layer of pre-cast blocks was then placed on top of the first layer but with the holes offset to create an interlocking structure. More cement was applied (well before the first cement application had started to set). A third layer of blocks was then added with another cement pour. The cement was allowed to harden for several days and the form was removed.

BLOCK SPECIFICATIONS

The resultant block was very square with flat sides that were visually perpendicular to the top and bottom. Measurements with a builder's square showed a small variation from true squareness estimated at about 1 to 2 degrees at most.

There were also small imperfections in flatness of about an eighth of an inch or so. The length of the square sides was very close to the desired 45.75 inches. These length variations were only about +/- 0.25 inches, maximum. The thickness of the block was about 24 inches with a peak in the middle of the top where extra, left-over cement was added. Since this side is not in contact with the quarter circles, this side's shape was not important. Overall, the block was very close to the intended size and shape.

The weight of the block was determined by weighing the materials that were used to build it. It was assumed that bags of cement were actually 80 pounds each, as labeled by the producer. Added water was taken to be eight pounds per gallon and the amount of water used was estimated by the specifications on the cement bag, which were followed in mixing the cement. Different types of pre-cast concrete blocks were used (corners, runners, half-blocks). A sample of each type was weighed and this weight was applied to the number of blocks used. Added water to wet the blocks before applying the cement was not included. The cement coating that remained in the mixing pan was ignored. (All possible cement was removed from the pan. It was up-ended over the form and well-scraped.) The measured volume of the block (using 45.75 inches per side and a height of 24 inches) was 29.07 cubic feet. The measured weight of the materials was 4200 pounds. Typical concrete weighs about 2400 kilograms per cubic meter (Portland Cement Association 2006) which corresponds to about 145 pounds per cubic foot. Using this typical value and the actual size of the block provides a second estimate of the block weight of 4215 pounds. Thus the 4200 pound measured weight of the block is independently verified by its volume.

BUILDING THE QUARTER CIRCLES

Initially, old railroad ties were selected to be used for the quarter circles. These are made from a hard, dense wood (often oak) that was expected to make reliable, solid quarter circles. Unfortunately, working this wood proved to be very difficult. It was too big and heavy for the band saw available. Additionally, there were stones embedded in the wood. This created safety concerns. A chainsaw was also considered, however it was not felt that the necessary precision could be obtained with a chainsaw. Safety was again an issue.

For these reasons ordinary dimensional lumber (kiln-dried pine) was used for constructing the quarter circles. Figure 5-2 shows the basic construction approach. Three pieces of ordinary 2" x 10" lumber were cut and covered with 9/16" plywood to form a single quarter circle. (Note that the actual dimensions of the 2" by 10" board are 1.5" by 9.25".) The width of the quarter circle is about 8" and was chosen somewhat arbitrarily. It was found that the plywood had enough flexibility to bend to the curve without much difficulty. Three rows of annular-ring nails (ridged steel nails, often used for gypsum wall board) 1.5 inches long were used (one row per 2" by 10" quarter circle shape) and spaced about 6 inches apart. These nails were chosen primarily because they have a very thin head (about 0.05") when compared to ordinary nails. The weight of a single complete quarter circle was about 23 pounds.

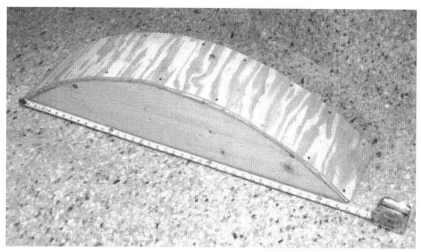

Figure 5-2: Quarter circles were built with common lumber. Only two rows of nails are shown.

It was possible to use five pieces of lumber, side-by-side, to create a "solid" quarter circle and eliminate the plywood covering. However this was felt to be wasteful of materials. Even the third/middle piece was probably not necessary but was included to be conservative and to increase safety.

Ten quarter circles were built. This would provide a track of about 16.75 feet in length using two parallel quarter circles for stability (as described previously). This would allow a full 360 degree rotation of the block with some extra margin.

Step 3: Experimentation

With the experimental components fabricated, the testing could proceed. It was late November of 2003.

The selected site was a section of a parking area that appeared flat. This section was concrete (5 inches thick with wire reinforcement) and was known to have supported very heavy vehicles in the past without difficulties.

First Tests

The quarter circles were placed in two parallel tracks about eight inches apart. The tracks themselves consisted of five quarter circles abutted to each other. The block was slowly and carefully rotated onto the first set of quarter circles. Two problems were noted very quickly.

The first problem was that the quarter circles moved too easily. The light weight of the dry lumber and the flatness of the concrete made them very easy to dislodge from their position. It proved impossible to maintain their proper position while maneuvering the block. There was not enough friction between the smooth concrete surface and the smooth dimensional lumber to hold them in place.

The second problem was that the block slipped on the plywood covering the quarter circles. Again, the smooth concrete of the block and the smooth plywood covering did not provide enough friction for them to hold together during the rotation.

Modifications

The first modification was to mount the quarter circles on a dimensional lumber receiving plate (2" by 10" by 8 feet). This was accomplished with screws (to "tack" the quarter circles in place) and with 1/2 inch steel pins that were inserted through the bottom of the plate. Two pins were used for each side for a total of four pins per quarter circle. This resulted in four sections of track, each eight feet long. These were to be connected together to form two independent tracks of 16 feet. Note that a quarter circle overlapped the receiving plates such that two pins were in one plate and two pins were in the other plate. This, and metal screw plates, held the receiving plates together to form a single track.

Additionally, two "starter" quarter circles were added to aid in aligning the block (one for each track). These were partial quarter circles and consisted of only about the first foot of a quarter circle curve and were abutted to the beginning of the first whole quarter circle. This created a "V" where the corner of the block could be placed without concern of the block shifting position at the beginning of the test. These starter quarter circles were fabricated from three pieces of 2-inch lumber sandwiched together. Two ½-inch pins per starter were used to hold them in place on the receiving plate.

In order to eliminate the slipping between the block and the plywood covering of the quarter circles, a rubberized roofing material was bonded to the plywood. This material was mineral-covered, like an asphalt shingle, and was known to offer high friction. The material itself was only about 1/16" thick. The thickness was a concern because it would change the dimensions of the quarter circle. However, 1/16" was considered to be within the range of tolerance. Additionally, it was suspected that the weight of the block would flatten the rubberized material as it rolled over it. This would mean that the dimensions of the quarter circle would not be affected very much. However the rolling resistance would probably be increased by some undetermined amount. Nevertheless, this solution appeared to be the best choice.

The rubberized roofing material was pre-glued on one side (covered by release paper). Since this glue alone perhaps might not be sufficient to maintain the proper positioning of the material as the block rolled over it, contact cement was also applied to both the plywood and the already pre-glued side of the roofing material. Additionally, the material was nailed to the quarter circle with three rows of 1.5 inch annular-ring nails spaced about three inches apart that penetrated through the plywood and into the dimensional lumber underneath.

It was felt that these changes were reasonable compared to the setting that the ancient Egyptians addressed. Their quarter circles were solid pieces of wood, that were not kiln-dried; thus they were far heavier. Nor was this wood finished to a very smooth surface. There would be no need to do this. In fact, it has been seen that a smooth surface is not useful. Quarried stone blocks would not be as smooth as a cast concrete block. The Egyptian quarter circles would be placed on a roadway or bed that would be designed to maintain their position. Even when used on the pyramid proper, the much heavier quarter circles would be resting on rough, quarried blocks which would provide significantly more friction than smooth, finished wood on smooth, finished concrete.

Second Tests

A second test was performed with the modified quarter-circle tracks. This became a valuable learning experience.

Note that all tests were video-taped and performed by a single 52-year-old man weighing about 135 pounds. The block was maneuvered into the starting position with a hydraulic jack and fulcrum blocks and great care. However, the 4200 pound block resting on a corner between a full quarter circle and "starter" quarter circle did not appear to be a safe position. It was therefore pushed so that it was resting on top of the first full quarter circle, with the bottom of the block parallel with the ground. This looked much more stable. It was noted that this was hard to do, but clearly manageable by a single person. The block rested there for a few minutes while safety checks were made of the track. The block was then pushed again. There was apparently some twisting of the block because as the corner dropped into the next "V" between the quarter circles, it bound up due to a slight change of the block's orientation. Further movement of the block was not possible by a single unaided person and a large iron pry was employed to re-align the block.

This re-alignment resulted in the block being positioned on a corner between the first two sets of full quarter circles. It was again pushed and the block rotated properly. However, the rotation could not be maintained. This was partly due to the necessity of standing on the quarter circles to push because the space between them was too small for the convenient placement of the feet. After several stop-and-go rotations the block reached the "V" between the last two quarter circles and was stopped, resting on a corner.

It is important to note that a single person moved a 4200 pound block over stabilized quarter circle track on the very first session.

The modifications to the quarter circles were shown to be adequate. There was no slippage of the block on the quarter circle and the tracks were stable. The weight of the block held the receiving plates firmly to the concrete.

Another test was performed moving the block back over the quarter circles. In this case, the helpful experience of walking on the quarter circles became apparent. The block was moved in one continuous motion a full 360 degrees past the starter quarter circles and onto the holding platform. The total time required from a stationary position to the end of the test was about 12 seconds. Additionally, the block was accelerating in the second half of the test. Figures 5-3 to 5-6 are still frames taken from the video tape of the test.

There were some notable points. The first is that resting the block on the top of a quarter circle may appear more stable than resting it on a corner between the "V" of the quarter circles but, of course, it really isn't. Because there is no center of mass amplitude variation during the rotation, any position is equally stable and safe (or unsafe). However, there is a drawback to resting the block on top. The problem occurs when starting to push the block. If the force is applied off center the block can twist and bind in the next "V". This was seen in the first part of the test. However, by starting the block in a "V", the block is forced to maintain the proper registration, at least at the start.

Walking on the quarter circles is awkward but did not require much time to learn. The test block was fairly narrow, only 24 inches wide. Making the block wider would provide more space between the tracks, which could allow a person to walk on the ground instead. However, at certain points of the rotation, the downward angle of the quarter circle provided an excellent platform for exerting pressure to the block. Although the opposite happened at other points of rotation, this was a clear benefit because it is easier to push in bursts with good footing than continuously while walking. It was also seen that once the block began to rotate, it maintained that rotation with less effort. This was noted by the acceleration of the block during the second half of the second test.

Public Demonstration

At this point it was felt that a public demonstration was needed to provide credibility and an unbiased confirmation of the technique. A press conference was announced and interested persons were invited to the demonstration on Friday, December 5, 2003. Approximately a dozen people were present including members of the press representing The Buffalo News, The Amherst Bee and WIVB TV (CBS Buffalo affiliate).

Prior to the demonstration the block was set in place at the starter "V". However, it was decided to add a bit of drama to the test by rolling the block completely off the quarter circles and onto a wooden pallet. To make this convenient, the block was rolled to the other end of the track as the starting position. This was done slowly and single-handedly and without any difficulty. It seemed much easier than the previous time (perhaps the rubberized covering was flatter because of the previous passages). The block was parked in the "V" between the last two full quarter circles for about two hours before the demonstration began. (Note that the two parallel tracks were independent of each other. They were not cross-connected.)

After about 20 minutes of introduction and background information, the demonstration was performed. There was a subtle but significant difference in the procedure when compared to the previous test that was not apparent until later. The public demonstration was successful. The block was moved from a stationary position, over about 15 feet of track, in about 9 seconds. This was a full 3 seconds faster than the previous test, which was a significant improvement. Additionally, the block was much easier to move and it was accelerated throughout the whole demonstration. The block rotated off the "starter" quarter circle and landed in the pallet with a satisfying crash. (It should be noted that one 2" x 3" member of the hardwood pallet was cut in two by the point of the block.) The track was much too short to determine what the maximum obtainable speed of the block could be. The results of the demonstration were published in the *Buffalo News* on Saturday, December 6 (Elmer Ploetz), *The Amherst Bee* on Wednesday, December 10 (Jodi Sokolowski) and broadcast on WIVB on Friday, December 5 (Mylous Hairston).

The difference in the tests was not realized until well after the demonstration had been performed and the video reviewed. The difference was ergonomic.

Figure 5-3: Maximum leg power is applied at this point. Note very good ergonomic position.

Figure 5-4: Both arm strength and weight is used here. Block approaches horizontal.

Figure 5-5: Block is horizontal. Pushing while moving to the next set of quarter circles provides little power.

Figure 5-6: Block nears figure 5-3 position. No more power is applied until the corner comes up into position.

In the first tests, the block was initially pushed to rotate it. In the demonstration, the block was lifted to start the rotation. Pushing the block required the worker's body to be at a significant angle to the ground to get good leverage. This was awkward and stressed the back.

However, if the worker stood close to the block at the start, the corner could be lifted much more efficiently. In fact, the ergonomics of that position closely resembles that of a weight-lifter's position. Instead of putting stress on the back, the legs were used to provide the lifting power. This provided more power and less body strain simultaneously. It is difficult to see how to ergonomically improve such starting conditions. This suggests that the size of the block may have been chosen for that very reason. Also, as noted above, it was quickly, and unconsciously, learned that standing on certain positions of the quarter circles provided excellent body position to exert the most force in the most efficient manner.

Step 4: Analysis of the Experimental Results

Fundamentally, it was shown that a single 52-year-old man weighing about 135 pounds could move a 4200 pound concrete block about 15 feet over wooden quarter circles in about 9 seconds from a stationary starting position. At the start, full exertion was necessary for less than a second to get the block moving. However, once it was rolling, less effort was needed to accelerate the block along the length of the track. At the end of the public demonstration, it was beginning to be difficult just to keep up with the block while walking over the quarter circles. The total physical exertion for the block movement was negligible; it was roughly equivalent to jogging for about 20 seconds. It may not be possible to provide this level of energy indefinitely (one cannot jog indefinitely) but it was clearly not a problem in the short term. (The work output per person will be discussed in more detail in a later chapter.)

Moving the block 15 feet in 9 seconds corresponds to 1.67 feet per second as an average speed over that distance. However, the block was accelerating from a stationary position. This means that the maximum speed achieved was in excess of 1.67 feet per second. There was no direct measure of the final speed of the block, but it can be estimated. If it is assumed that the acceleration was constant the final (maximum) speed of the block was exactly double the average speed or 3.3 feet per second or about 2.25 miles per hour. (The assumption of constant acceleration was based on the observation of the video.) It is also useful to note that virtually no practice was used to achieve this speed. It seems reasonable to suggest that more practice would improve performance. This is especially true for learning to move faster over the quarter circles. It is also important to note that the short track length did not allow for the block to reach the final maximum speed. It was still accelerating as the track ended.

Nevertheless, the observed average speed and calculated maximum speed can be compared to the estimates provided in Chapter 4. In Chapter 4 it was stated that the quarter circle should be so efficient that: "The quarter-circle method should allow a single worker to move a block at about 2 feet per second." This was observed. The average speed over the track was 1.67 feet per second with the maximum speed being considerably more. "The conservative estimate is that three workers will require twenty minutes to roll one block 1500 feet." This corresponds to the very slow rate of 1.25 feet per second. If one person can roll a block at 1.67 feet per second (average speed), surely three people can perform the same task in 36% more time. It is seen that the initial estimate (made before the experiment was performed) was accurate and that the "conservative estimate" was indeed extremely conservative.

The walking speed for an average person is four feet per second (TranSafety, 1997). It was stated that three workers should be able to roll a block at about walking speed (Fonte, 2000). This statement was met with significant skepticism, as noted at the start of the chapter. However it is seen that the maximum speed (calculated) achieved by a single man was 3.3 feet per second over a very short track. It is plainly reasonable to suggest that three times as many workers could improve the rolling speed of a block by a mere 21% over a long track.

Step 5: Discussion

In the experiment, the shape was referred to as a quarter circle rather than a catenary. The reason for this is because the relationship to catenary was not known at that time. The catenary shape is that of a hypercosine and is actually a fairly common family of curves. A rope or chain suspended between two equally high points above the ground (e.g. a clothesline) creates a catenary shape. Technically, the rope, chain or cable should be completely flaccid, with no support added by that material. In practice, everything creates some support. Therefore if the cable is long, when compared to its thickness, and reasonably flexible, the catenary shape is more closely approximated. Changing the tension changes the angles but not the catenary shape. The main cables of a suspension bridge are catenaries. Hanging power lines have the catenary shape. The St. Louis Arch is an inverted catenary. The equation for the catenary curve/hypercosine function is: $\cosh z = 1/2 \, (e^z + e^{-z})$ (Weisstein 2005).

As noted previously, the catenary road has many useful features. Two of the more subtle and useful features are that it allows the blocks to be moved over the pyramid itself with little difficulty and also that the road itself can be moved very easily. This became much more apparent during the experiment. Moving the road was simple and efficient. All that was required was for one person to pick up a quarter circle and move it to a new location. If the new roadway was close to the old roadway (which was exactly the scenario on the pyramid itself) this operation literally takes just seconds per quarter circle.

This suggestion needs clarification. Suppose it takes a person 15 seconds to pick up one quarter circle and move it over about 4 feet for the next row of pyramid blocks. How long will it take to move a whole roadway? (Note that 15 seconds is a very conservative value. The author performed this operation slowly and it required less than 8 seconds to complete.) With a pyramid about 765 feet long and the quarter circles about 3.6 feet long, there are about 424 quarter circles in a road spanning the whole length of the pyramid. At 15 seconds per quarter circle that comes to 6360 seconds, or less than two man-hours (3600 seconds per hour) to reposition a road that is about 1/7 of a mile long. This converts to about 12 man-hours per mile of road. This value is simply astounding. One mile of quarter circle road can be repositioned/rebuilt by a single person in a single day! Again, the efficiency of the quarter circle road cannot be overstated. And again, the genius of the ancient Egyptians cannot be overlooked.

Block Moving Scenario

It is now possible to describe a likely method for moving the blocks from the quarry to the pyramid as well as moving the blocks on the pyramid itself. The lifting of the blocks to the proper layer of the pyramid is discussed in the next chapter and the quarrying of the blocks is presented in a later chapter. The discussion will be limited to the lateral movement of the blocks from the quarry to their proper position on the pyramid.

Gross Movements

At this point the gross movement of the blocks is fairly well defined. They move from the quarry on a semi-permanent quarter circle road to the pyramid. Once on the pyramid, they move again on a quarter circle road. However much of this road is temporary, servicing only one row of blocks. For the next row of blocks, the road must be displaced an appropriate amount that corresponds to a standard block or about four feet. Since the pyramid is square, the road will incorporate crossed quarter circles to allow the road to change direction by ninety degrees (see Chapter 4).

A reasonable road design is shown in Figure 5-7 (other designs are certainly possible). There are a number of feeders in the quarry that supply blocks to the main collection road that intersects with the semi-permanent road that goes to the pyramid. This quarry-to-pyramid road terminates at the main distribution road on the pyramid. From here the blocks are moved to their proper location on the pyramid via the supply road(s). The pyramid distribution road is moved every time a new course is built. The pyramid supply roads are moved every time a row is completed.

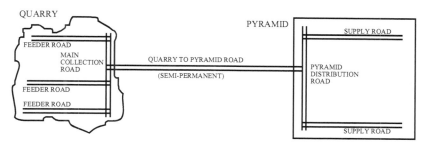

FIGURE 5-7: A suggested site design for quarter-circle roads. Blocks are quarried and placed on feeder roads to the main collection road. From there they travel over the quarry to the pyramid. At that point, the blocks are moved over the pyramid proper to their appropriate location via the pyramid distribution road and supply road. All roads except the quarry to pyramid road are moveable.

The collection road in the quarry may or may not be semi-permanent. That depends upon a number of factors and choices. The quarry feeder roads must be moveable in a manner similar to the on-pyramid roads. This is because the quarry changes its size and shape as the pyramid grows. The roads must be placed close to the point where the blocks are first cut away from the bedrock. Otherwise the efficiency of the quarter circle road is lost.

It is useful to estimate the volume of traffic on the main quarry- to-pyramid road to determine if a single road is adequate. The number of blocks is already defined to be about 2.5 million. The construction calendar time has not yet been derived. Therefore we will presume that the pyramid is built in the shortest possible time, or one year. A one-year construction time-frame means that about 6850 blocks will have to be moved along the road every day. This corresponds to 570 per daylight hour or about 10 per minute, or one every six seconds. If the speed of a block is four feet per second (walking speed) then the on-center spacing between blocks (and workers pushing them) becomes about 24 feet (6 seconds times 4 feet per second). If the blocks are four feet and the people require four more feet of space to push (for a total of eight feet), there will still be 16 feet between a block and the feet of the workers pushing the next block ahead. However, if the stated conservative rate of 1.25 feet per second is used, the spacing becomes only 7.5 feet and there is not enough space on the road to service the traffic volume and a second road must be built.

Realistically, a single main road is probably adequate. If it is assumed that four calendar years are needed to build the Great Pyramid, then only about 142 blocks per hour are needed. This corresponds to about 2.4 blocks per minute or about one block every 25 seconds. This provides an on-center spacing of 100 feet if the block speed is a reasonable four feet per second. If the conservative 1.25 feet per second speed is used, than the spacing becomes 31 feet. This indicates that only a single quarry-to-pyramid road is necessary. Of course, that does not mean that the Egyptians didn't choose to use two or more roads. It has been shown how easy and efficient these roads are to build. It means that from an engineering standpoint, a single road is sufficient to service the expected traffic.

FINE MOVEMENT

A number of issues arise when considering the fine movement of the blocks. The basic problem is that the base of a quarter circle is about 88% of the length of a block's side, or about 5.5" over the four foot length of a typical pyramid block. This creates minor positional alignment errors of +/- 0.5 blocks or about +/- two feet (worst case). This error occurs during the loading of a block on a quarter circle road, when a block is placed in its final position on the pyramid, and in the placement of distribution and collection roads. While this error averages only 8 feet per block over 1500 feet, or about 0.5%, it means that the manual movement of blocks without the quarter circles is necessary. It also translates to about 3800 miles for 2.5 million blocks. So while this error is insignificant when compared to the traditional pyramid construction methods, it becomes more important when highly efficient methods are used.

It appears easier to work backwards from the final placement of the block to loading the block onto the road. Once the block reaches the end of the road, it is on its edge and must be tipped over on its side. This action is trivial. A very simple method to accomplish this is to position a small tipping stone (about 6 inches high) such that as the pyramid block rotates off the end of the road it falls onto this stone. By placing this stone on one side, the block will automatically tip over towards the other side.

Once this pyramid block is placed, the last set of quarter circles is removed (and off-set by one block to create a new road for the adjacent row of blocks). This means that the next block will rotate to a stop 12% too far. It can't be tipped over as it is without contacting 12% of the edge of the previous block. This is the fundamental problem with the shorter quarter circle base.

One very simple solution to this is with the use of a slide-plate. This is just a flat surface that moves over low-friction surfaces (lubricated) or perhaps rollers or smooth wooden rails. While rollers are not practical for moving blocks over large distances, they are certainly suitable for short distances. In this case the maximum error is only four feet. Since the quarter circle road elevates the block, getting the block onto this slide-plate is not a problem. It simply and automatically rotates onto it when the road ends. Then the plate is moved the short distance necessary to properly align the block and then the block is tipped off the plate. Note that this method cannot easily use the tipping stone as described above. However, the slide-plate can be made such that about a third of the block hangs off the side of the plate. This makes tipping the block much easier because a third of the weight is already off the plate. This effectively narrows the block and reduces its tipping weight by two thirds (the one third of the block that is unsupported exactly balances one third of the block that is supported).

However, this technique can be improved. It was implied above that the block stopped 12% past the proper alignment point and was moved backwards. It is not necessary to do this. Instead the block can be loaded onto the slide-plate before the proper position. This has the minor effect of changing the alignment error from +/- 0.5 blocks to +0/-1 blocks. That is, the block is stopped up to one full block-length before the final position. The advantage to this is that the block's rolling inertia can be used. Its forward speed and inertia are considerable, and its own momentum can be used to push the slide-plate. The experiment clearly showed that this momentum is substantial. It certainly appears that there is abundant inertial energy to carry the block the few feet necessary for proper alignment. This adjustment to the slide-plate technique can eliminate the manual time and effort needed for fine positioning of the block. But must the block still be tipped manually?

No. As noted earlier, a tipping block was used to force the block to tip over. A similar idea can be used here. Instead of raising one side of the block, we will lower the other side. This can be accomplished by reducing one side of the slide-plate's rails. In this way the slide-plate will tilt when it reaches this point. Additionally, because the block is moving downward, little or no energy may be required. By properly aligning this depression, the block can be made to automatically tip at exactly the proper position. Therefore, the final precise positioning of the pyramid blocks can be achieved without any additional time or effort if a simple slide-plate mechanism is employed.

A similar problem occurs when moving a block from the pyramid distribution road to a row supply road. Again the pyramid rows are not the same size as the quarter circle base. A similar slide-plate technique can be employed here but a few minor changes are required.

The technique is as follows. The block is first turned 90 degrees from the distribution road to be parallel to the supply road, using a crossed quarter circle. Then the block is rotated onto a slide-plate. This slide-plate also has quarter circles on it, so it is essentially a continuation of the road. Once the block is on the slide-plate, the assembly is moved laterally as required (+/- 0.5 blocks) to align it with the row road. Then the block is rotated off the quarter circles of the slide-plate and onto the quarter circles of the row road. The movement of the slide-plate must be performed manually. This distance is only a maximum of about two feet, over a well-lubricated device, so it should be reasonably fast and efficient.

As noted in Chapter 4, about 1,000 pounds of force are required to move a 5,000 block over a track with a sledge. If three men each employ a wooden lever with a 5:1 ratio, each man would have to provide about 67 pounds of effort on the lever. With a 6-foot-long lever, moving from 45 degrees to 90 degrees, the block can be moved about 4 inches before the levers have to be reset. Therefore about 6 leverage actions will be needed to move the block the worst-case error, or two feet. The average required movement is exactly half of this, or 3 leverage actions. A reasonable time estimate for experienced workers is probably about five seconds per leverage action. This is especially true if the slide-plate is built with sockets to receive the levers. In order to be conservative, a value of 10 seconds per leverage action will be taken. Therefore, the average time needed to manually align a slide-plate is about 1.5 man minutes (three men, three leverages each at 10 seconds per leverage).

There is one additional consideration. Because quarter circles are on top of the slide-plate, the thickness of slide-plate increases the overall height of the quarter circles. This means that the center of mass of the block must be raised this thickness. A minimum reasonable thickness of these boards is probably about an inch. This assembly will have to slide over lubricated rails/tracks. The minimum thickness of these rails/tracks is also about an inch. (Note that these rails/tracks can be wooden boards placed on existing pyramid blocks. They do not require any structural strength because they are essentially flat bearings.) Thus, the height of the slide-plate assembly is about two inches higher than the rest of the quarter circle road.

This is not a significant problem. The momentum of the block can again be employed. Simply raise the crossed quarter circle (or make the ordinary quarter circles before this into a two-inch ramp). In order to roll up such an incline without additional energy, the speed of the block must be 3.2 feet per second. Since three workers can move a block at normal walking speed of 4 feet per second (see above), this requirement is met. The block has enough forward momentum to roll up a two-inch incline without additional energy requirements. And, because the slide-plate is higher, when the block is rotated off the plate and onto the lower row road, this energy can be recovered. There is no real energy loss.

A similar slide-plate approach can be used when moving the blocks from the quarry supply road to the quarry collection road. The difference is that the block must be aligned before being moved onto the collection road. The mechanics are the same but the order of operations is reversed. The block is rolled onto a slide-plate with quarter circles and the slide-plate is aligned. Then the block is rotated onto crossed the quarter circles of the collection road and turned 90 degrees. The height difference is also present here and the solution is the same. The time required to perform the manual alignment is also the same.

Manipulating a block from the quarry onto a quarter circle road is a special case. This will be discussed in detail in the chapter on quarrying.

The slide-plate technique is clearly within the technical and conceptual abilities of the Egyptians. However, no archaeological evidence has been found or identified as yet to support the theory that they used a slide-plate device. This is also true for crossed quarter circles.

CONCLUSION

An experiment was performed using a 4200-pound concrete block of approximate pyramid size with quarter circles that were copied from artifacts found at pyramid sites. The results of the public demonstration were exactly as predicted. A single person could move the block with relative ease over a quarter-circle road. The average speed was measured at 1.67 feet per second and the calculated top speed was 3.3 feet per second. However the maximum speed possible could not be determined because the track was too short.

Additional practical information was gathered that illustrate that the quarter circle roads are even more useful than previously thought. With the addition of a simple slide-plate mechanism, the Egyptians would have had all the tools necessary for gross and fine movement in the placement of pyramid blocks. It has been determined that the use of the quarter-circle road allows movement of blocks on the pyramid proper. Fundamentally, the incorporation of quarter circles as a means of transporting blocks increases the efficiency of block movement by a fantastic amount.

CHAPTER 6. LIFTING BLOCKS

INTRODUCTION

The question of how to lift 5,000-pound blocks to a height of nearly 500 feet or about 40 stories is something that has piqued the imagination of countless people. Many theories have been proposed. Some are wildly creative. Some are mundane. And some of these will be examined in more detail in a later chapter. However, few are practical and fewer still are compatible with the technical abilities of the Egyptians and the evidence found at the pyramid sites. This chapter will address only two methods of lifting blocks: ramps and levers. The primary focus will be on Energy Management or the most efficient use of manpower.

RAMP PRINCIPLES

It is certain that ramps were used by the ancient Egyptians. It is certain because some of them are still in place. Additionally, any inclined plane can be called a ramp and there are many surviving examples of these, as well. Common sense and evidence found at the pyramid sites suggest that ramps were certainly used in pyramid building. However, the extrapolation that large ramps were used to lift the blocks to the highest levels poses some serious complications. In fact, the evidence will show that a large ramp cannot have been used for lifting at the Great Pyramid.

In terms of Energy Management ramps can be anything from very efficient to very inefficient; it depends largely upon their height. It takes energy to build ramps. Low ramps that can service many blocks for the lower courses of a pyra-mid and that are easy to fabricate are very efficient: the energy-per-block expen-diture is very small. However, a large ramp would service few blocks and would take a large amount of energy to build. The result is that the energy-per-block expenditure is enormous. This is because the geometry of a ramp is very similar to that of a pyramid in that most of the mass is located at the base.

Large ramps cannot be made with vertical side walls; they will fall over. Building a ramp with sides steeper than the Great Pyramid would be a concern to the Egyptians for two reasons. The first is ramp failure. Additionally, they would be mindful of the problems at Maidum as well as with the Bent Pyramid. The secondary concern is that if a large ramp failed it could cause significant damage and possibly ruin the pyramid. Therefore it seems unlikely that any large ramp built for the Great Pyramid would have sides of greater than 50 degrees. Yet the smaller the angle of the ramp's walls, the more material is required to build it. Steep-sided ramps are not as stable but take less material to build. This is a typical engineering trade-off: stability versus volume.

In order for the ramp to reach higher, the base must be widened. A simple way of visualizing this is to "lift" up the existing ramp and add material below it. In this way it is seen that a larger and larger volume of material is needed to raise the top of the ramp while maintaining the existing angles. As we saw with the geometry of the pyramid, the volume varies with the cube of the height (an 8:1 ratio). The same is true for a ramp. However, the number of pyramid blocks serviced by a ramp decreases by the cube of the height (assuming equally sized blocks). The result is that the efficiency of a ramp decreases by a factor 64:1 when building a pyramid. This is measured by the energy needed to build the ramp compared to the energy needed to lift the blocks.

This is more clearly seen when estimating the dimensions needed to build such a ramp. Smith (p. 164) estimates that a single long ramp to the top of the Great Pyramid would be "more than a half-mile long" and require more than "three times [the material] of the pyramid itself." A relatively short ramp that rises about 100 feet and services 50% of the blocks would incorporate 45% of the volume of the pyramid (Smith, 164). Lepre (p. 253) discusses a steeper ramp (probably not feasible) 1000 feet long that needs more than 50% of the volume of the pyramid. This adds significantly to the effort of building the pyramid. What's more, this material must be removed. At such a scale, the removal effort becomes nearly equal to the building effort. Incorporating this energy requirement for dis-assembly into the ramp-height efficiency ratio doubles it from a factor of 64:1 to a factor of 128:1 (for every doubling of the ramp height). Large ramps are simply not an energy efficient approach.

There is also the problem of the quarry size. Lehner (p. 206) states that the volume of stone removed from the quarry is calculated to be 97.5 million cubic feet. The Great Pyramid uses about 94 million cubic feet. This leaves about 3.5 million cubic feet as lost or wasted stone. But a ramp that used just 50% of the Great Pyramid's volume would require about 47 million cubic feet of additional stone, or about 44 million cubic feet more than the quarry can supply. No one to this date has explained how 141 million cubic feet of stone can be removed from a quarry that only holds 97.5 million cubic feet of stone. (This problem is significantly exacerbated if the traditional quarrying methods are used. This topic will be addressed in later chapters.) Then there is the question of where this ramp material is removed to. It seems difficult to hide or disperse a mass of stone debris that is 50% as large as the Great Pyramid.

All that aside, the efficiency of actually moving a block up a ramp can be extremely high. There is virtually no inherent energy wasted when a ramp is used. Consider a quarter-circle track on a ramp. The additional energy required to roll the block up the ramp is nearly identical to the actual increase in potential energy the block gains. This is because the rolling friction has already been accounted for. The lifting energy is nearly 100% efficient. No other method can match this. Simple mechanical lifting machines, like levers, can be expected to lose 10% or more energy. (This energy loss will be discussed in more detail below.) The more complicated the lifting machine is, the more inefficient it becomes because there are more sources of friction and more play in the parts.

A Practical Ramp

The evidence suggests that a ramp was used for the lower five courses of the Great Pyramid. These layers are very thick when compared to the other layers. "The height of the first five courses are, respectively, 58", 45", 44", 42" and 40". But from the sixth course on the stones average 36" (sic)" and gradually decrease to a 20" height." (Lepre, 254). (Note: the actual average height of the remaining courses is calculated to be 27.294".)

This illustrates an important fact. While large ramps become inefficient by a factor of 128 as they grow in height, the reverse is also true. Ramps become more efficient by a factor of 128 as they get smaller. A ramp that services these five overly-large courses would account for 229" or about 19' of the entire pyramid. Referring to Appendix 2, it is seen that the lower 19' of the Great Pyramid contain about 13% of the entire volume of the pyramid. Additionally, every higher block can be raised by this amount before being lifted further (by another method). This ramp has the effect of shortening the pyramid by 19 feet. Recalling that the number of blocks in a pyramid varies by the cube of its height, this modest ramp is seen to be extremely energy efficient.

A simple design exercise in building a ramp for the first courses is useful. The first course (58") is placed directly on the ground so no ramp is needed. The second course needs a ramp that rises 58". Presume that the width of the ramp is 20 feet for the top-most section and that a side angle of 45 degrees is used. This makes the base-width of the ramp 58 feet wide. For numerical convenience, this width will be maintained for the full length of the ramp (others narrow the ramp at the low end). The inclination angle is fairly arbitrary. Smith (p. 163) suggests an incline of 9.5 degrees which is quite steep. Lehner (p. 215) actually built a ramp and used 4 degrees for the NOVA experiment. "Conservative highway designs attempts [*sic*] to limit grades to 6 percent or less" (Smith, 163). A 6% grade is about 3.4 degrees. Since quarter circles will be incorporated with the ramp, it is useful to keep the angle small. With too high a ramp angle, the blocks could be difficult to control. Therefore a choice of 3 degrees for the incline will be used (this is an incline of about one foot over a length of nineteen feet). A 3 degree ramp that rises 58 inches will have to be about 92 feet long and contain about 12,000 cubic feet of fill. This will service only the second course. To work on the third course, the ramp height will have to be increased by 45 inches (see Figure 6-1).

Level	Added Height	Total Height	Added length	Total length	Added Fill cu. ft.	Total Fill cu. ft.	Force Needed to Offset Gravity
1	58"	58"	92 feet	92 feet	11,798	11,798	394 lbs. (45" block)
2	45"	103"	72 feet	164 feet	21,455	33,253	386 lbs. (44" block)
3	44"	147"	70 feet	234 feet	27,167	60,420	368 lbs. (42" block)
4	42"	189"	67 feet	301 feet	28,087	88,507	349 lbs. (40" block)
5	41"	230"	65 feet	366 feet	25,642	114,149	262 lbs. (*ave. block)

Figure 6-1: The table of design characteristics for a 3 degree ramp that is 20 feet wide and has 45 degree sides. Note that the actual force needed to roll a block is one half of the value shown because of the mechanical advantage when a block is rolled (see Chapter 4). Rolling friction is not included.

*An average block is 30" tall and weighs 5,000 pounds.

The use of quarter circles can greatly enhance the building effort here. Instead of using fill for the ramp, use blocks. As shown in Figure 6-2, employing 45" blocks eliminates a substantial amount of fill. A four-foot square block that is 45" high contains 60 cubic feet of "fill." Only about 250 blocks are needed to cover the existing ramp, which is about 75% of the addition. Fill would only be required in front of these blocks. As shown, an additional fill of about 6,000 cubic feet is needed. Of course, there is no need to limit the height of the blocks to 45 inches. A half-height block could be used to eliminate even more fill. And, of course, this approach could have been used on the first part of the ramp as well (see Figure 6-2).

What emerges is a simple and efficient ramp-building process that requires a relatively small amount of fill and manpower. Rolling blocks on quarter circles has already been shown to be extremely efficient. Using this technique speeds up ramp construction significantly. (Consider the comparison of rolling several tons of fill in seconds versus hauling buckets of fill manually.) Blocks provide an extremely stable and durable ramp that requires little maintenance. It appears that solid stone blocks on solid stone bedrock would provide better support than a ramp comprised of rubble. Lastly, the disassembly of the ramp can be speeded up by rolling the blocks away on quarter circles. (Short block-filled ramps like the example can also have steeper sides.)

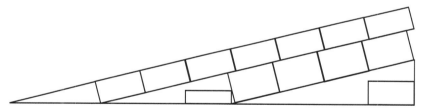

Figure 6-2: Building a ramp is very easy when blocks are used instead of fill. They are simply rolled into place with quarter circles. Fill is only needed to form the angle of the ramp. Additionally, some of this fill can be from smaller blocks rather than rubble. Not to scale.

The amount of effort needed to roll a block up such an incline can be calculated. A 3 degree incline requires about 5.25% of the object's weight to compensate for gravity. For an average 5,000 pound block this is about 264 pounds in addition to level-ground rolling requirements. However, these 45" blocks are much larger and weigh about 7500 pounds. They will require about 400 pounds of force to roll them up the incline. Is this possible?

These blocks are about 4 feet wide when placed on quarter circles. This provides enough room for three or four workers, at the most, to push the block. Generally people can push/lift with about half their weight without too much effort.

If the workers average 150 pounds in weight then only about 225 to 300 pounds of effort can be expected. However, recall the two-to-one mechanical advantage obtained when pushing a wheel (Chapter 4). This means that the additional rolling effort appears to be only 200 pounds. Thus three or four workers can supply enough power to push these overly large blocks up a 3-degree incline. Of course, a shallower ramp can be employed to reduce the effort required. The important consideration is that this method is possible and practical. What's more, by applying reasonable ramp design criteria a reasonable amount of manual exertion is calculated for the observed/measured block size. It seems unlikely that this is a coincidence.

Nor is this effort continuous. The ramp is a fraction of the whole road. At the worst case the ramp is 366 feet, or about a quarter of the total length of 1500 feet. If a speed of one half of normal walking speed is assumed (or 2 feet per second), then it will take about 3 minutes to push the block up the ramp on quarter circles. (This additional time is lifting time and not transportation time.) Also note that this value is slightly inflated. The lower-level blocks will not have to be pushed up the full length of the ramp because the ramp is shorter for these courses. In order to come up with a conservative estimate, the worst-case value is used for all courses.

In order to compare this to other lifting methods, this value must be standardized. The standard used here is the man-hours needed to lift an average block the average height. An average block must be lifted just about 100 feet (Chapter 1). Since the ramp is only 19 feet high, the ramp time must be calculated for 100 feet, a factor of 5.26. This time comes to 16 minutes. If four workers are needed to roll the block up the ramp, then the total lifting time is 1.05 man-hours for an average block the average height (0.79 man-hours if three workers are used).

This value is incredibly small. Referring again to Smith (p. 172), who suggests that 14 men can move a block on a sledge up a ramp at 10 feet per minute (0.17 feet per second), or Lehner (p. 209) who requires 20 men to do the same, we see a startling comparison. Traversing just the 366 feet of the ramp takes Smith 8.54 man-hours, or 12.2 man-hours for Lehner. Standardizing these values for the average block, lifted the average height, gives 44.9 man-hours for Smith's estimate and 63.56 man-hours for Lehner's. This is a factor of about 50 times the time needed for the ramp/quarter circle combination.

SIMPLE LIFTING MACHINES

The simplest lifting machine is the lever. It is something everyone has used and is familiar with. It is natural to consider a lever as a first choice for lifting the blocks. However, ordinary levers do not help much when lifting pyramid blocks. Lehner (p. 209) tried and abandoned simple levers. The fundamental problems he had were that he could lift only one side of the block at a time, so the stone had to be "rocked" and supported in many steps; the fulcrums had to move upward as the block was lifted; and the long levers created work-space problems. Besides these practical problems he cites safety concerns as well. However, Lehner is an archaeologist and not an engineer. His approach was to take some wood and give it a try. This is not the proper engineering technique. (In a future chapter we will examine other proposed lifting machines.)

The typical engineering method is to design a machine according to a set of specifications. In this case the specifications are rather clear. The lifting machine must: 1) lift at least 5,000 pounds (an average block) 2.5 feet (one average course), 2) be able to lift to the course above the base of the machine, 3) be simple in terms of operation and construction, 4) be efficient, 5) be safe and ergonomically sound.

There is a simple lever design that has the potential for meeting these requirements. The structure uses a raised fulcrum. The basic design is shown in Figure 6-3. It consists of a simple but stable wooden frame that holds a cross-piece. This crosspiece is the fulcrum for the lever. The lever rests on this fulcrum and raises the block from the top, rather than from the bottom (as Lehner attempted). The lever has the potential to lift 5,000 pounds to the course above the one that the base is on. It is simple, safe and should be quite efficient. The question is whether it is a practical approach. The method for determining this is a fairly straightforward engineering problem.

DESIGNING A PRACTICAL RAISED FULCRUM LIFTING MACHINE

Engineering is often accomplished by a somewhat step-wise, trial and error approach. Usually, an idea is proposed and a design is created. This design is often nothing more than a set of calculations. These calculations can show flaws in the approach. These flaws are then addressed with a new and improved design. Then this new design is analyzed numerically. If flaws are again found, then another design is made. Generally it quickly becomes apparent if the basic idea is valid. If the revisions to the design clearly result in better performance, then the idea is probably a good one. If the revisions cause worse problems or more problems, then the idea is probably not useable. At this point, it will be assumed that a suitable frame to hold the suspended fulcrum is available. The analysis will only examine the physical requirements of lever itself.

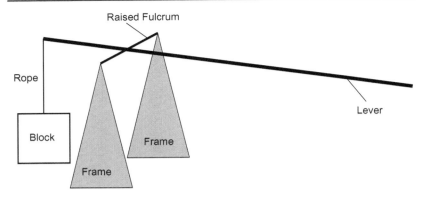

Figure 6-3: The basic concept of a raised fulcrum lever. The lever is above the weight rather than below it.

The first design approach is to design a suspended lever such that a single person can lift a 5,000 pound block 2.5 feet. The angular movement of the lever will be chosen to be 90 degrees (+45 degrees above horizontal to -45 degrees below horizontal). This has the convenient characteristic that the starting and finishing positions are exactly vertical. This means that the minimum length of the block-side of the lever must be 1.77 feet.

Archimedes' celebrated quotation, "Give me a place to stand and I will move the earth," seems to be an appropriate first step. What are the physical characteristics of a lever that allows a single person to lift a 5,000 pound block 2.5 feet? Assuming that the person weighs 150 pounds, it follows that the person-side of the lever must be 33.3 times the length of the block-side (thus generating equal foot-pound ratios). Since the block-side is fixed at 1.77 feet, the person-side must be just about 60 feet long. It also means that the fulcrum must be positioned about 41 feet off the ground for the needed angular movement. Obviously, this is an impractical design. However, it provides information on how to improve the design.

A practical lever must be significantly shorter. Additionally, people pulling on a rope cannot be expected to exert more than about one-half of their weight for extended periods of time. Quite simply, human arms weren't designed to do that. Therefore, ten people will be employed to pull down on the lever for this design iteration. Ten people weighing 150 pounds each can exert 750 pounds of force with their arms. This allows for the person-side of the lever to be reduced to 6.67 times the length of the block-side, or 11.8 feet. It also allows the fulcrum to be raised only 8.34 feet off the ground. Clearly, this is a far more practical design.

The number of people is reasonable, the size of the lever is reasonable and the height of the support frame is also reasonable.

The lifting time for an average block can be roughly estimated. Coordinating the efforts of ten people is somewhat involved. There will have to be multiple ropes and places for the workers to stand, for example. Presume that it takes five minutes for ten people to lift one block. This corresponds to 50 man-minutes per 2.5 feet or 33.3 man-hours (2000 man-minutes) to raise an average block the average height. This is better that Smith's estimate of 44.9 man-hours and Lehner's estimate of 63.56 man-hours (above), but not remarkably so. Can this method be refined to provide a more efficient lever?

The two main problems with this design are the need for many people to coordinate their efforts and the limitation of using 50% of the weight for the workers' arm strength. In theory, the weight of five workers would balance the weight of the block. For the next iteration, two major changes will be made: only three workers will be used and the lift height will be decreased by 50% to one-half a course (or 1.25 feet). This reduces the block-side lever length by 50% (to 0.885 feet) and reduces the person-side lever length to 9.83 feet. However this approach also requires the full weight of the workers to offset the weight of the block. This is done by having the workers climb up a ladder and "stand" on the lever. They won't actually stand on the end of the lever; however, they could certainly employ rope foot-loops and lie across the lever (many other variations are also possible). This approach also requires two lever actions to raise the block a full course. After the first action, the block must be supported at the present height and the lever reset and the rope adjusted for the new length. Then the workers must climb up the ladder again and transfer their weight to the lever. This is somewhat like a two-step jack.

Initially, this seems to be overly complex. However, it uses leg muscles to climb rather than arm muscles to pull. Additionally, only three workers are needed to perform the task. Therefore, there is the potential for much better coordination and a corresponding time savings. A Time-Motion Analysis of this procedure was performed (Appendix 3) and the results were surprising. Using very conservative values, it was found that three workers could perform both lever actions in just under three minutes. This corresponds to nine man-minutes per course or only six man-hours (360 man-minutes) per average block raised to the average height. Recall that Smith requires 7.5 times this value and Lehner needs 10.6 times this value. (Note: an important point in this time-motion analysis was the fact that the quarter-circle road allows lifting ropes to be easily passed under the block.) The use of three workers as a counterweight appears to be the most efficient number. Curiously, this matches the use of three workers to roll a block.

LEVER DETAILS

The lever above is a "perfect" design. There is no accounting for friction or other practical considerations. For example, it is expected that the lever base will be positioned one course lower than the working course. It is also assumed that all the lifting will be done on the side of the pyramid that faces the quarry. The lever itself will be parallel to the side of the course. This allows the block to be rolled up to the lower course and attached to the lever. The lever lifts the block and it continues on a straight line one course higher. The lever frame must provide a clear path for the block to be moved into the lifting position and also out and onto the next course. The "perfect" design does not allow this, as the legs get in the way (see Figure 6-4).

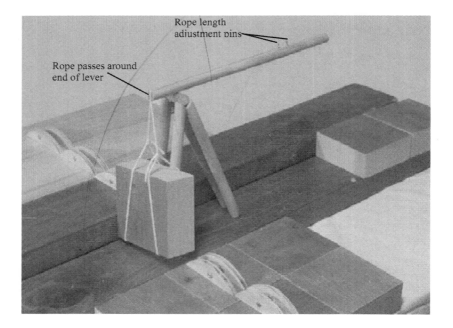

Figure 6-4: A simple model shows that the support frame legs interfere with easy block movement. Note that the lifting rope passes around the end of the lever and that two pins are used to adjust the rope length for the two lifting actions. Approximate height of the lifting machine is only about 8 feet.

The simplest solution is to use a cantilevered design. This eliminates any interference problems but it means that the frame in inherently unstable. It will tip over under load because the fulcrum extends beyond the frame base. However, all that is required is a method to hold down the legs of the frame. If the cantilevering is two feet and the full length of the frame leg is 16 feet, then there is an 8:1 weight ratio between the hold-down weight and the block weight. Since there are two legs, each leg requires only 1/16 of the block weight to stabilize it. This is only 312 pounds per leg for an "average" 5,000 pound block. This can be easily accomplished with tie-down ropes or stone weights (see Figure 6-5).

Unlike the original frame which had all the forces of the block oriented downward, the cantilevered design puts considerable lateral force on the joint where the vertical support and the cantilevered support meet. This is also not a difficult problem to overcome but it must be addressed.

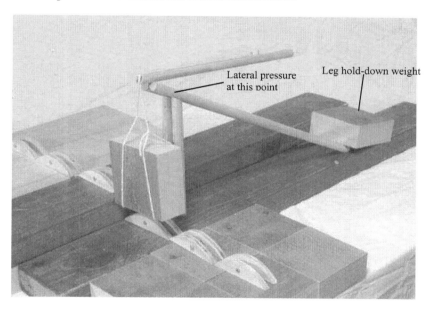

Figure 6-5: The use of a cantilevered design eliminates the interference problem between the frame legs and the block. However this design is not stable and requires a hold-down weight, as shown. (The actual hold-down weight is only 312 pounds per leg and a pyramid block is not likely to be used.) There is lateral pressure applied to the vertical support.

Another point to consider is the fulcrum. Since there is a great weight applied to the fulcrum, it cannot be a point. Presumably it will be a round piece of lumber. A diameter of about six inches appears adequate to support 5,000 pounds. If it is presumed that the lever is flat where it contacts the fulcrum, it is seen that the actual fulcrum position changes as the lever moves up and down (see Figure 6-6). This change is about 4.75 inches, which is considerable when compared to the initial block-side length of the 0.885 feet, or 10.62 inches, for the proposed lever. The lever ratio changes from about 11:1 to about 7.4:1 during operation. This means that up to 225 pounds of additional weight is needed as the load is lifted. This corresponds to an average person-side weight of 562 pounds rather than the 450 pounds initially specified. This makes the lever only 80% efficient; 20% additional weight is needed.

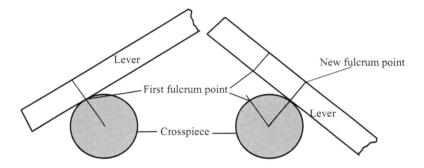

Figure 6-6: As the lever rotates over the crosspiece the fulcrum point changes position. With a very short block-end portion of the lever, this change can be significant.

This can be improved by increasing the overall length of the lever. In this way, the fulcrum change can be made smaller in relation to the whole length, thus increasing the efficiency. The block-side length will be increased to 1.0 feet. The block-side length and person-side length ratio will also be slightly increased to 12:1 to provide a greater force on the person-side. (The theoretically perfect lever above will actually balance horizontally like a scale because it would be precisely balanced.) This new ratio only requires about 417 pounds (instead of 450 pounds) to offset the 5,000 pound block and provides about 37 pounds extra, or about 8% more, than the perfect design. This is a more pragmatic lever.

The fulcrum movement remains the same because it is dependent on the diameter of the fulcrum. Thus the fulcrum changes from 12 inches to 16.75 inches measured at the block-side. The resulting ratio becomes 9.3 to 1 and the maximum weight needed is 537 pounds. The average weight needed to counterbalance the block now becomes 477 pounds, which is about 14% more than the theoretical value. This improves overall efficiency by about 30% in addition to providing a more realistic lever. (Note that this is the lever design used in the Time Motion Analysis found in Appendix 3.)

However there is another practical problem with this approach. The lever rotates over the fulcrum, and there is nothing to prevent the lever from shifting its position. This would mean that the lever would need constant re-positioning to maintain the correct registration with the fulcrum. The solution is to hold the fulcrum in place by "captivating" it (see Figure 6-7). This has the advantage of maintaining the precise lever ratio over the full 90 degrees of rotation (which eliminates the inefficiency because of the change in the fulcrum position). The disadvantage is that it exchanges very efficient rolling friction for not-so-efficient sliding friction. If the increased friction is less than the increased weight required because of the change in fulcrum position then there is a net increase in energy efficiency.

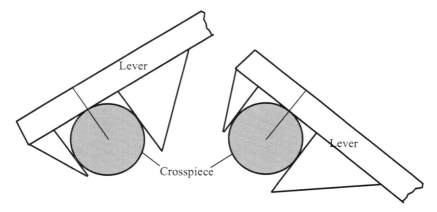

Figure 6-7: The problem with the shifting fulcrum position can be fixed by captivating the crosspiece. This can be done by adding parts to the lever. This increases friction by changing the motion from rolling to sliding. This is a primitive bearing.

This seems certain to be the best model. There is about 14% waste due to the fulcrum position change as noted above. The simplest slide bearings are much more efficient. It also must be remembered that the Egyptians understood and used lubricants (Lepre, 242). A smooth and well-lubricated wood-to-wood slide bearing should have a very low friction, requiring less than one percent of the total weight. Thus, the captive bearing approach with the new, practical lever provides about 99% efficiency or only about a 1% loss. Moreover, as designed, three workers provide 450 pounds of force where only 415 pounds is necessary. This is about 8% more than required.

To be conservative this additional weight will be maintained, making the overall efficiency of the lever about 90%. This inefficiency is not only related to weight but to height. It is always necessary to lift slightly above the desired final height. There must be sufficient clearance to maneuver the block. The 10% inefficiency includes this clearance factor.

This bearing idea can certainly evolve further. The wood-to-wood lever will cause wear mostly on the lever because that point is rubbed over the larger area of the fulcrum. This will result in a concavity forming on the lever. This will increase rapidly because of the high friction applied to a small surface area. However as the concavity increases, the area increases as well. This works to slow the rate at which the concavity grows. Eventually there will be a point where the indentation will grow extremely slowly. This is the proper size for the bearing. Seeing this, the Egyptians could have cut the lever to this shape to begin with. That is, they certainly could have designed a simple bearing from observing the wear over time.

It is also clearly evident to anyone examining friction that smooth surfaces slide better than rough surfaces. It is also clear that a copper sheet can be made very smooth. It would not be beyond the Egyptians' reach to place a smooth copper sheet on the round fulcrum. This would have had two useful effects. The first is that it would reduce the friction and increase efficiency. However, this is probably of little practical significance since friction is so low that it can be ignored. This second reason is that the bearings would last longer. The decreased friction between a metal to wood contact (well lubricated) reduces wear. The hardness of the metal also means less wear.

Thus it is seen that practical experience and considerations can drive the development of the important concept of compound bearings. This is a useful technological principle. We have no direct or indirect archaeological evidence for these bearings; but it appears that no one has looked for this evidence. As noted previously, wheels were not used in Egypt at the time of Khufu. However, if it can be shown that the ancient Egyptians understood and applied the principles of compound bearings, then it strongly suggests that they fully understood the concept of the wheel as well.

Up to this point, the weight of the lever has not been considered. However a beam of wood 13 feet long has considerable weight. Typically wood has a weight of about 75% that of water, or about 45 pounds per cubic foot. This is quite variable depending upon the water content and the type of wood. The thickness of the beam has not yet been specified. It appears that a 6 inch by 6 inch square beam is the minimum reasonable choice. This means the 12-foot-long person-side of the beam would weigh about 135 pounds. This will have to be lifted in place from above by two workers (see Time Motion Analysis, Appendix 3). Since one side of the beam is supported by the fulcrum, only one half of the weight, or 67 pounds, is presented to the workers (Chapter 4 discusses this mechanical advantage). This means that each worker must lift about 34 pounds from above. This is quite reasonable. It starts to become unreasonable when the weight becomes about a third of the body weight (50 pounds) and unacceptable at one half of the body weight (75 pounds). Additionally, this weight aids in lifting the block by providing an additional 67 pounds of downward force. Since there is no significant energy loss in raising a beam and then using that weight to help lift the block, the overall efficiency of the lever system remains at about 99%. That is, the lever could be shortened by the appropriate amount, if desired.

Note that these ergonomic estimates are based on observation and experience. For example, many construction items in use today weigh about 50 pounds and are carried by one worker fairly easily (for example, a box of nails). Heavier items such as a bundle of asphalt shingles or an 80-pound bag of cement are more difficult for one person to move on a continuous basis. The NIOSH (NTIS1994) lifting standard suggests 23 kilograms (51 pounds) for the maximum safe weight for repeated lifts with optimal body positioning that will not lead to physical damage (over time) in nearly all healthy men. The "Snook Standard" (Snook and Cirillo 1991) presents lift/carry values of about 30 kilograms (66 pounds) for average males. Therefore the generalized statements on human factors seem reasonable. It is also assumed that the average Egyptian worker of the time weighed an average of 150 pounds.

Finally there is the issue of the lifting ropes. These are the ropes that attach to the block and to the lever. The first issue is that significant rope wear will occur at the base of the block where the ropes make a 90 degree turn while under great tension. The edge of the block will act like a knife and cut the ropes quickly. A simple and easy solution is to protect the ropes with leather or to place a rounded wooden piece between the rope and the stone. Other methods work as well also. The second issue is that the rope must be shortened by 1.25 feet for the second stroke of the lever and returned to the original length for the first stroke. There is also a simple solution to this. The person-side of the rope can be made into a loop and the lever fitted with pegs (or the equivalent) so that the loop can be easily slipped over one or the other (as shown in Figures 6-4 and 6-5). This makes changing the rope length trivial and quick.

The last issue is a bit more complicated. The rope must pass around the end of the lever (refer to Figures 6-4 and 6-5). This raises the issue of rope wear again as well as the issue of rope positioning. The edge of the lever can't be square or else the rope will wear quickly. The end of the lever certainly could be rounded to eliminate this concern. However, the problem of rope positioning is worsened with this solution. It is clear that the rope could easily slide off to one side of the lever and require re-positioning. At the least, this is annoying and time consuming. At the worst, it could allow a block to fall. The first idea is to notch the wood to hold the rope in place. Unfortunately this technique cannot be used here because of the great weight applied to the rope. If the wood is notched, then it will tend to split under load. The rope will act as a wedge, pushing the grain of the wood apart. (And it is obvious that the lever must have the wood grain running parallel to its length to maintain any strength.) Therefore, the end of the lever must be rounded and protected in some manner.

Supporting Evidence

Unfortunately, unlike the quarter circles, no levers have been found or identified as such. There is some secondary evidence, however. "The ancients were fond of employing ropes and counter weights in their building projects," says Lepre (p. 254). And the Greek historian Herodotus reported: "This pyramid was made after the manner of steps, which some call "rows" and others "bases": and when they had first made it thus, they raised the remaining stones with machines made of short pieces of timber, raising them from the ground to the first stage of the steps, and when the stone got up to this it was placed upon another machine standing on the first stage, and so from this it was drawn to the second upon another machine; for as many as was the courses of the steps, so many machines there were also...." It must be noted that Herodotus visited Egypt 2000 years after the Great Pyramid was built and many of his statements are inaccurate (Lepre, 255). But this passage is a clear and precise description of the use of a raised fulcrum lever system.

However, there is a significant piece of evidence in the form of a "mystery tool" described by Lehner (pg. 211) and reproduced in wood as shown in figure 6-8. This artifact, which is made from a hard stone like granite, has been found at the pyramid sites in Giza.

Forensic Analysis of the Mystery Tool

A number of important facts can be gleaned from a close examination of the mystery tool.

1) The first apparent fact is that it must have been inserted into a wooden tool. It can't be inserted into limestone because limestone is a soft stone and the tool is a hard stone. Presuming that pressure was applied with ropes, the soft limestone would fragment and wear quickly. Nor is it likely that it would be

inserted into a hard stone. Quite simply, it would be much easier to fabricate a whole stone piece with the appropriate rounded end rather than make two separate pieces and fit them together. A single hard-stone tool would have superior characteristics as well.

Figure 6-8: The Mystery Tool. This hard stone artifact (replicated here) has been found at pyramid sites. A lot of forensic information can be gleaned from examining this. Lehner suggests that it could have been used as a "proto-pulley" (Lehner, 211); however this seems highly unlikely. Granite has a rough finish. Pulling a rope under load across such a stone would shred it quickly. It must have had a different function.

2) The grooves were for ropes. There is nothing else that the Egyptians had that would fit this.

3) The ropes were stationary. As noted above, rope cannot be pulled under load across a rough stone like granite without shredding. In theory, granite could be polished and made smooth enough for the wear to be minimized. However, there is no evidence that these stones were polished. Nor is there evidence that the Egyptians had the capability to polish hard stones to the required finish. If they needed something that smooth, they did have the capability to employ smooth copper. Using copper would certainly be easier than trying to polish granite. Since copper was not employed it can be inferred that a smooth finish was not required.

4) The tool was used under a great load. There is no need to use a hard stone if the load is light. Wood is capable of enduring considerable pressure. Wood is much easier to work.

5) The number of grooves does not necessarily indicate the number of ropes employed. The three-groove tool shown can accommodate three, four, five and possibly six ropes. This is because multiple ropes tend to overlap each other rather than spreading out individually. This is especially true if the ropes are

bundled together. Bundling is not unexpected when employing multiple stationary ropes and heavy loads.

6) Multiple grooves are used to prevent rope wear. A single deep groove is easier to fabricate but will wear the edges of the rope when the load is applied. The rope will be pressed deep into the groove and the rough stone sides will abrade it. This is another indication that the load was great.

7) The tool is used inverted as well as with and without load. The hole in the stem is only required to hold the tool in place when there is no load and when the tool is pointing down. Making this hole requires considerable effort and is done for a reason. If the tool is always pointing up, gravity will hold it in place. If the tool is under load, the load pressure will hold it in place. The only time the tool will not be held in place is when it is pointing down and there is no load. In such an instance, it will fall out of the wooden socket. The hole allows a holding pin to be inserted through the wooden socket and through the tool.

These characteristics of the tool are exactly the specifications required by the lever-end protection requirements identified above. It is a perfect match. Additionally, this tool supports the notion that a multiple step lever was employed. As described, a multiple step lever requires the rope to pass around the end of the lever. If a single step lever was employed, the rope could simply be tied at or near the end of the lever because a single step lever does not require repositioning the rope. It is this repositioning of the rope that forces the rope to be passed around the end of the lever and this in turn forces the protection of the lever end. This mystery tool provides strong evidence that a multiple step lever was employed by the Egyptians to lift the pyramid blocks.

MISCELLANEOUS POINTS

Moving the raised block from the lever to the working course is a fairly simple task because the block is initially on quarter circles and already raised above the lower course. This means that when it is raised it will be above the higher working course by an amount equal to the quarter circle height. This is exactly the proper height to roll onto the quarter circle track. Therefore, it is a simple matter to place elevated quarter circles under the raised block and roll it away onto the working course. These elevated quarter circles can be implemented with a number of different methods and will not be discussed further.

It is seen that differences in course height and corresponding variations in block weight can be accommodated with minor variations in the lever design. It seems likely that there was at least one lever per course with multiple levers being used for the lower courses. As defined in chapter 3, the delivery rate for a minimum time, one-year project, is ten blocks per minute. The Time Motion Analysis (Appendix 3) requires three minutes to lift one block. In order to maintain this rate, thirty lifting levers must be employed simultaneously at the lowest levels. Restating this in somewhat more direct terms: only ninety workers are needed to lift at a rate of 2.5 million pyramid blocks in a year. (Additional workers are needed to raise the blocks higher, but that number, like the number of blocks, decreases by the cube of the height.)

Figures 6-4 and 6-5 show that the lever frame is located entirely on the course below the working course with only about four feet of width. This does not have to be the case. The frame legs can be extended at a greater angle and placed at different courses. Additionally, only when the course is practically finished is it required to be narrow. Normally there is a great deal of room on the course below the working course. The Figures show the worst case situation.

The Time Motion Analysis (Appendix 3) assumes a fixed ladder of some sort for the workers to climb up in order to reach the top of the lever. This seems like the most likely method. However, an alternative approach provides a curious scenario. Suppose that instead of climbing a fixed ladder, the workers "climbed" a rope ladder. The workers' weight would keep them on the ground as the lever lifted the block. This might be faster because the "climbing" and lifting occur simultaneously. (This was not analyzed because benchmark values for rope climbing were not available.) The most curious part is when two workers abandon the rope ladders at the same time, leaving the third worker standing on a rope ladder. (With 2.5 million blocks this event is almost certain to happen.) It seems that the result is a trebuchet form of catapult. All the fundamental components of the trebuchet are present. And, while there is no evidence that the Egyptians employed the trebuchet, like the wheel, they may have understood it.

Time Estimate

Two methods for lifting blocks have been presented, ramps and lifting machines. The standardized man-hour value employing a ramp to lift an average block the average height is 1.06 man-hours. The simple cantilevered raised fulcrum lever requires 6 man-hours for the same task. It is presumed that the first five courses, or 13% of the volume of the pyramid, were lifted with a ramp. Additionally every higher block could use the highly efficient ramp to be raised the first 19 feet. However, to simplify the calculations and to be conservative, only the less efficient lifting lever value will be used which is 6 man-hours per average block (5,000 pounds) lifted to the average height (100 feet).

CONCLUSION

Ramps are an extremely efficient method of lifting blocks if the ramps are small. When used to build a pyramid, their efficiency drops by a factor of 128:1 the higher they are. This is because the amount of fill needed increases by the cube of the height and the number of blocks serviced by the ramp decreases by the cube of the height. Additionally, large ramps require substantial time to dismantle. The conventional approach of using large ramps, as proposed by Lehner and Smith, require 50%, or more, of the volume of the Great Pyramid itself. This presents a serious problem because the quarry is too small to provide this additional volume of material. Additionally, there is the question of where this material went after the pyramid was completed.

A simple two-step lever system was designed that employs a raised fulcrum with a cantilevered support frame. Such a design is clearly within the technical and intellectual capabilities of the ancient Egyptians. This device allows three workers to lift an average block an average height in only 6 man-hours (using conservative values). This compares to 44.9 man-hours for Smith and 63.56 man-hours for Lehner which are less efficient by a factor of 7.5 or 10.6, respectively.

The strongest evidence for the use of this type of lever comes from Lehner's "Mystery tool" (Lehner, 211). These stone artifacts are a necessary (and predicted) part of the lever. Their physical characteristics leave little doubt as to their function. Additionally, this type of simple machine is typical of the devices the Egyptians used.

In reference to the standard large ramp method of lifting blocks, Lepre's (p. 254) comment is apt: "Surely, the architect of the first built and last remaining of the Seven Wonders of the Ancient World was capable of devising a more sophisticated system than we give him credit for."

Chapter 7. Quarrying Blocks

Introduction

The last major operation in building the Great Pyramid is quarrying the blocks. The quarry for the vast majority of stones is very near the base of the pyramid. Only the decorative outer casing stones and the handful of special granite stones for the chambers were quarried elsewhere. Nevertheless, cutting 2.5 million blocks out of solid bedrock is no trivial matter. This chapter will examine the tools and techniques that most archaeologists believe were employed by the Egyptians. It will be found that these approaches are inefficient and do not match the evidence found at Giza. There are other methods that match the evidence, in addition to being much more efficient.

Limestone

Limestone is a sedimentary rock that is generally believed to be formed by the collection and compression of the shells and bones of once living organisms. Thus limestone consists of mostly calcium carbonate (sometimes called calcite). Calcium carbonate is quite common. Some over-the-counter antacids contain calcium carbonate as their main ingredient for soothing an upset stomach. Ordinary blackboard chalk is generally calcium carbonate (however, modern sticks of chalk are usually a compressed powder form). Calcium carbonate is highly reactive with most acids.

Depending upon the amount of other materials in the stone and the porosity of the stone, different limestones can have different physical properties. Typically limestone is listed with a hardness of 3 on the Mohs hardness scale. The Mohs scale needs some explanation. It was developed in 1812 by geologist Friedrich Mohs. He created a system for measuring the relative hardness of minerals. A rock or mineral with a higher Mohs value will scratch a rock or mineral with a lower rating, but not the other way around. As such, the scale has little relationship to the absolute hardness of a material. Additionally, since there are relatively few extremely hard or extremely soft rocks, most of the scale is used for the more common minerals. A copper penny has a hardness of about 3.5; a fingernail is typically about 2.5. Limestone is soft stone. It should not be confused with a hard stone like granite, which has a Mohs value of 7. Additionally limestone can change its hardness depending upon factors such as water content. Since Lehner (NOVA) demonstrated that copper tools could work Giza limestone reasonably well, it will be assumed that the Great Pyramid limestone has a hardness of 3 on the Mohs scale.

PRACTICAL LIMESTONE INFORMATION

A discussion and tour of several western New York limestone quarries with Gary Nelson, the geologist for Buffalo Crushed Stone Incorporated, provided useful and practical information. Limestone is much more variable than is suggested in the references. Limestone used for roads (in concrete and asphalt) must meet hardness requirements in New York State. The limestone in some quarries has a hardness of up to 7 on the Mohs scale. Stone with a hardness as low as 3 is not suitable for roads.

Limestone is always found in beds or layers. These layers can be as small as an inch or so thick. "Massive" beds are several feet thick or more. It seems apparent from the descriptions and photographs that the Giza limestone beds would be classified as massive beds. Multiple limestone beds are typically separated by thin layers of a different material or a different type of limestone and are easily distinguished visually. Sometimes there is a natural break that occurred during the deposition of the limestone due to variable sedimentation rates or other reasons. The adhesion of the rock varies at the bed boundaries. Typically it is less than the limestone itself. This means that there is a natural tendency for the rock to break or cleave at the bed boundaries. Some modern quarries with massive limestone beds use a small black-powder blasting charge to shock the beds to unbind the layers. In this way very big blocks of limestone (pyramid-block sized and larger) could be removed easily with just vertical cuts. No difficult undercutting is required.

A sample of soft limestone was obtained from the quarry and is shown in Figure 7-1. It weighs slightly more than five pounds and is roughly 6 inches by 3.5 inches by 4.5 inches. It scratches a fingernail and is scratched by a copper penny. Therefore, its hardness test is presumed to be at about 3 on the Mohs scale, which is similar to the Giza limestone.

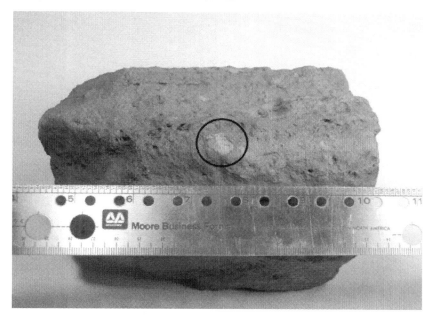

Figure 7-1: An example of limestone with a hardness of 3. This is a very soft stone. The circled area shows the damage the rock sustained when dropped about two inches onto an iron vise.

This rock is incredibly soft and is reminiscent of rotten wood: it looks solid but falls apart at the slightest insult. The circled area shown in Figure 7-1 is the result of deliberately dropping the stone about 2 inches onto an iron vise. There is damage of about a half of an inch in diameter. Several other blemishes can be seen as well which resulted simply from normal handling. Taking two common rocks and striking them together (without excessive force) usually produces a clacking noise and no damage. Taking two of these limestone rocks and striking them together in the same manner results in a thudding sound and pieces of stone are broken off. A stone with a hardness of 3 is simply much softer than any stone one is normally likely to encounter by chance.

AVAILABLE TOOLS

The Egyptians had a variety of stoneworking tools available to them. Their primary metal was copper, which had been in general use for hundreds of years before the first pyramid was built (Lepre, 236). Numerous copper chisels and artifacts have been found. It appears that they also employed iron, to some degree. The evidence for this includes a piece of wrought iron discovered imbedded in the Great Pyramid itself by Colonel Howard Vyse (Lepre, 245). However, it is usually accepted that there was no widespread use of iron in those times. Ancient copper mines have been found in Sinai (Lepre, 237). But there are no indications of ancient iron mines. There is always the possibility that whatever iron that was available came from meteoric origin.

The Egyptians used various types of saws for cutting stone. Typically, these were made from copper; however copper was not the actual cutting material. This can be determined from the simple fact that sawn granite artifacts have been found. In particular, the Khufu's sarcophagus is made from rose granite and demonstrates clear saw marks (Lepre, 92, Smith, 83). As noted above, granite is very much harder than copper so it is difficult to imagine how a copper saw can cut through it. The apparent method was to use the saw with a slurry or paste that included sand. Sand is typically made up of quartz particles, which are extremely hard. In this way the sand, rather than the copper, abraded the granite. The copper saw became a "holder" for the sand. Quartz and granite have about the same hardness. Therefore about an equal amount of sand and granite would be powdered in the sawing process. However, sand was plentiful.

The Egyptians also used a wide variety of hammers that were typically made from a hard stone (Lepre, 238) such as dolerite (not to be confused with dolomite, which is a soft stone). These were usually funnel-shaped (but solid) and were used by holding the narrow end and striking the larger end. Pounders were just rounded pieces of stone that were held in one or two hands. There are illustrations of smaller stones held in place with two wooden pieces (Lehner, 211) that approximate the modern hammer.

The Egyptians also had drills made from dolerite and may even have employed diamond drills (Lepre, 238). Some of these drills were at least 3.5 inches in diameter (Lepre, 91). Drills were sometimes used in conjunction with wood to split hard stone. The procedure was to drill or notch hard stone and then insert dry wood into these openings. Water was then added to the wood, which would expand and exert great pressure, splitting the stone (Lepre, 237). This is yet another example of the intelligence of the Egyptian builders.

There are some tools that the Egyptians apparently did not possess. They did not use pulleys, winches or screws (Lepre, 238). Lepre suggests that they did not use cranes. And there is certainly no evidence that anything resembling a modern crane was employed. Typically modern cranes use pulleys to lift the load and include a method of rotation to move the load laterally. This appears to have been beyond the Egyptians' abilities of the time. However, the cantilevered, raised-fulcrum lever presented in Chapter 6 does have some basic crane-like properties.

QUARRYING BLOCKS USING THE STANDARD METHODS

Most archaeologists' theories conform to one general method for quarrying the limestone blocks at Giza (Lehner, 207, Smith, 146). The technique is called channeling; it consists of creating blocks by excavating channels around the stone. Typically there was a long back channel and then right angle channels were created to define the sides of the block. The height of the block in the quarry matched the height of the course in the pyramid. That is, the block was quarried with the largest side down. The channels were wide enough for a worker to stand in (Smith, 145). Smith (p. 146) defines this size as "about two hands wide." Lehner (p. 207) provides several photographs and it is estimated from these that the channel was about 10 inches wide. The bottom of the block was broken by cutting slots, inserting wedges and hammering them until the rock split (Smith, 146). Another possibility was to insert dry wood into these slots and add water so that the expansion would break the rock at the base (Lehner, 206). The block thus detached was then levered or pulled out from its position by about 20 men (Smith, 146; Lehner, 206).

The evidence for this approach comes from some observations made at various quarry sites and from techniques used today at Egyptian limestone quarries (Lehner 206). However, it will be seen that are problems with this evidence. Additionally, the procedures in use today do not necessarily represent what the ancient Egyptians did. Lehner (p. 207) provides a photograph of channels cut in a bed of limestone and uses this to support the standard theories. Unfortunately his quarry is not the source of pyramid stones. The quarry in the photograph is one close to the Sphinx and is not generally associated with the Great Pyramid. The apparent distance between the channels is estimated to be about seven feet. This is considerably larger that most pyramid blocks and because of the size of the block and position of the quarry, it seems unlikely that this was an actual pyramid block. Instead, as suggested by Lehner, it was probably intended to be a component of one of the many other structures at Giza. Since these structures are several orders of magnitude smaller than the Great Pyramid, it is reasonable to believe that different quarrying methods were employed because of the differences in the engineering scale factors (Chapter 3).

Lehner also presents a photograph (p. 206) that shows a large granite slab (at Aswan) with two closely-spaced parallel grooves worked into it, shallow and wide. He suggests that these grooves are the "beginnings of such channels." However, why would the Egyptians place two channels so close together? From an engineering perspective this makes no sense. They must have had a reason for making these cuts, because granite is a hard stone and very difficult to work. They would not have made that much effort without a good reason. But it is just as clear that this cannot be an example of channel quarrying. (A different possible use for this stone is presented in the next chapter). It would be horribly inefficient and wasteful of materials and manpower.

Smith (p. 144) includes a photograph of a partially cut block that exhibits five relatively large rectangular openings at its base (estimated to be about 6 inches by 18 inches). He suggests that wedges or levers were used to in these cavities to release the block from the bed. He describes the location as "the old" quarry, which may or may not refer to the quarry for the Great Pyramid. There is no scale to the picture but it appears that the block is over eight feet long, making it much larger than a typical pyramid block. Therefore it cannot be assumed that this procedure was the typical method for quarrying pyramid blocks. Again there are the considerations of scale factors to weigh.

There is also the issue of when these artifacts were created. There is no way to be sure that they were worked at the time of the Great Pyramid. It is possible that these stones reflect the quarrying activity of other people who wanted limestone for some completely different reason, hundreds or even thousands of years after the Great Pyramid was built. Virtually all of the casing stones of the Great Pyramid were stolen. Most of the casing stones, as well as a number of underlying stones, of Khafre's pyramid were also stolen. So it does not seem unreasonable to consider that someone may have worked the quarry well after the early pharaohs. Limestone blocks apparently had value.

Another problem with the standard theory is the amount of stone that is lost/wasted with the channeling technique. The amount of this lost/wasted stone can be estimated numerically. For these calculations it will be assumed that an average block 4 feet square and 2.5 feet high is to be removed. The block will be oriented with the large face down, with the front face and one side face open. This is the orientation that is encountered when quarrying a number of blocks in a row. The channel size will be set at ten inches (see above). Two channels will be needed. One will be four feet long. The other will be four feet and ten inches long. The channels will be 2.5 feet deep. This corresponds to 18.4 cubic feet of lost/wasted stone per stone.

There is also the wastage due to the cut-outs at the bottom of the block. The existing stones visible used in the Great Pyramid do not show these cutouts. Therefore, if this method was used, it must be assumed that then these blocks were trimmed to provide a flat face. This results in six inches of lost/wasted stone from the base. However the base must also include the width of the channels. Instead of four feet on a side, the base wastage becomes 4 feet 10 inches on a side or 23.4 square feet. If the height of these cutouts is six inches (see above), then the volume of material lost from the base cut is 11.7 cubic feet lost/wasted.

Combining the lost/wasted volumes for the sides and base results in a lost/wasted volume of 30.1 cubic feet of stone per average block. The average block (4' x 4' x 2.5') is 40 cubic feet. Therefore for every block about 75% of the volume of the block is lost/wasted. Since the Great Pyramid is known to possess about 94 million cubic feet of stone, at least 164 million cubic feet of stone must have been quarried, if this was the method used. But the quarry has been measured and been shown to have had about 97.5 million cubic feet of stone removed (Lehner, 206). Quite simply, the quarry is too small by nearly 70%.

The quarry problem was noted previously when we considered large ramp construction. In Chapter 6 it was noted that large ramps would have required an amount of stone equal to a considerable fraction of the pyramid's volume as well. The smallest ramp proposed by Smith (p. 171) uses 29% of the volume of the Great Pyramid. This results in 99% of the Great Pyramid's volume in lost/wasted stone. In that case, the quarry it too small by a factor of two.

Then there is the issue of where all this wasted material went. It seems difficult to hide or disperse such a huge amount of rock and stone without a trace.

The rate of block production using these methods can be approximated. In Lehner's NOVA experiment, twelve men produced 186 blocks in 22 days of work (Lehner, 206) (the number of hours per day was not specified). This corresponds to 8.5 stones per day for twelve men or 0.7 blocks per man-day or 1.4 man-days per block. If it is assumed that there were ten productive working hours per day then it took 14 man-hours to quarry one block. This will be the benchmark value used for quarrying blocks with the standard methods.

Note that the value of ten productive hours per day is very high. There was no indication of lights in any of Lehner's photographs of the site. Therefore is assumed that no work was performed in darkness. It is further assumed that there were twelve hours of daylight available (the time of year was not specified, but at thirty degrees of latitude the day length is not as variable as at higher latitudes.) Workers generally cannot perform manual labor for extended periods of time, day after day. There must be breaks for eating and personal needs in addition to rest periods for physical recovery. This value is chosen because it represents the maximum practical work product in one day.

ALTERNATIVE QUARRYING METHODS

There are two major considerations for quarrying. The first is efficiency in the work product which reduces man-hours and the second is efficiency in the quarrying process which reduces lost/wasted stone. Both of these can be addressed if the channels used to separate the blocks can be made very small. This obviously reduces the amount of loss/wasted stone. However, it should also reduce the work required because less stone must be broken. Fundamentally, quarrying requires energy to break the binding force between the limestone particles. If fewer particles must be broken, then less energy is needed. Less energy translates to faster quarrying.

The standard theory requires channels large enough for a man to stand in. Why? Apparently because of the belief that short-handled tools were used. Lehner's workers used a pick with a handle estimated to be about two feet long (Lehner, 207). With such a tool, a wide channel would be needed to reach areas lower and farther back. The Egyptians had equivalent tools. Unfortunately, making the handle of a pick long enough to cut the difficult areas makes it very unwieldy. It is very difficult to precisely control such a tool with a six- or eight-foot handle. Lifting a pick from the end of a long handle also requires considerable strength. Extending the handle is thus not a good solution to the problem.

A second reason given for the wide channel in the back was to allow workers to room to use large wooden levers to remove the cut block from its position (Lehner, 206; Smith, 146). Therefore any alternative method must address this issue as well.

The Egyptians had chisels and drills. These can be used to make narrow cuts but cannot be used for the deep cuts necessary to quarry blocks. The problem with drills is that the debris from the drill cannot be removed from the hole. This would result in binding of the drill or simply a huge increase in friction. Long chisels do not suffer from the debris problem if the cut is started from an edge. In this way the waste can be swept along the cut to the outside. Unfortunately, hammering long copper chisels is not an efficient way to remove rock. If a long chisel made from soft copper should bend even slightly when hit, much of the energy would be lost. Should the chisel actually be bent, hammering it will only worsen the defect and make it nearly useless. Long copper chisels would probably be easy to bend. Additionally, small hand chisels are inefficient in that they have to be held with one hand while the other hand strikes it with a hammer. This limits the applied force to that of one arm.

A "spear-chisel" would be a possible alternative. Basically this is a copper chisel with a long wooden handle. It is used vertically, without a hammer. The worker holds the shaft with both hands and pounds the rock between his feet. The weight of the tool and the whole upper body strength of the worker are applied to the point. The action is similar to using a modern post-hole digger or ice chopper. The wooden shaft is resilient and transfers the force to the copper point of the tool. Such a tool can be quite long and can work deep and difficult-to-reach areas with precision. It can be used horizontally to undercut the blocks as well. Horizontal cuts can be facilitated by using a "table" to carry and align the tool. This table can be a very simple support. The spear chisel seems to be a natural tool to develop.

In theory, the tool could be made from solid copper. However, this would probably make it too heavy (about 2.8 pounds per foot at one inch in diameter). Additionally, while copper was in general use, it certainly wasn't cheap. It is presumed that the optimal weight of the spear chisel would be in the five- to ten-pound range. This is the typical weight of most tools of this sort. A one-inch diameter spear-chisel with a twelve-inch-long copper chisel point and a ten-foot wooden handle would weight just about five pounds. The useable cutting depth for such a tool would be about four feet, leaving six feet extending for the worker. If desired, additional weight could be added to the handle near the top so it would not interfere with the kerf (tool-wide cut). This tool would cut channels with about a one-inch kerf.

A one-inch kerf clearly results in much less lost/wasted stone. Using the same block specifications as above, the amount of lost/wasted stone employing a spear-chisel is 3.07 cubic feet. This is about an order of magnitude less than using the standard methods (30.1 cubic feet lost/wasted).

Spear-Chisel Performance

The easiest point to analyze is the amount of lost/wasted stone. This is 3.07 cubic feet for an average block. There are about 2.5 million blocks in the Great Pyramid; this calculates to 7.68 million cubic feet of lost/wasted stone. Adding the volume of the Great Pyramid to the amount of lost/wasted stone gives a value of 101.68 million cubic feet of stone required. That is still somewhat greater than the quarry size of 97.5 million cubic feet. However the values are much closer in agreement, differing only by about 4%. If the diameter of the tool were reduced to 0.5 inches in diameter, the values would agree precisely. But such a thin tool is probably not practical. It would be too light and flimsy. Alternatively one could argue that the measurements of the quarry size could be in error by a few percent.

There is another factor that has not yet been discussed because it is a "second-order" factor. In engineering a second order factor is one that does not usually need to be considered in the preliminary analysis of a problem. The initial analysis generally focuses on the "first-order" concerns. In this case the second order factor is the volume of the Great Pyramid.

It turns out that the Egyptians did not start with a perfectly flat base. The limestone bedrock has a bulge which was incorporated in the design. This hump under the Great Pyramid comprises about "225,000 cubic meters" (Smith, 160) or about 6.4 million cubic feet which is about 6.8% of the original estimate of the volume. So, although the Great Pyramid's volume is 94 million cubic feet, only 87.6 million cubic feet of blocks were used. This reduces the actual number of number of blocks from 2.5 million to 2.33 million. With 3.07 cubic feet of lost/wasted stone applied to only 2.33 million stones, the lost/wasted value comes to 7.15 million cubic feet. Add this to the pyramid's block-volume of 87.6 million cubic feet and the second-order estimate of the volume of material needed for the Great Pyramid is 94.8 million cubic feet. This is comfortably less than the calculated volume of the quarry, which is 97.5 million cubic feet.

The next issue is that of speed. The amount of material removed with the spear-chisels is about 10% of that using the standard methods. But which is faster? It can be seen that the amount of material removed is not necessarily related to speed. However it is a good indication that there is the potential for faster operations. The key issues are the amount of energy applied to the rock per stroke and the relative rate of the strokes. This is because a certain amount of energy is needed to overcome the binding forces of the stone. Therefore it is necessary to compare the amount of energy deposited as well as the amount of material removed.

A pick can create a very large amount of energy at the point with a full round-house swing. However, such swings can not be employed when the channel is fairly deep. In this case, the half-swing usually starts with the hands directly over the head of the user. Much less force is applied, but the pick is easier to control. An estimated maximum rate, based upon personal experience, is about one swing of a pick every three seconds. This rate cannot be sustained over more than a period of a minute or so. A reasonable sustained rate would probably be about ten strokes per minute. "Sustained" is defined as a rate that can be maintained for about 15 minutes before a rest period of a few minutes is required.

Picks have an annoying characteristic, too, that bears mentioning: the fragments fly backward and often strike the user.

The spear-chisel cannot provide as much energy per blow as a pick. This is seen by the short, vertical stroke and relatively slow speed of the point. However, many more strokes per minute can be applied to the stone with a spear-chisel. The estimated maximum rate is about two strokes per second and a sustained rate of about 60 strokes per minute.

The energy comparison is probably best achieved by examining the source of the energy rather than the expected results of individual strikes. The pick half-swing uses most of the upper body muscles, especially those of the arms and shoulders. The spear-chisel uses these same muscles. The actions are not identical but they are similar. This leads to the inference that the amount of energy that can be supplied to either tool is approximately equal. One person can provide a limited amount of muscular energy. If two tools use the same muscles then it follows that the overall energy applied to the point must also be the same. The pick provides more energy per blow but the blows are relatively slow. The spear-chisel calls for less energetic blows but at a higher rate. The factor that defines the speed is the amount of material removed. It takes more energy to break up 30 cubic feet of stone than it does to break up three cubic feet.

There is a second-order consideration here, too. The size of the rock fragments can affect the energy requirements. The energy required is directly related to the surface area of the rock that is broken. Removing large chunks uses less energy than powdering the stone. This is because no energy is needed to break the binding energy within the chunk. The size of the fragments depends mostly on the size of the point. Larger points usually create larger fragments. For the purpose of this exercise the pick's point is estimated to be about two inches and the stated point size of the spear-chisel is one inch. Thus it is expected that the fragments created by the spear-chisel will be somewhat smaller than that of the pick. This means that the spear-chisel will be less efficient than the pick in terms the amount of rock binding energy that must be overcome. But this is small when compared to the actual amount of rock removed.

The conclusion is that an ergonomically designed spear-chisel can provide a similar amount of energy to the stone as a pick. Thus, because the amount of stone removed with this method is an order of magnitude less than with the pick, the procedure should be significantly faster. A direct ratio suggests that 1.4 man-hours would be required to cut a typical pyramid block. This seems much too short. To be conservative, a somewhat arbitrary value of 5 man-hours per block will be used.

Removing the Block

Once the block is freed from the bedrock it must be moved onto quarter circles for transport. This raises two issues: how are the blocks initially moved from their resting place and how are they placed on the quarter circle track? For the following discussion it will be assumed that the block has three open sides: the top, side and front and is detached from the bedrock. This is the expected geometry when blocks are harvested in a row.

Lehner and Smith suggest that a wide channel is needed in the back of the block in order to place large levers to pry the block out (Lehner, 206; Smith, 146). However, this is not the case. There are simple techniques that allow the removal of a block with a small kerf.

The procedure starts with quarrying the blocks on end. That is, the four-foot-square side is vertical. (The blocks shown in Lehner, on page 207, are quarried with the large side down.) This vertical orientation has several benefits. The most important benefit is that the center of mass is higher. This makes the block easier to manipulate (as shown below). Another benefit is that only a small side needs to be undercut. (Undercutting certainly appears to be the most difficult cut to make.) A side of 4 feet by 2.5 feet must be undercut instead of a side four feet square. This reduces the undercutting from 16 square feet to 10 square feet. Additionally, the undercutting length is reduced from 4 feet to 2.5 feet.

The easiest method for obtaining complete access to all four of the sides of the block is to simply tip it over. With the block on the narrow side with a high center of mass, this is a fairly simple task. It only requires about 880 pounds of force applied to the top edge to tip a block. One method is to drive thin wooden wedges (like cedar house shingles) into the back kerf with a heavy mallet. A lubricant can be used on the wedges to improve efficiency and reduce wear. For best performance, the wedges should only contact wood. This means that thin wooden shims should be placed in the kerf beforehand. As the kerf is widened, spacers are employed to hold it open as thicker wedges and shims are used. Once the opening is extended a few inches, wooden pry bars can be inserted and the block can be tipped easily.

There is another method that appears to be faster and simpler. This is shown in Figure 7-2. The procedure is to wrap several loops of rope around the top of the block. Then place a wooden pole that is sixteen feet long between the block and the rope. With a rope attached to the top of the pole, only 125 pounds of lateral force is needed to tip the block. Two men can provide this force with no difficulty. This technique places the lever at the front of the block instead of at the back of the block. There is no need for a large channel at the back of the stone.

A time estimate for looping the rope, inserting the pole and tipping the stone is fifteen minutes for two men. This equates to 0.5 man-hours to extract the block. (Realistically, it should take much less than fifteen minutes for two workers to loop a rope around the block, insert the pole and tip the block. This value is chosen to be conservative.)

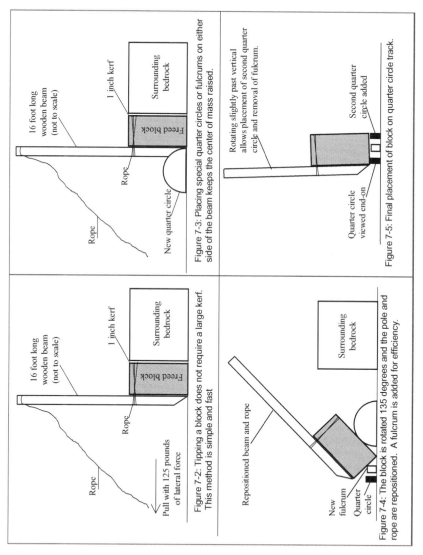

Figure 7-3: Placing special quarter circles or fulcrums on either side of the beam keeps the center of mass raised.

Figure 7-5: Final placement of block on quarter circle track.

Figure 7-2: Tipping a block does not require a large kerf. This method is simple and fast

Figure 7-4: The block is rotated 135 degrees and the pole and rope are repositioned. A fulcrum is added for efficiency.

The last issue is placing the block on the quarter-circle track. Figure 7-3 illustrates how this can be accomplished. Instead of allowing the block to fall completely flat, incorporate another quarter circle for it to roll over (fulcrums

119

could also be used, albeit with less efficiency). This quarter circle is not exactly the same as those used for the tracks. This is because the rotating shape is a rectangle rather than a square. This new quarter circle is taller in the middle. The block is rotated 135 degrees over the special quarter circle. This places the block at the side of the quarter circle track with a 45 degree list (see Figure 7-4) and the raised edge is 21 inches off the ground (for an average block). The height of the quarter circle track is 9.9 inches. At this point a fulcrum slightly less than 9.9 inches is placed under the block as far as possible. For safety and stability this fulcrum is the full length of the block. The rope and pole are re-attached and the block is pulled slightly past vertical so that the second quarter circle can be placed under the newly raised edge. Once the second quarter circle is in place, the fulcrum can be removed (see Figure 7-5). The block is now on the quarter circle track.

The time necessary to perform these tasks is similar to that for tipping the block. There are the additional actions of placing the special quarter circles and rolling the block once over them. This should take less than a minute. Then there is the placement and removal of the fulcrum.

This should take less than a minute as well. (Note that these tools will be on hand, because the blocks are expected to be quarried in order.) The second tipping of the block should take the same amount of time as the first tipping; perhaps less, if the rope loops can be shifted into position rather than loosening and re-tying them. The time estimate for the first tipping of the block is conservative and these extra actions of placing and removing the quarter circle and fulcrum are very quick. Therefore the time estimate for the second tipping will be 18 minutes for two men or 0.6 man-hours.

One final action remains to be incorporated into our time estimate. This is the fine-placement of the block in order to register it properly with the quarter-circle track. This was discussed in detail in Chapter 5. In this case, the block must be moved +/- 0.5 block lengths or +/- two feet (worst case) for an average block. The slide-plate technique can be used here. As noted in Chapter 5, this procedure will take about 1.5 man-minutes. Generally it is always more difficult to start an alignment than it is to maintain it. For this reason the fine-placement time will be inflated to 6 man-minutes per block.

Miscellaneous Notes

Because limestone is formed in layers, it is possible that the Egyptians took advantage of this characteristic to aid in removing the blocks. As noted above, the layer boundaries are often weaker than the limestone itself. If the blocks were quarried with the layer boundary at the base of the block, undercutting may not have been required. Once the vertical cuts were made, the block could be "shocked" with something like a battering ram to release it from the bedrock. This is far faster and more efficient than undercutting.

There is no direct evidence that the Egyptians used spear-chisels. That is, none has not been found or identified as such. However, many different types of copper chisels have been recovered from the pyramid sites (Smith, 83). Additionally, copper points survive better than wood handles. The main evidence for these tools is circumstantial and indirect. It is based upon the quarry size. Spear-chisels are the only proposed tool that allows the small amount of lost/wasted stone necessary to match the volume of stone removed from the quarry.

There is an interesting photograph provided by Lehner (p. 211) that shows a side of a block of "Turah-quality" limestone at the North Pyramid at Dashur (also called the Red pyramid and identified as Lepre's number 66 in Appendix 1). This is a large pyramid, about one half the volume of the Great Pyramid, and was built by Sneferu, who was Khufu's father. Lehner points out that the block "still retains thumb-width chisel marks." However this appears inappropriate. Why would the Egyptians use ordinary hand chisels when they had a tool that was about equivalent to a pick? A pick is clearly a superior tool for removing large amounts of stone when compared to a hand chisel.

Lehner (p. 211) also states that for dressing and finishing the casing stones, chisels of only a 1/3" wide were used. (This is certainly not "thumb-width" in size.) He further states that: "Wider blades of soft copper simply will not work on stone [for dressing and finishing]." From this, it seems clear that the "thumb-width" chisel marks were not the result of dressing the stone but rather the remains of cutting the stone. The photograph showed many, many parallel strike marks several inches long. This is not what would be expected if a pick-like tool was used. A photograph of a NOVA block that was quarried with a modern pick is also provided (Lehner, 208). The work marks are completely different.

A spear-chisel with a one-inch point is just about the width of a thumb. It would be expected to leave hundreds of parallel strike marks on the stone. While the block was not part of the Giza pyramid, it does appear to have been a part of a massive pyramid built by the same pharaoh, Sneferu, that initiated the concept of huge structures. The marks on the block are exactly what would be expected if the spear-chisel was used. The spear-chisel is a practical tool that the Egyptians could have developed without much difficulty. They were most certainly practical builders.

First-Order Time Estimate to Build the Great Pyramid

At this point all of the primary or first-order operations have been defined and time estimates calculated. These actions are: cutting the block, extracting the block, transporting the block and lifting the block. Additional tasks such as finishing the outer casing stones, order of assembly, positioning the top-most blocks and other functions are relatively minor and have little impact on the overall time estimate for building a pyramid. These factors will be discussed in the next chapter and the time estimate will be refined at that point. The first-order tasks for an average block are listed below along with their time estimates and the chapter in which they were developed. (Note: values stated initially as man-minutes have been converted to man-hours.)

1)	Gross block movement*	Chapter 4	1.0 man-hour
2)	Fine block movement (four operations)	Chapter 5	0.1 man-hours
3)	Lifting the block*	Chapter 6	6.0 man-hours
4)	Quarrying the block	Chapter 7	5.0 man-hours
5)	First block tipping (extraction)	Chapter 7	0.5 man-hours
6)	Second block tipping (loading onto track)	Chapter 7	0.6 man-hours
7)	Fine block placement (track alignment)	Chapter 7	0.1 man-hours

Total time required to quarry, lift and place an average block = 13.3 man-hours.

Time to quarry, lift and place 2.5 million blocks = 33.25 million man-hours.

Converting man-hours to man-days (10 hours per day) = 3.325 million man-days.

With 10,000 workers, the calendar time is 332.5 days.

(* very conservative values; for details refer to the chapters)

Discussion

When first calculated, these results were quite surprising. It was clear that these methods were more efficient than those discussed by previous writers, but the degree to which this was so was startling. The individual values can certainly be argued. Some choices were fairly arbitrary but were based on observation and measurement. Inflating the numbers by even 50% to 100% will produce a result that is still incredibly small. And it must be recalled that throughout the development of these figures, conservative choices were consistently made. In particular the gross movement and lifting values are still reasonable if reduced by 50%. This would decrease the time required by over 25%. This calculation also presumes that 2.5 million blocks are used. However, it was seen above that only 2.33 million blocks are really necessary because of the bulge in the bedrock. This reduces the effort by an additional 6.8%. If non-conservative values are used and the actual block-volume is incorporated, the calendar time for 10,000 workers could be reduced to about 225 days. If the typically accepted number of 25,000 workers is used in conjunction with the non-conservative estimate, the Great Pyramid could have been built in 90 days (in theory).

Realistically, it seems doubtful that the Great Pyramid was built in less than one year. Quite simply this is not the way people work (although other theories that have been advanced require this super-human effort). There is written evidence that states that 4000 workers built the Great Pyramid (Lehner, 225). Given this value and adopting a relatively leisurely work effort, it will be shown that a calendar time of four to six years is probably a more reasonable estimate. This is discussed in more detail in a later chapter.

CONCLUSION

There is a significant and fundamental problem with the standard theories offered as to Egyptian methods of quarrying. The quarry is simply too small to supply the volume of material needed, once we take account of the lost/wasted stone that goes with the channel technique. This wastage is about 75% for the quarrying operations alone. If a large ramp is also used then an additional 25% to 50% of stone volume is called for. This difficulty has not been addressed or even acknowledged in the available literature. Nevertheless it is an inconvenient fact that cannot be ignored.

However, the spear-chisel tool provides a simple solution to this awkward situation. It reduces the amount of lost/wasted stone by an order of magnitude. Then the quarry could have provided more than enough stone for the Great Pyramid. Additionally, this approach appears to be faster. This tool is something simple that would be naturally developed because of the need to create deep and narrow cuts in the soft limestone. It is certainly well within the scope of the Egyptians of the time. In fact, upon reflection, it seems that this tool is something they could not have failed to develop.

Quarrying the blocks is the last of the first-order tasks necessary to build the Great Pyramid. A time estimate was calculated and the surprising result was that 10,000 workers could have built the Great Pyramid in about 332.5 days. This estimate used conservative values. However, it is more likely that about 4000 men spent about 4-6 calendar years working at a more leisurely pace.

CHAPTER 8. ADDITIONAL CONSTRUCTION DETAILS

INTRODUCTION

The major tasks for building the Great Pyramid have now been addressed. This chapter will discuss the second-order construction details. These issues include shaping the outer casing stones, positioning the top-most blocks, fabricating the major tools, order of assembly, and an examination of the wood requirements. There are simple and logical methods for addressing these issues. The time estimates for these actions are less precise. Because they comprise such a small part of the whole, precise estimates are not mandatory. However, for the sake of completeness, the whole process should be examined to eliminate any possible unforeseen problems.

Often times in an engineering project, seemingly small problems can become major obstacles. These are humorously termed "gotchas" because they are unanticipated and become apparent only when the project is well under way. These unforeseen problems can necessitate the re-evaluation and redesign of the whole project. The classic gotcha is building something too big to fit out of the door; although most are more subtle than that. A more typical gotcha is when a part or procedure fails to perform as expected and there is nothing else available to replace it with. The likelihood of encountering a gotcha can be reduced or eliminated by attention to detail from the very start of the project.

THE GREAT PYRAMID'S INTERNAL DESIGN

The time required to build the corridors and rooms in the Great Pyramid will not be estimated. This is because it is clearly so small, when compared to the whole, as to be insignificant. The mechanism by which the huge granite stones that make up the King's chamber and other structures are raised will be discussed in the "order of assembly" section. Some of these are estimated to weigh 80 tons (Lehner, 108). It is important to provide a reasonable means to accomplish this task within the framework of the already detailed construction methods. Otherwise it could be a gotcha.

FINISHING THE CASING STONES

There must have been about 80,184 outer casing stones (calculated, Appendix 2) originally incorporated in the Great Pyramid. Only a very few remain. These were fabricated from high quality Tura limestone (Smith, 104). The precision by which they were made is simply incredible: "the jointing between them was barely discernable to the naked eye, resembling hairlines rather than joints of masonry" (Lepre, 65). Smith (p. 160) calculates that there were 98,000 casing stones. Lepre (p. 65) suggests that 144,000 casing stones were used but does not provide details concerning this estimate. Regardless of the estimate chosen, there were a lot of casing stones to finish.

It is important to realize that five of the six sides of the casing block must be suitably dressed to fit properly. The top, bottom and both sides must be perfectly square or else there will be gaps that would be very apparent. "The casing stones are without parallel, having been so perfectly cut and squared that their corners were found to be true 90-degree angles to 1/100 of an inch [over their length]" (Lepre pg 71). "On the exterior faces of the pyramid, the final dimensions of the stones were extremely accurate, so that joints could be made in fractions of a millimeter" (Smith, 90). The front face must be angled precisely at 51.9 degrees in order to match with the adjacent casing stones. The height of adjacent stones must also be identical, otherwise obvious gaps in the joints would be visible. How is this precision possible?

Creating a single perfect block by hand is reasonable to consider. The pharaoh's sarcophagus was often made from a single block of stone. But to create 80,000 to 100,000 perfect blocks by hand does not seem reasonable or practical. Again there is the consideration of waste. It is impossible to believe that every block was precisely formed. Human beings are not perfect. It stands to reason that if every block was hand finished, there would be many mistakes. Tura limestone was special and had to be imported from miles away. This made it expensive, and waste would have to be minimized. The Egyptians had every incentive to develop techniques to allow the rapid fabrication of these casing stones to the precision required.

The answer is that the blocks were machined. This is not as fantastic a notion as it first appears. Without suggesting that complicated mechanisms were constructed to automatically turn rough-hewn stones into perfect blocks, it is safe to say that there are simple methods that can be applied to guide cutting tools with repeatable precision. Casing stones can be fabricated quickly, simply and precisely, without the need for special skills. Some of these general methods are still in use today.

The first task in squaring a block is to make one side flat. This is not a big chore because the blocks coming out of the quarry were already fairly rectangular. Additionally, limestone is formed in layers, which can help. One simple method to flatten one side is to drag the block over a hard flat stone to scour the bottom (like reverse sanding). The great weight of the block combined with the softness of the stone would make this operation relatively quick and effective.

Unfortunately a flat stone, while easy to understand conceptually, is probably not the best practical choice. Quite simply it would be difficult to keep clean. The fine particles of limestone trimmed off the block would be forced into the surface of the flat stone, reducing its effectiveness (like clogged sandpaper). It would require constant brushing to clear the debris. A better design would be to incorporate ripples or ridges perpendicular to the direction of travel of the block. This would place very high pressure points at the tops of the ripples, which would act more like a scraper than a sander. This would be much easier to keep clean. The debris would tend to accumulate in the troughs and could be simply swept away when necessary.

Curiously, Lehner (p. 206) provides a photograph of just such a tool located at Aswan. It is a large flat granite slab with shallow, closely-spaced, parallel furrows. He suggests that this demonstrates the beginnings of channels used for quarrying. However, as noted in the previous chapter on quarrying, placing two channels so close together is inconsistent with channel quarrying. However, it is perfectly reasonable and useful to have such closely-spaced "channels" for use as a bottom-scraper.

MACHINING THE BLOCKS

Once there is a smooth flat side to the block, it can be machined in a number of simple ways to create precise flat and square faces. One of the simplest techniques is to use a parallel planer. This is conceptually shown in Figure 8-1. It consists of a base that is flat and a pendulum bar that is parallel to the base. The pendulum is fairly massive (a hundred pounds or so) and incorporates cutting blades, probably of copper, but a hard stone is also a possibility. The pendulum will automatically cut through the block only until the proper amount of stone is removed because the ropes limit the lowest point of the arc. The block is then moved incrementally so that the pendulum can work on the next section of block. After the block is passed completely through the planer, the top and bottom sides will be flat and parallel.

It is presumed that the block will be on some type of slide-plate similar to that described in Chapter 5. It was shown that moving a block incrementally on a slide-plate is easy to do with simple levers and two or three workers. It should also be noted that the "pendulum" aspect of the planer is only for the limiting the vertical movement of the cutting tool. The energy comes from workers swinging the pendulum back and forth. The large mass of the pendulum has the effect of storing the workers' applied energy until the tool contacts the stone, whereupon it is expended. This increases the efficiency of the tool. Note that the workers are using the whole of the upper body in swinging the pendulum. This certainly provides much more energy than using a simple hammer and chisel. In this case, the speed with which the block can be machined is directly related to the amount of energy supplied to the work-piece. As noted previously, the binding energy of the rock must be overcome in order to break it. For the casing stones, the particle size is about equal for either hand-chiseling or pendulum-machining. The amount of material to be removed is also the same. Therefore the technique that can apply the most effective work energy to the surface of the block will be faster. It is expected that the energy efficiency of the pendulum-plane approach is about three times better than that of the hand-chisel method (two arms and upper body versus one arm).

Note that the cutting tools in the pendulum cut in both directions. For that reason, and because of the large momentum of the pendulum, they do not need to be chisel-shaped. A wide, flat-bottomed shape (rectangular-bar shape) would work well. There is no need for the tool to have a sharp point. This means that the cutters will last longer before they need to be replaced or re-sharpened. The actual cutting tools could be a hard stone or copper.

The two requirements for this technique to succeed are modest and well within the grasp and understanding of the Egyptians. Fundamentally the base and pendulum must be straight and parallel to within 1/100 of an inch (about the thickness of a business card). A simple straight-edge tool can be used to measure the base and pendulum for flatness. Placing one straight-edge against another can easily show variations of 1/100 of an inch. Once the base and pendulum are known to be straight, they can be adjusted to be parallel with a measuring rod. This "spacer" rod is cut to the precise height desired between the base and pendulum. Then it is placed vertically between the base and pendulum and then the pendulum (or base) is adjusted to just touch the rod. This operation is repeated for at least two points along the pendulum and base, at which time the pendulum is known to be parallel to the base. Given a fixed rod, it is not difficult to adjust two objects to within 1/100 of an inch. The length of the rod is somewhat arbitrary. The rod length (or finished block size) is not as important as is the repeatability of the machine.

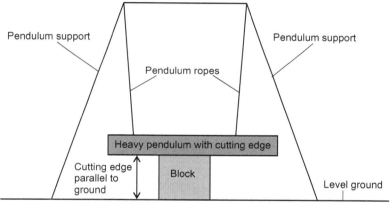

Figure 8-1: A simple plane is similar to a playground swing. The ropes limit the bottom of the arc and the height of the block. Incremental movement of the block through the plane results in a top face that is flat and parallel to the bottom.

A number of variations on the pendulum-plane theme are possible. The method shown in Figure 8-1 indicates that the pendulum is swung parallel to the block's movement through the device (like a child's swing). Alternatively, the pendulum could be swung side to side, or perpendicular to the block's movement. This action mimics the use of a two-man saw. With this alternate design many small blades perpendicular to the cutting direction would be used instead of one long blade running the length of the pendulum.

Ropes probably aren't the best choice for supporting the pendulum. They would allow rotation of the pendulum, which would affect its height. Instead wooden rods with small rope loops only at the ends to connect the pieces together is probably a better design. This would reduce the possible twisting movement. In this instance the ropes are actually acting as simple bearings.

As noted the pendulum-plane provides two useful characteristics: it automatically limits the cutting depth and the momentum aids in applying energy to the block's surface. However there could be a slight scalloping of the surface as a result of the arc of the pendulum. It is not known if this is would be a significant factor or if it would take too much effort to eliminate by manual smoothing. This scalloping can be completely eliminated with a different plane design that is shown in Figure 8-2.

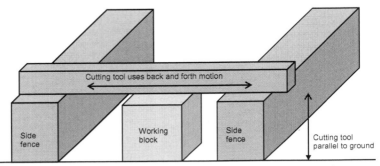

Figure 8-2: Another simple plane uses side fences made from stone or wood to limit the downward cutting distance. The tool does not contact the side fences until the block is the finished. The cutting motion is back and forth like a two-man saw.

This approach eliminates the pendulum so that scalloping cannot occur. Instead the cutting tool rests on the block and is moved back and forth over the block to remove excess material (like a two-man saw). The side-fences automatically limit the depth of the cut. Obviously, the height and straightness of these fences are critical. But it has already been shown that measurements to within 1/100 of an inch are not unreasonable. The side-fences are not used support the cutting tool so there is no wear on them. They are only used as a means for measuring the proper height. There are many variations on this theme as well.

SQUARING THE SIDES

At this point the block has flat and parallel top and bottom sides. (Note that the first side could have been smoothed by planing it instead of dragging it. The choice is somewhat arbitrary.) The next step is to smooth a side such that it is at a right angle to the top and bottom.

This turns out to be a fairly simple task. The Egyptians were known to possess tools that allowed them to measure horizontal flatness, verticality and squareness (Lepre, 238; Smith, 74; Lehner, 210). Even without unearthing these tools, this is abundantly clear by simply looking at their remaining works. They could not have been built without the availability of such measuring tools. Additionally, there are many simple methods that allow the fabrication of these measuring tools.

The first step in squaring the block is to level the ground (or slide-plate) under the plane so that it is horizontal. The cutting bar is adjusted as necessary to be parallel to this. Then the block is tipped onto one of its non-finished sides and adjusted to make the planed and parallel sides vertical. The top of the block is then machined with the plane. The result is that this new horizontal side is perfectly square with the previously finished two vertical sides to the limit of the machine. This process is repeated for the remaining three sides, creating a finished block with sides that are parallel and square.

This does not produce a cube. It produces square angles, parallel sides and rectangular-shaped blocks. A long rectangular block could be passed through the machine without difficulty. Additionally, as noted at the start, only five of the sides need to be finished. The sixth side that faces inwards can be rough and non-square.

However, the result so far is a rectangular block. The casing stones have the front face at 51.9 degrees rather than 90 degrees. The solution to this problem is to build a cradle for the block that holds it at precisely 51.9 degrees. This face would probably be worked last, so that the cradle would hold finished and square faces. This would make alignment easier. Once the block is set to the proper angle, it is passed through the plane for a finished face. It is presumed that the block will be roughly dressed to this angle before machining. Rough dressing would be faster than removing all of the rock by machining. (Chunks of rock would be removed, instead of powder.)

The finished blocks will be smooth with no significant chisel marks. They will be flat and square to the limits of the settings of the machine. It was seen that 1/100 of an inch is not unreasonable for the precision of such settings. More importantly, they will be of precisely the same height and have precisely the same face angle. These aspects are critical for properly fitting the blocks. Very minor discrepancies here would result in misalignments that would be very apparent visually.

It may be that additional polishing of the blocks is required. This would probably be done by hand. The tool would likely be a hard stone with a flat face shaped something like a small brick. It would be rubbed over the surface to remove minor imperfections (like sandpaper). Water might also be used. This would tend to create a slurry that would enter minor voids. Upon drying, the block would have a smooth and polished appearance. It is imagined that it might even create a shiny sheen (which would be visually spectacular).

There is no definitive evidence for these machines other than the fact that a very large numbers of perfectly formed blocks exist. One can choose to believe that these were all hand fabricated and attribute to the Egyptians stone-working skills that are beyond understanding. Or one can attribute to the Egyptians the intelligence and common sense to develop simple stone-working tools to assist them in making precise and repeatable operations. Given their fantastic engineering accomplishments, the latter appears more likely.

POSITIONING THE TOP-MOST BLOCKS

One of the more enduring questions is how the final, top-most blocks were placed. They could not have been installed last because there was no place for the workers to stand. The steep angle of the finished pyramid sides makes that impossible. Positioning them early in the assembly procedure suggests that the faces were finished from the top down. This would require hand-finishing all of the casing stones in place and without error because there would be no way to replace one if things went wrong. This is difficult to accept. Ramps are the classic answer to this problem. It is clear that a ramp can be built to reach the top of the pyramid in order to place the last casing stones. However, as was shown in earlier chapters, large ramps cannot have been used. Instead, the idea of "big steps" can be applied.

The pyramid without the outer casing stones is very much like a staircase with steps of about 2.5 feet tall and four feet deep. The width of these steps spans the side of the pyramid at that height. Manipulating large and heavy blocks on such a narrow platform is difficult and dangerous. Figures 6-4 and 6-5, photographs of the lift-lever models, illustrate the difficulty. The steps are simply too shallow. However, if the steps could be made deeper, then it would be easier and safer to maneuver the blocks and casing stones.

Figure 8-3 provides a simple solution: add a block to the lower course to make a step that is eight feet deep and five feet tall. The width of this step can be made as long as the pyramid side. If eight feet is still too narrow, add two more blocks to the next-lower course to make the step 12 feet deep and 7.5 feet tall. Twelve feet deep certainly appears to be adequate. A width of 20 feet, or five average blocks, also appears adequate. Building a 20-foot by 12-foot platform requires only 15 additional blocks. Only 70 of these big steps are needed to reach the top of the pyramid. A total of 1050 additional blocks is required, which is an insignificant 0.04% of the volume of the pyramid. Only one series of big steps is required but multiple series can be used if desired.

The lift levers are certainly capable of lifting 7.5 feet. Instead of two lever operations to lift a block one course, six operations would be required to lift the three courses. This would require three times as many man-hours but the height raised is also three times greater. Therefore, the per-course time to lift a block is the same as in the Time-Motion Analysis (Appendix 3). The only modifications required for the levers are the addition of four more block supports of different heights and four more rope-length tie points.

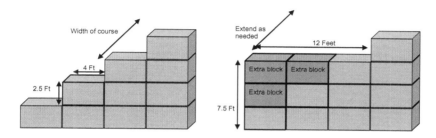

Figure 8-3: The basic pyramid is like a set of stairs with steps 2.5 feet high, 4 feet deep and as wide as the course. This is shown on the left. It is difficult to manipulate heavy blocks on such a narrow platform. Adding just three blocks (shown on the right) creates a platform 12 feet deep, 7.5 feet high and as wide as necessary. A width of five blocks makes the platform 20 feet wide which seems adequate. Fifteen blocks are needed for this big step and only 70 big steps are needed to reach the top of the pyramid.

ORDER OF ASSEMBLY

With the tools and techniques described, a basic order of assembly can be defined. There are many possible variations. The simplest one follows.

The pyramid is completed layer by layer. Generally, each layer is finished, including the casing stones, before the next layer is started. The far-side finished casing stones are placed first and then fill blocks are added, working towards the front ("front" is defined as the side closest to the quarry). Side and front casing stones are placed as required. The exception to this is where the big steps will be needed; which is presumed to be on the front face. The finished casing stones are not placed here. This provides a route (perhaps multiple routes) for workers and materials when nearing completion. When as many blocks as possible have been placed, the big steps are built. At this point, only the top-most blocks need to be put in place. The back and sides are finished with the casing stones placed. The front face is finished with the casing stones except where the big steps are.

The top-most blocks, including the top casing stones, are placed with the aid of a wide "big-step" working platform. These top-most blocks are relatively small, about 20 inches high (Lepre, 254) instead of the 30-inch average, and weigh about a ton (Smith, 102) instead of 2.5 tons. The casing stones are smaller than that. Once these top-most blocks are in place, the big steps are replaced with the final blocks and casing stones. This last task is finished from the top down. The lift-levers allow placement of blocks above the course the base is on, so these blocks can be replaced without a problem. And because of the big steps this replacement activity is not too dangerous or awkward.

The very large blocks that are used for the King's chamber and Queen's chamber are raised layer by layer as the pyramid grows. They are placed in the middle of the pyramid field at the very start. As the course reaches that point during construction, the large blocks are lifted one course. Core blocks could be moved underneath them or else they could be shifted onto the new course to make core block placement easier. (If they are shifted to the new course then they may be initially offset to compensate for this lateral movement.) This approach allows significant room to incorporate many lift-levers. For an 80 ton block, 40 tons of lift must be applied to raise one end. This requires 16 standard lift-levers and 48 workers. Special extra-large levers could be built to reduce the number of levers and workers, but this is may not be efficient because of the very few large blocks that must be raised.

WOODEN TOOL QUANTITY

Wood is the material used for quarter circles, lift-levers and block planes. In order to create estimates for tool-production time and the amount of wood required, we must first calculate how many of each of these tools are likely to have been used. Most importantly, it must be shown that the amount of wood needed was actually available. For simplicity, it will be assumed that 25% of the wood is wasted during fabrication. This is a large amount of waste, but cutting square beams from round wood will waste about 10% just to start. The legs of the lift levers and block planes can be round, without any problem. The quarter circles require a flat bottom and would probably have been cut from squared beams. Proper layout of the quarter circles can reduce the waste but curves do not make efficient use of material.

The number of quarter circles required depends upon the number of quarter-circle roadways. The simplest design will be chosen. It will consist of one quarry feeder road, one quarry collection road, one main road, one pyramid distribution road and one pyramid supply road (see Figure 5-7). Each of these roads is about

750 feet long. The base of the quarter circle is 40.3412 inches (calculated, see Figure 5-1). About 450 quarter circles are needed for each road, for a total of 2250 quarter circles. If the quarter circles are made six inches wide, then each quarter circle requires about 1.105 cubic feet of wood. (The three pieces of dimensional lumber that were used to fabricate the quarter circles mentioned in Chapter 5 summed to 4.5 inches wide. They were separated with spaces for a total width of about eight inches.) The quarter circles require just about 2,500 cubic feet of wood.

The amount of wood needed by the block planes is quite variable depending upon the design chosen, the quantity desired, and the pyramid schedule. Presuming 100,000 casing stones are needed and only one can be machined in a day, then about 275 planes are needed for a one-year schedule. This is the worst case situation. If a simple tripod is used to support each end of the pendulum and these tripods are made up of four-inch diameter wooden legs, each six feet long, then each plane uses about 3.14159 (!) cubic feet of wood. This totals about 865 cubic feet of wood. This value is correspondingly less if the schedule is lengthened.

These dimensional values were chosen simply as workable values and are fairly arbitrary. But the result is *Pi* that is accurate to six places. One could choose to attribute special meaning to these dimensions and propose all sorts of imaginative implications. This was discussed in Chapter 2. However it is truly enlightening to see such a coincidence occur in a context that supports the view that there is nothing numerically extraordinary about the base-to-height ratio of the Great Pyramid.

The number of lift levers also depends upon the schedule. Placing 2.5 million blocks in one year requires one block to be placed every six seconds (on average). If it takes three minutes to lift one block, at least 30 levers are needed to maintain the pace for each course, for a total of 6300 levers. Unfortunately this value is not reasonable because it is based on an average rate. The placement of the blocks will be faster at the low courses and slower at the higher courses. (Thirty levers are not needed to place the capstone.) This is just common sense. It is possible to create complicated formulas based upon various assumptions. However, the point of this exercise is to determine a rough estimate of the number of levers needed. A different approach may prove useful.

The Great Pyramid consists of 210 courses (see appendix 1). At least one lever will be needed for each course. Will 210 levers be adequate to service the pyramid, assuming that they can be supplied with blocks at the required rate? The first course needs no levers. The second course can be serviced by all 210 levers for a rate that is seven times the average. The third course can incorporate 105 levers per course for a rate that is 3.5 times the average, and so forth. At the eighth course, the rate is exactly the average. Since 50% of the blocks are placed at course 44, this is the point where the average should be — not at course 8. Working backwards provides a value of about 1200 levers. This is still a very large value and is based on an arbitrary schedule of one year. However, in order to be conservative, this number will be used.

The lever consists of two main supports each about eight feet tall, two cantilevers about 16 feet long (see Figure 6-7) and the actual lever which is about 13 feet long. The lever was already specified at six inches in diameter in chapter six. The two sides of the lever only need to support half that weight so four inch diameter wood can be used for the support and cantilevers. They require about 3.67 cubic feet of wood, together. The lever is comprised of about 2.5 cubic feet of wood. Thus the whole lever uses about 6.2 cubic feet each. About 7440 cubic feet of wood is needed for all the levers.

The sum total of wood required for the levers (7440 cubic feet), the block planes (865 cubic feet) and the quarter circles (2,500 cubic feet) is 10,805 cubic feet. This is an extreme worst case value based on a one year schedule. A more realistic value of five years reduces this requirement to about 4150 cubic feet. (These values do not include wastage.)

AVAILABLE WOOD

Egypt does not possess native wood of sufficient quantity and quality for the levers, planes and quarter circles needed. However, it is known that Sneferu (Khufu's father) sent a fleet of 40 ships to Lebanon for cedar wood (Lepre, 257). (It should be remembered that Sneferu was the pharaoh who actually built the first very large pyramids.) The Egyptian vessels of that day had "capacities of at least 100 metric tons and perhaps as much as 1,000 metric tons" (Smith, 84).

In Chapter 6 the density of wood was set to be about 75% that of water or about 45 pounds per cubic foot. Therefore the "smallest" ship of 100 metric tons (2240 pounds per metric ton) could carry just about 5,000 cubic feet of cedar. The worst case estimate of the wood requirement is 10,805 cubic feet plus 25% waste, for a total of 13,500 cubic feet. Only three ships out of the forty would be needed to provide 15,000 cubic feet of wood. It can be seen that the large pyramids require a substantial amount of wood. Sufficient wood was clearly available for all of these large pyramids plus substantially more left over for other efforts that would use wood (ship building, for example). (It is interesting that Lepre (p. 257) was puzzled by this large quantity of wood. He was unable to find a use for it.)

ADDITIONAL TIME REQUIRED FOR MINOR TASKS

The time necessary for these second-order tasks can now be estimated. These numbers are not precise but variations of 100% or more will make little difference in the overall schedule. Note that many other researchers do not include tool-making in their time estimates for building the Great Pyramid.

The first and easiest estimate is for the big steps. This requires the placement of additional blocks. It was shown that about 0.04% of the pyramid's volume was added. This involves quarrying, moving and lifting the stones just like ordinary pyramid blocks. These blocks must be removed, as well, and an equal time will be allotted for this. Thus the time required for this task is 0.08% of the basic total of 3.325 million man-days, or an additional 2660 man-days.

The 275 planes and 1200 levers are of about the same complexity and volume and will be presumed to require equal construction time. (These values are inflated because of the arbitrary one-year schedule.) They are very simple to build and it should not require much effort to cut and assemble six or eight pieces of wood. An estimate of three man-days per lever or plane will be used. This seems very conservative. The total additional time allotted for this is 4425 man-days.

About 2250 quarter circles are required. It is hard to believe that it would take one man more than a full day to cut one piece of curved wood. Copper saws were reasonably efficient with wood. The Egyptians may even have designed a tool to assist in the mass production of these "precision" pieces. The block-plane with side fences (see Figure 8-2) could be easily adapted to this task. Instead of flat and level fences, quarter-circle fences could be used. The result is a simple pantograph that fabricates identical quarter circles one after another. (However, sharp copper cutters would be needed.) To be extremely conservative, a full man-day per quarter circle will be allocated for this task. The total additional time required for this is 2250 days.

Casing stone finishing is the final chore to be estimated. Since there are 80,000 to 100,000 blocks to consider, it is fairly important to come up with a reasonable value for this. (This is a true second-order factor. The previous items can be seen to be third- or fourth-order considerations. The time required for their completion is totally insignificant to the whole.) There are three main sub-tasks for the casing stone job: moving the block, planing the block and rotating the block. We showed earlier that moving a block on a slide-plate takes only about 0.1 man-hours (Chapter 5). Tipping a block with ropes, levers and fulcrum blocks takes longer but is still only estimated to take 0.5 man-hours (Chapter 7). Planing one side of a block is less well-defined. However, the stone is soft and two men can apply a considerable amount of energy to the face of the block. A rough estimate of two man-hours per face will be chosen. To process one block, five faces must be planed; this requires five tippings and five passages of the block (the plane works the block in either direction). This equates to 13 man-hours or 1.3 man-days per block (10 man-hours per man-day) for a total of 130,000 man-days (for 100,000 casing stones.)

SECOND-ORDER TIME ESTIMATE TO BUILD THE GREAT PYRAMID

It is now possible to provide a second-order estimate of the time required to build the Great Pyramid. It will start with the conservative first-order estimate that was defined in Chapter 7. The minor tasks discussed in this chapter will be added to that base to create the new estimate.

1) Previous first-order estimate (Chapter 7)	3,325,000 man-days
2) Casing stone finishing (100,000 stones)	130,000 man-days
3) Big steps (placement and removal)	2,660 man-days
4) Quarter circle fabrication	2,250 man-days
5) Lever and block-plane fabrication	4,425 man-days
Second-order estimate total	3,464,335 man-days
With 10,000 workers the calendar time becomes:	346.4 days

REALISTIC SCHEDULE

It is not realistic to suggest that the Great Pyramid was actually built in one year. While it is theoretically possible, that would not have been a practical approach. In particular, during the lever fabrication examination it became apparent that a higher rate of quarrying is needed at the start. Upon reflection this makes sense. More blocks are used at the lower levels and they can be placed faster than the higher blocks. Unfortunately, many pyramid-building theories that have been proposed do not consider this. (Modern-day managers often make a similar mistake in thinking that a project can be completed in any calendar time as long as the total man-hour requirement is met. The engineer's standard, if crude, response to such wishful thinking is: "You can't get a baby in one month by making nine women pregnant today.")

Lehner (p. 225), citing some ancient graffiti found in Menkaure's Pyramid at Giza, suggests that two crews of 2000 workers each built the Great Pyramid. This is a very reasonable number. A straight ratio creates a calendar time of 866 days or 2.37 years. However, this is not a reasonable schedule either. These workers were not slaves and could not be expected to provide 10 productive hours per day, every day, for over two years straight (even considering the conservative time estimates used). A more realistic value is six hours of physical labor per day. This is still a large amount of daily physical labor, but it is a more acceptable number. It corresponds to 42 productive hours per week. Using this value the calendar time inflates to 3.95 years. This seems to be a much more rational calendar time figure.

This still presumes that the workers labored every day of the week for four years. While it is possible, this also seems unlikely. Those people were just like people of today. They had their own families and interests and certainly would not want to spend four years laboring constantly. Therefore it will be taken that they worked an equivalent of five days per week or 260 days per year. An additional 20 holidays per year will be added for various religious and other social events. This reduces the work year to 240 work-days and increases the calendar time to six years. This relatively leisurely schedule is much more human. It also happens to coincide very well with large building projects of today. For example the Hoover Dam (AKA Boulder Dam) employed an average of 3500 workers (Smith, 88) and took five years to build (two years ahead of schedule).

CONCLUSION

An examination of the second-order factors involved in pyramid building has not revealed any significant problems. The application of defined tools and techniques was adequate for all of these tasks. Simple tool-guiding machines were designed that allowed the precise finishing of the casing stones to within 1/100 of an inch. Additionally these machines eliminated the need for super-human skills in the consistent fabrication of the 80,000 to 100,000 perfect casing stones that were used in the Great Pyramid. The question of available wood was easily solved with the realization that Sneferu sent 40 ships to Lebanon for cedar.

The first-order schedule was modified to account for these extra tasks. It was found that the first-order estimate only had to be increased by about 4% from 3,325,000 man-days to 3,464,335 man-days to cover them. Evidence suggests that 4000 workers were employed to build the Great Pyramid. Using this number and applying a realistic construction schedule results in a calendar time estimate of four to six years to build the Great Pyramid.

Chapter 9. Social Considerations

Introduction

The Great Pyramid was not built as an isolated structure. It was not separated from the people who built it. Nor was it the only pyramid built. The Great Pyramid was only one piece of a large social, political and religious structure. In order for this (or any such) structure to succeed, certain fundamental social principles must be understood and applied properly. It is unfortunate that these principles are not often discussed in any detail because they help to explain how the Egyptians were able to build the pyramids. The pyramids were built by people. If these people cannot be understood then the true mechanism for building the pyramids cannot be understood, either. The pyramids emerge from the character of the Egyptian society.

Egyptian Psychology

People were no different 4500 years ago. The social structure was different, but the people were not. Egyptians laughed, cried, told jokes and were envious if their neighbor had more goats then they had. *Homo sapiens* has not changed in any meaningful way in the last 4500 years.

People then had the same amount of native intelligence as people have today. Education and intelligence are not necessarily correspondent. Clearly, the average Egyptian did not have our level of scholarship and technology. But they had at least as much curiosity and imagination. They could and did analyze things logically and with astute perception and insight.

What they didn't have was a well-documented history and a large population. Modern society builds on the advances of the past, and schools and new information technologies make vast amounts of information available to the public at large. The ancient Egyptians certainly had writing in the form of hieroglyphics. But "books" were not commonly available. There was no method of mechanically reproducing records. Copies were made by hand. Few records were available and were precious. Illiteracy was the rule.

The relatively small population, estimated to be between one and two million people (Smith, 206), could support proportionally fewer scientists and artists than a larger population. Fewer scientists will generally result in fewer scientific discoveries. However it is clear that the ancient Egyptians valued both the sciences and the arts. Their dedication to the arts is clearly demonstrated by their beautiful sculptures, paintings and designs. Their science astounds us today with their architecture and mummification techniques. It is generally accepted that before they built the Great Pyramid the Egyptians invented the decimal system, paper, copper plumbing, an alphabet, and surgery.

It seems apparent that their social attitude was one of enlightenment. The people enjoyed their lives and their society. This pharaonic civilization endured for over 3000 years. No other method of government on earth has existed for even 1,000 years. In comparison, the Roman "Empire" as such lasted a mere 300 years. This fact suggests that in Egypt there was a mutual respect between the ruling class and the people. Perhaps it was like a paternal relationship. The successful character of this social organization is not something that can be ignored. It is woven into the substance of their culture. It is important to consider this when postulating how major public works were managed.

Available Population Problem

When considering a massive project like the Great Pyramid it is clearly necessary to determine what the available worker population is. It will be presumed that the population of Egypt of that time was about 1.5 million people. This is half-way between the estimates of one and two million and is the same value that Smith (p. 206) accepts (Lehner, p. 7, suggests 1.6 million). Smith (p. 206) suggests that the potential workforce was about 375,000. His rationale is that 50% of the 1.5 million people were female and a further 50% of the men were not capable of working on the pyramid (without explanation). He goes on to suggest that 50% of the remaining 375,000 available workers were farmers, who were required to provide crops, which reduces the available workforce to 137,000.

This estimate does not appear to be reasonable. The Egyptian society was primarily agrarian. It seems very likely that a much higher percentage of them were farmers. Typically other references indicate that about 90% of the people were farmers (Dollinger 2006). As late as 1700, about 90% of the people in America worked in agriculture (Doyle 2006). If the same ratio is applied to the Egyptians then only 37,500 people (out of 375,000) were available as workers. Smith specifies a peak workforce of 26,100 people (p. 230). Taking two-thirds of all the available workers for three years and a somewhat lesser number for ten or more years is simply not plausible. It implies forced labor. This conflicts with the apparent essence of the Egyptian society of the time. (Note that Smith provides very different workforce values in different places in his book. This is discussed in more detail in the next chapter.)

Smith (p. 207) also suggests that additional workers were available during the annual flooding of the Nile. The idea is that the farmers would be idle during this time. This suggestion does not seem reasonable, either. Farmers do not simply tend crops. The chores are never ending on a farm. Animals must be fed and watered every day. During the flooding, this can be more difficult than normal. Food must still be gathered and processed in order to be able to eat. If fresh crops are not available, then other food sources must be found. This can include hunting and fishing. The competition for fish and wildlife must have been higher during the flooding, when more farmers are doing the same thing. Clothing must be woven, seeds must be gathered for the next season, drinking water must be hauled, fires must be tended and so forth. Just because there are no crops to tend does not mean that the farmer is idle. Tending the crops is only one of many tasks that require a farmer's time.

There were additional chores that accompanied the annual flood as well. The Egyptians understood and practiced irrigation. During the flooding the water was diverted into basins for later use. This required considerable labor throughout the flooding season in the construction and removal of dikes and ditches. The control of water supplies was critical to the success of the next season's crops. It must always be remembered that Egypt was a desert. The deposition of fertile soil contained in the floodwater sediment was critical. It is not credible that these crucial factors would be ignored by the people of the time. Their lives depended upon arable land and flourishing harvests. The annual flood brought life to the Nile valley. It was a time of vital importance for everyone's survival. Water was the only thing that kept the desert at bay. The flood season is actually the least likely time that additional workers would be available to build the Great Pyramid.

The standard method suggested for pyramid construction leads to an untenable situation. There aren't enough available people to build the Great Pyramid. The idea of conscripting a very large percentage of available men to labor continuously for many years challenges the character of enlightenment that the Egyptians seem to have possessed. Governments generally do not last too long if the populace is bitterly unhappy. Societies that celebrate art and science are not usually oppressive. Art is a manner of self expression. Science is a form of truth-seeking and it forces changes. Strict and regimented governments habitually have difficulty with self expression and with changes in the status quo. They often dismiss and discourage science and art. These are conflicting social characteristics.

Lastly it is difficult to imagine tens of thousands of men working in social isolation for ten or twenty years. These people were human. It is not reasonable to believe that they would readily give up their families and friends to spend the rest of their life working on a pyramid. At the very least, wives and children would have had to be brought to the pyramid site. This would have created additional significant problems. The pyramids were not built on fertile ground. Therefore the workers, as well as their families, would have to be fed and cared for. This more than doubles the number of people to support. During the decades of pyramid construction, families would be created and would grow. People would come to think of the site as home and it might be difficult to de-populate the area after the construction was completed. Re-locating tens of thousands of families is not an easy task. Nor is it one that would place the pharaoh in good stead.

Volunteer Workers

A small workforce of about 4000 men with a construction schedule of four to six years can harmonize with human nature and the prevailing social conditions instead of conflicting with them.

It is natural for near-adult men to yearn to escape from the confines of their parents' homes. It is also natural for young people to imagine accomplishing great things in their adult life to come. However, they may not be prepared to live entirely on their own. One solution is military service. The recruit spends two to four years away from home but in a structured setting that includes guidance and oversight. The young man may learn a new skill. He certainly will be indoctrinated into the accepted social setting. Upon completion of the enlistment period the new adult returns home with a freshly found sense of social values and self worth. If the youth was involved in a significant project, a feeling of accomplishment is also present.

How many young men were available? In order to determine this, an examination of the age distribution of the ancient Egyptian population is necessary. With a population of 1.5 million people, it will be assumed that 750,000 are males. Since about 50% of the children did not live to their fifth year (Dollinger 2006), the age range will be from 5 years to 70 years. It will be assumed that no Egyptian lived more than 70 years and the average life-span was about 40 years (Dollinger 2006). This defines two points on a curve, showing that 100% of the population was alive at 5 years old and 50% was alive at 40 years old. The last detail is to determine the death rate for people from 5 years old to 40 years old. For simplicity a straight-line rate from 5 to 40 will be used. This is the age range where humans are the heartiest, so a linear death rate seems plausible. Other death rate curves can be used, but the results will be quite similar. With these assumptions the teen-age population distribution can be estimated. The calculated male population value for ages 17 through 21 (five years) is about 90,000.

It seems practical to consider that five to ten percent of these 90,000 young men living at home would be willing and able to spend several years at a job that paid reasonably well, held great prestige (working directly for the pharaoh), created breathtaking monuments, and offered the real possibility of learning an important and profitable trade. With this approach to recruitment it seems very reasonable that there would an abundance of volunteers.

This program is not exactly like military service because there is the potential for considerable personal danger associated with the military. In fact, there does not seem to be a comparable social policy in place today. It has facets of the Peace Corps as well as the Army Corps of Engineers. Perhaps a modern comparison would be something in the form of an academic scholarship/internship with a salary, available to any young man. However it must also be realized that the pharaoh was seen as nearly a god. He had fame and fortune that transcended those of modern day movie stars, sports figures and teen idols. It certainly appears that there would be considerable competition for volunteer positions.

Instead of clashing with human nature, the volunteer approach embraces it. The close association of the youths with the center of power bonds them to the pharaoh. It fosters loyalty and respect at a time when a young person is pliable. The great public works become a source of pride for the workers as well as the community. Working together creates social skills and connections that are important for any group to be effective. Simply, the pyramids and other fantastic monuments become a major cohesive element for the Egyptian society and government. They were not chores to stoically endure; they were a celebration of a jubilant and proud society.

The Big Picture

The most significant problem with the standard theories on pyramid building methods is that they present an inherent dissonance that is instinctually apparent to most people. The theories call for tens of thousands of people to renounce their humanity for decades in constructing the huge pyramids. There are the Dr. Jekyll and Mr. Hyde aspects to the pharaoh, who alternately forces workers to perform at an inhuman pace while he is being honored by the populace (although there are modern instances of this). The beauty of the artwork contrasts with the idea of forced labor. These pieces, and many others, simply don't fit together.

However, it is now possible to assemble all of the disparate facts and clues and pieces of evidence into a form that is internally self-consistent and matches both the physical and social aspects of the ancient Egyptian society. All of this relies on nothing more incredible than what develops from the degree of creativity and intelligence among of the Egyptian engineers that enabled them to reduce the labor requirements of the huge pyramids to a minuscule amount.

The following is a speculative re-creation of how the projects might have been accomplished.

At regular intervals (perhaps yearly), the pharaoh would tax the people. This tax might be in the form of food, grain or services. At least some of the grain would be stored for distribution to the populace in the event of a poor harvest, because grain was the only foodstuff that could be kept for a significant period of time without going bad. At the same time as the taxation, a request for young male volunteers would also be made. If this was done on a yearly schedule, only about 1000–2000 men would be needed. These work positions would be for a period of several years. The young men would labor for the pharaoh on major projects. This combination of taxation and youth benefits would tend to offset the acrimony of taxation alone.

Since there were always ongoing projects, the workers were employed for a specific period of time rather than for a specific project (although there certainly could be exceptions). The Necropolis at Giza is more than just the Great Pyramid. Khafre's pyramid is nearly the same size. There are numerous small pyramids as well as Menkara's pyramid, which is over 200 feet tall. There are dozens of other stone buildings; many of which incorporate huge stone blocks. And more buildings, canals and mastabas are being discovered on a regular basis.

Lastly, the Sphinx is at Giza. The work at the Giza Plateau clearly took decades to complete.

The constructions at Giza are attributed to the pharaohs Sneferu, Khufu and Khafre. But Sneferu, in particular, also built the Bent Pyramid and the Red Pyramid at Dashur (along with associated structures there). Those two pyramids combined contain more stone than the Great Pyramid. It seems logical that a corps of workers would be maintained by these pharaohs to work on the various different projects that were continuously being constructed.

A "permanent" workforce of about 5,000 at Giza (Smith, p. 130) is a natural outgrowth of maintaining this corps. The individuals would only be present for a few years but the corps would have existed at least throughout the reign of the three pharaohs, or about seventy years. Other sites would have had "permanent" facilities for the workers as well (Smith, 131).

It would not be surprising if the organization resembled that of the military. Lehner (p. 225) describes how a "Crew" of 2000 men is broken down into two "Gangs" of 1000 each. A Gang is further sub-divided into five named "Phyles" of 200 men, comprised of twenty groups of ten men (or ten groups of twenty men). This regimentation is useful in maintaining the organization of the whole when individuals and small groups come and go. It also fosters a powerful sense of belonging and social acceptance when a new recruit is given a place and a name.

Pride and acceptance of the group would invariably lead to competition between the groups. This is a natural state for young men and can be encouraged and used by the organization to improve performance. Males of this age are very willing to endure significant hardships for the good of the group. Success of the group creates a feeling of success for the individual. This is the fundamental concept behind teamwork and a good society.

The building of the Great Pyramid, while astounding, was not technically difficult and could be understood by the average person. (Contrast that with the specialized training of today in fields such as medicine or engineering.) Everyone could comprehend the order of operations, the techniques to be used and what the various pyramid building tasks were. This allowed individuals to perform different tasks at different times, which provided work variety and helped to alleviate boredom. Boredom is an invitation for carelessness and accidents. Obviously, when working with multi-ton objects, safety is an issue.

However, work variation can also be seen as cross-training. Some of the machines already described allow a non-skilled worker to perform precision operations (like casing-stone finishing). This diversity of labor is a benefit to the worker, who learns different aspects of the project. It also provides the opportunity for personnel to demonstrate their abilities over a wide range of jobs. If they excelled at something, then they might be given the chance to develop that talent to a greater degree and become a skilled worker rather than just a laborer. Skills were certainly appreciated at that time and could easily provide greater rewards than farming.

Generally, wherever isolated young men work, a community will develop to provide them with goods and services for a price. It seems difficult to imagine that ancient Egypt was an exception. There is considerable evidence that other people lived at the outskirts of the Giza plateau in "pyramid towns" (Lehner, 231). This secondary commerce is common today with any large and time-consuming project and at many isolated military bases. People, then as now, saw an opportunity to benefit from the situation and did their best to do so. Thus an additional subtle commercial infrastructure grew around these huge engineering projects that supported a substantial number of people. These people's livelihoods depended upon the pharaoh's stonework. It is natural that they would exhibit a strong loyalty to the pharaoh, too. Pyramid-building is seen to have a much wider range of social effects than first imagined.

Not all of the projects at Giza were pyramids. But, relatively speaking, these other building projects were very much smaller; often by three or more orders of magnitude. For that reason no significant infrastructure was necessary for optimizing the energy management (refer to Chapter 3). In these cases the task was to provide sufficient work for all of the men rather than minimizing the effort required. The standard methods of sledges and small ramps would certainly be adequate for these projects. The men would work relatively harder on a per-stone basis but the elimination of the infrastructure would simplify the process.

After a period of about three years, the young man might or might not return home. If he did return to his home, he would be rightfully proud of his accomplishments. He would speak well of the pharaoh. The young man would understand teamwork and social values much better. His rebellious years, that would normally be a difficult time for his family and neighbors, would be past. Instead a solid citizen with a deep loyalty to the both the ruling government and the social fabric would have blossomed. Obviously, this is a good thing for everyone.

Or perhaps the young man would have already started a new life. Perhaps he had a new skill. Perhaps he had a wife. But he clearly had the experiences that he obtained by working for the pharaoh. These characteristics would be a considerable factor in his personality, shaping his future. The teamwork and pride that he enjoyed for the previous three years is not something that can be ignored. He would be one of the few special people whom the pharaoh trusted to build the world's greatest temples and pyramids. Confidence and a feeling of self-worth are the keys to any individual's success in life.

Later pharaohs built fewer and smaller pyramids. For the next two thousand years, only two pyramids would approach 10% of the volume of the Great Pyramid. This could mean that these later pharaohs had fewer resources. Or it could mean that the engineering concepts of the quarter-circle road were forgotten. Without the quarter circles, a pyramid about 10% of the Great Pyramid might very well have taken the same amount of time and people to build. However, in a larger sense, these considerations are not really important. What is important is that pyramid building was a consistent part of Egyptian society for 2800 years out of 3000 years (Lehner, 15). It does not seem reasonable that such a practice would endure if it was a significant hardship to the populace. However, it does seem likely that a mechanism for creating loyalty to the pharaoh and imbuing accepted social values in young men would play an important stabilizing role in any community.

Human nature has not changed since the time of the pharaohs. And it is clear that governments and societies that embrace human nature last longer than those that reject it. It has been shown that the ancient Egyptians were astute architects and engineers. They created incredible buildings that have lasted 4500 years. But it also appears that they were brilliant students of social psychology. They created a government that lasted 3000 years. It is this second fact that displays their real genius. Perhaps there is something that can still be learned from them: government as a true symbiote.

A Question of Timing

The casing stones of pharaoh Menkara's pyramid at Giza have a very unusual feature. The bottom casing stones are made from hard granite, which is not common. However, the most unusual feature is that these stones are not finished (photographs: Smith, 201; Lehner, 41, 221). Why is that?

Granite is an extremely hard stone, about 7 on the Mohs hardness scale. It is very difficult to work. Copper chisels are completely ineffective. Since they were put in place before they were finished, saws could not be used. It seems that the only tool that was available to dress granite was the dolerite pounder (Lehner, 211). This is a pear-shaped stone weighing about 10 pounds and it is used by smashing it against the granite. If used properly, small granite flakes will be removed. Lehner (p. 207) tried his hand at this and spent five hours removing about 0.8 inches from a one-square-foot area of stone. This corresponds to a removal of about 23 cubic inches of stone per hour (which is little more than the volume of a baseball). Clearly this is a difficult and tedious task.

This laborious job cannot have come as a surprise. The Egyptians had considerable experience in working with granite. They would have certainly known precisely how much labor would be required to complete the chore. So why wasn't it completed? The pharaoh's pyramid was his final resting place and had great social, personal and religious significance. It seems very unlikely that any pharaoh would willingly give up on finishing any part of his own pyramid. It was his legacy as well as a monument to his reign. It is out of character and it conflicts with human nature. The most obvious speculation one can draw from this is that pharaoh Menkara died before the pyramid was completed (Lepre pg 160). If so, it was the next pharaoh, Shepseskaf (Lepre, 145) who decided to abandon this time-consuming work.

This leads to another, admittedly very unconventional, thought. Perhaps all the pyramids were built after the deaths of the pharaohs; more like memorials rather than legacies. It is formally accepted that the pyramids were built during the reign of the pharaoh. But this presumption assumes that they required decades of effort. If the build schedule can be reduced to a few years, the idea that they were built after the demise of the pharaoh becomes less objectionable. There is also the time it takes to mourn and mummify the body. The mummification process is still not well known and it is possible that some processes required substantial time. And considering that the mummified remains have survived for millennia, waiting several years for the pyramid to be built is not inconceivable. This seems an unlikely scenario, but it may be worthwhile to ponder.

CONCLUSION

It is seen that the people and society of Egypt had an intimate relation to the pyramids and other monuments of the time. They built the Great Pyramid because they had the means to do it efficiently and speedily. It was not built to crudely demonstrate the power and authority of the pharaoh. Rather it was built to subtly cultivate respect and pride in both the worker and the community. The Great Pyramid and the other projects bound the workers to the pharaoh by exploiting (rather than fighting) human nature. These projects developed loyalty and confidence in young men at a time at an age when these traits are the most important and most pliable. It is not a coincidence that the longest living civilization also had the most numerous and most spectacular public works.

It is unfortunate that few writers examine the human aspect when considering these fantastic creations. It is often the case that the ancient Egyptians are presented as being dim-witted, dull, with plodding intellects that are incapable of any creative thoughts. But this image is entirely incompatible with the magnificent monuments and breathtaking buildings that these frail and unassuming human beings left as tributes to the longest living social structure in mankind's history. The pyramids were built because ancient Egypt had visionary artists, scientists and engineers. They also had brilliant leadership. The pharaonic rule operated with the mutual respect of the pharaoh and the people. The pyramids reflect the genius of the Egyptians at many different levels.

Chapter 10. Other Approaches

Introduction

Much has been written and many ideas proposed to explain the building of the Great Pyramid, perhaps more than any other structure on earth. The concepts range from variations on the traditional methods to proposals that are literally out of this world. Part of the reason for this is because the traditionally-accepted methods of sledges and ramps require such an inhuman a level of effort as to make that theory unbelievable. The idea of 25,000 laborers working every day for 23 years is certainly difficult to accept. So it is not all that surprising that other, admittedly fanciful ideas appear somewhat more credible when compared to this. Nor is it all that unexpected that some suggest that the pyramids were not built by humans at all.

Most of the authors of these unconventional approaches are neither archaeologists nor engineers. This in itself does not necessarily mean that their concepts are poor; rather it means that they rarely consider the archaeological evidence and/or fundamental engineering principles. Naturally, this can put their ideas in conflict with established facts. Unfortunately, it is often the case that facts do not have the power to dissuade these people from their beliefs. In fact the reverse is common. Once such a person "believes" in the idea, the mind closes and no rational discourse is possible. For that reason none of the more outrageous suggestions will be discussed. It is felt that no real purpose would be served.

This brief review will focus on three fairly modern and popular approaches: 1) the standard methods as proposed by Dr. Smith and Dr. Lehner, 2) the kite-lifting technique championed by Dr. Maureen Clemmons and 3) the cast-in-place concrete concept proposed by Dr. Joseph Davidovits. These procedures will be examined from practical engineering and Energy Management perspectives. Additionally the physical implications of their approaches will be identified and examined. The purpose of the discussion is to show that all of these methods fail to consider certain basic factors, are internally inconsistent and/or do not match the evidence found at the pyramid sites. It is difficult to entertain any pyramid building theory as valid if these points are not satisfied.

Cast In Place Concrete

In 1988 Dr. Joseph Davidovits (a chemist) published a book titled *The Pyramids: An Enigma Solved*. In it he proposes a very unconventional suggestion that the pyramids were not built from blocks of stone but were formed out of a "geopolymeric" cement. He states that the Egyptian workers carried wet cement up the sides of the pyramid and dumped their loads into wooden frames to form blocks. He proposes that the composition of the cement was about 93% limestone rubble and about 7% cement.

On the surface, this approach has a number of interesting and useful features. There would be no need for workers to struggle with lifting large blocks. The workers could carry as much material as practical. Different people could certainly carry different amounts. This would allow children and others not normally considered suitable for pyramid building to contribute to the effort. Casting in place would also apparently account for the precise fitting of the casing stones. As noted previously, manually chiseling about 100,000 pristine blocks to the required precision is certainly a daunting task. But if the stones were actually liquid, then a perfect fit should be easy to accomplish. The blocks would not have to be quarried as blocks. All that would be needed is a source of "rubble" (which is normally called "aggregate" in modern cement).

This idea eliminates the problems associated with the standard methods of moving large blocks, lifting large blocks and quarrying large blocks. Additionally, because there is no stone wastage/loss concern (as there was with the standard method of quarrying), there is no problem with the volume of the quarry. The cast-in-place theory also disposes of the need for a large ramp. This simplifies the whole pyramid building procedure and removes the need to dismantle the ramp when the pyramid is completed. Unfortunately, there are a number of insurmountable practical and theoretical problems with this concept.

Lehner's NOVA project showed that it took about 1.4 man-days to quarry one block. This required the removal of about 30 cubic feet of stone (as waste) for each block that was about 40 cubic feet in volume (see Chapter 7). Since the Davidovits procedure only requires stone bits, the estimate for removing a block can be used to determine the rate for producing rubble. In this case, since it requires 1.4 man-days to chip away 30 cubic feet, it will take about 1.87 man-days to create forty cubic feet or one average block's volume. This technique takes 33% more man-days than the standard method.

The effort of hauling the material up the pyramid in buckets (or their equivalent) can be estimated using the time-motion appendix, where it was measured that climbing 8.5 feet of stairs took 7 seconds at a normal rate and 12 seconds at a slow rate. (The actual value used for the time-motion study was a conservative 15 seconds.) It has also been stated that the weight limit for carrying objects is between 33% and 50% of the body weight. For a 150-pound person this corresponds to about 50 to 75 pounds. This is for carrying the weight over level ground. Hauling it up the side of a pyramid is significantly more difficult. When walking over level ground the weight is not lifted and it is held aloft with a locked, load-bearing leg. But when climbing, a single leg must lift the load (as well as the person) up each and every 2.5 foot tall step of the pyramid. A realistic maximum value for repetitive actions such as this is probably about 35 pounds. The time to climb will be increased to correspond with the total mass of the engine. This is sum of the average body weight plus the load which is 185 pounds. This is an increase of about 25%. Therefore the estimate for the time to climb 8.5 feet becomes 8.75 to 15 seconds. The approximate average of 12 seconds will be used (this estimate is a very small value for continuous and repetitive climbing operations with a load).

It will take about 2.3 minutes to climb the average block height of 100 feet. It will also take time to climb down. Obviously this is easier and faster, so an estimate of 1.2 minutes will be used for a total round-trip time of 3.5 minutes. (The coming-down time is probably closer to 1.5 minutes but, again, a very generous estimate will be accepted.) An average block weighs about 5,000 pounds, so about 142 round trips will be required to equal one average block volume. This comes to 500 minutes or about 8.3 man-hours. This is actually quite fast when compared to the standard methods of between 45 and 64 man-hours (Chapter 6).

However this doesn't include the mixing time. From experience it takes about 0.5 man hours to mix one 80-pound bag of cement. Mixing 5,000 pounds is the equivalent of about 63 of these 80-pound bags. Without a mechanized apparatus, mixing more than about 80 pounds in one batch is difficult for one person. Multiple batches can be mixed by multiple people, but the time per batch will remain about the same. Mixing is then seen to add over 32 man-hours to the task, which brings the total mix and lift time to about 41 man-hours. This is about the same as Smith's value of 45 man-hours.

But there are additional tasks. The frames must be built and removed for every block. This is not a trivial task when nails and screws are not available, although it may be possible to use ropes. It will probably take an additional man-hour or two per block if ropes can be used. Otherwise it will take a number of man-hours to assemble and disassemble the forms. It appears that there is no significant time savings with the cast-in-place approach when compared to the standard methods.

But there is a "gotcha" with this cast-in-place idea. How is one block placed adjacent to another? A square form must go all the way around the block in order to be held together either with ropes or some other means. This puts the cast-in-place block the thickness of a form-wall away from the adjacent block. When the form is removed, there will be a gap between the blocks.

It should be noted that, in practice, removing this frame piece would be a nearly impossible task in itself. Most typically the wood will absorb moisture from the cement and swell, creating great pressure. As noted earlier, this method was used to split solid granite. There are probably methods to ameliorate this problem but there would certainly be many instances where the wood could not be removed. It should be noted that Dr. Davidovits has been unable to indicate such an instance and, to the best of my knowledge, no trace of imbedded frames have been noted by the archaeologists examining the sites. It seems that such a situation would be something that would be remarked upon.

One could suggest a three-sided form (or a two-sided form for blocks meeting at a side and back — which is the most typical geometry). However, such forms are impossible to fabricate. This is because of the great weight of the cement, which is about 150 pounds per cubic foot. At the bottom of a very short 2.5-foot, form the lateral pressure of the cement is about equal to the weight of the height of the column of cement or 375 pounds per square foot. If the block is 4 feet wide, then this pressure is 1500 pounds along the base of the form. There is no practical method of building a wooden form or frame with only two or three sides that can sustain this pressure. (Building a concrete block is discussed in Chapter 5.)

A frame might possibly be made from solid stone but it would be oddly shaped, very heavy and prone to breakage. Worse, many of these "form-stones" would be needed. Over a 23-year period an average of about 300 blocks per day must be placed. Cement needs time to set. This setting time is at least a few hours for thin forms like sidewalks. For massive blocks, at least a day would be needed. So at least 300 very peculiar form-stones would be required (in reality probably many, many more than 300). None has been noted by archaeologists. This approach seems to be obviously impractical. (This unrealistic stone form alternative was proposed here and not by Dr. Davidovits.)

Additionally, maneuvering these big and heavy stone forms would take many men substantial time. It would probably take 10 to 20 men about 15 minutes to set the form in place and then another 15 minutes to remove it. This corresponds to about 5 to 10 additional man-hours per block. The total time to "lift" a block becomes 51 man-hours (compared to Smith's value of 45 man-hours) or an increase in required time of about 10%. Lastly, the surface of the cement must be kept wet as it dries. This is necessary to prevent cracking. Additional man-hours are needed for this task. Significant amounts of water from the Nile must be hauled and lifted.

All of this presumes that the Egyptians would attempt to cast tall blocks and attempt to employ two- or three-sided stone forms, which is highly improbable. It is self-evident to anyone who has actually used cement that the most efficient manner to build large objects is to employ relatively thin layers. A typical layer size might be 6 to 8 inches thick. This puts relatively little lateral pressure at the base, due to the plastic nature of the cement. (This plasticity is negligible at a depth of several feet.) A simple board, two or three inches thick and of appropriate height, with several backing stones of about 15 pounds or so, will provide a simple and sturdy form. (This could be two or three sided.) Nowadays, cement sidewalks three or four inches thick are often framed with simple pine boards and small stakes driven into the ground. Layers of a few inches dry faster (because of the increased surface area) and are less prone to cracking (because of less differential drying). If the Egyptians were smart enough to create a cement, it seems clear that they would have been equally smart in exploiting its benefits. They would not make the situation much more difficult than it already was.

This first part of the examination has taken the idea as given and explored its strengths and weaknesses. Matching the idea to the existing Egyptian evidence has not really been attempted. That will follow. The point of the above analysis is to show the inherent implausibility of the concept. The approach requires more time than the standard methods. But time and manpower are the two factors that are in short supply. Making the project take longer and/or using more men is counterproductive. And the idea founders on an impossible detail. Two- and three-sided wooden frames simply cannot be built as needed. Finally, the application of the idea is seriously flawed. Making large blocks from cement is not a task to embark upon casually. There is absolutely no reason why the Egyptians would choose that approach over relatively thin layers.

An unaddressed question is why they didn't simply make bricks out of the cement, if they had it. Carrying a brick up the pyramid is certainly much easier than hauling a bucket full of semi-liquid material. What's more, the forms could be laid out on the ground for much easier fabrication. Bricks were used throughout this 3000-year period for pyramids and mastabas. The Egyptians understood brickmaking well — they apparently invented it.

DAVIDOVITS VERSUS THE EVIDENCE

The blocks that are exposed on the Great Pyramid are not all the same size. The utility of the cast-in-place idea is significantly reduced when custom forms are required for every block. The Egyptians would not have used precious imported wood for one block and then discard it. No remains of wooden forms have been found. And it should be noted that wood that is covered by a concrete coating would tend survive much longer than plain, exposed wood.

There are many spaces between the blocks that Davidovits implies do not exist. A very conspicuous problem is that there are spaces below blocks. Obviously, if a wet cement mixture is placed over an open space, it will fall into that space. This is explicitly not the case in the Great Pyramid, where there are many instances of an upper block that straddles two lower blocks that have a distinct space between them. It also seems apparent that if there was any evidence of a "poured" rock it would be noticed and reported by the archaeologists. The use of mortar has been reported regularly (Smith, 90; Lehner, 202; Lepre, 238). But not a single reference has been found about a stone that sags between two lower stone. Additionally the actual use of mortar seems to contradict the whole idea of cast-in-place concrete. Smith (p. 182) provides a picture of mortar filling a space between blocks in the Great Pyramid itself. Why would this be found if concrete blocks were cast in place?

The exposed blocks display absolutely no indications of any imprints of any casting forms. Quite to the contrary, the exposed blocks unmistakably show chisel marks, indentations and many features that indicate that they cannot have been cast.

Then there is the subtle but significant problem of the granite stones that are used to make the King's chamber and Queen's chamber. The magnificent ceiling beams in the King's chamber weigh about 50 tons each (Lepre, 92). Since these are made from granite, the cast-in-place concept cannot be applied here. These stones must have been lifted in some manner to their present height. Davidovits provides no mechanism for this. If a ramp is proposed then the time to build and remove this ramp must be added into the overall time estimate. Additionally, it seems quite impractical to build such a large ramp for a small number of stones, even if they are very large. If a ramp is not used, then he should provide an explanation that addresses how the Egyptians lifted these massive blocks.

KITES

Dr. Maureen Clemmons has suggested that kites were used to lift the huge stones into position. This is certainly a creative approach and it has received considerable publicity in recent years. It has the advantages of eliminating the need to build huge ramps and allows easy lateral transport of the blocks. The process does not envision kites with long lines stretching from the ground to the top of the pyramid. Instead the kite would be tethered to the block and several people would control the block with short lines also tied to the block. The workers would then "walk" the block up the side of the pyramid with wind providing the lifting component. This is an ingenious concept and apparently is something that no one else has considered. She has succeeded in actually lifting a 6900-pound stone a foot or so off the ground using this technique (Tindol, 2001). On the face of it, this evidence suggests that the idea could have merit. However, upon close examination, the approach has considerable practical problems.

The kites that Clemmons used were nylon airfoils. These are typically designed with the aid of computers for maximum efficiency. The actual lift of the "mammoth" 30-foot kite was only 400 pounds (USATODAY.com, 2001) with a wind estimated to be about 15 MPH. An elaborate pulley system and fixed tower were additional parts of the experiment.

The ancient Egyptians possessed neither electronic computers nor nylon cloth and nylon rope. The utility of the idea wanes if a fixed tower is required. Also the Egyptians were not known to use pulleys at the time of building the Great Pyramid. The Egyptians did have sails and understood that power could come from the wind to push ships. It is not known if they had kites in any form (including toys).

A brief examination of the engineering requirements needed to lift an average block is a useful exercise. For simplicity the kite design will be a flat kite with two wooden cross members for support (like a child's toy). This is probably the most likely form factor and is seen all over the world. It also provides a fairly direct and simple analysis. Note that this is a "back of the envelope" estimate. This is common in engineering to determine if an idea is feasible. If it does not pass this analysis, it's "back to the drawing board."

The maximum calculated lift for an ideal "flat-plate" kite is estimated to be 0.02 pounds per square foot of kite area times the square of the wind speed. A toy kite with each side about two feet long provides about 4 square feet of surface area. Flown in a fairly stiff breeze of 10 MPH, the maximum lift is about 8 pounds. Note that this is the absolute maximum value and it depends upon many factors, including the angle of the kite. Also the term "lift" may be more accurately expressed as "pull." This is because the maximum force occurs when the kite is completely perpendicular to the wind. Since the wind normally blows horizontally, this means that the kite would have to be exactly vertical. This produces the maximum force on the string, or "pull," but zero vertical lift. The kite must be at an angle to the wind to fly. For simplicity it will be assumed that the kite is at a 45-degree angle to the wind and this reduces the maximum vertical lift to about 5.5 pounds. (This is why Clemmons required the complicated pulley system. It converted a lateral pull into a vertical lift.)

Paper is very good barrier to air and is a useful material for building small kites. But paper is also very weak. It cannot be used for large kites because it tears too readily. Large kites require cloth. Unfortunately, ordinary woven cloth allows air to easily pass through it. Air that passes through the cloth is not providing lift. This "leakage" reduces the effective wind speed. A rough estimate of this loss will be set at 50%, reducing the effective wind speed from 10 MPH to 5 MPH. Recalculating the lift with a 5 MPH effective wind speed and with a 45 degree angle provides a vertical lift of about 2 pounds for a flat-plate kite with an area of 4 square feet. This corresponds to 0.5 pounds of lift per square foot of kite area with an actual wind speed of 10 MPH. This will be the working kite parameters for the following examination.

In order to lift an average pyramid block of 5,000 pounds, the surface area of the kite must have 10,000 square feet providing 0.5 pounds of lift per square foot. This corresponds to a square kite that is 100 feet on a side and with a diagonal measurement of about 141 feet. Such a kite cannot be built out of wood and cloth. The 141-foot long wooden cross-pieces would have to be made from immense tree trunks just to support their own weight. And their weight would greatly exceed the 5,000 lift of the kite. Attempting to increase the size of the kite to offset this additional weight only makes the situation worse.

Since the lift of the kite depends upon the square of the wind velocity, doubling the wind speed to 20 MPH (10 MPH effective) will reduce the surface area required by a factor of four, to 2500 square feet. This shortens the wooden diagonal members to 70 feet. This is still clearly unfeasible.

If the wind speed is again increased by a factor of two, to 40 MPH (20 MPH effective), the kite area is reduced by a factor of four as well, to 625 square feet. This makes the diagonal members 35 feet long. At this point it might actually be possible to use a wooden beam for a cross member. However, it would still have to be very large to support its own weight. The absolute minimum estimate for the diameter of the cross member is about two feet! This corresponds to about 110 cubic feet of wood per diagonal. Assuming that the wood weighs 45 pounds per cubic foot (Chapter 6) then each member would weigh 4950 pounds. This weight still does not include the sail cloth or control ropes. It also seems unlikely that the wooden cross pieces would be strong enough to survive winds of that speed. Furthermore, 40 MPH is a gale force wind. That in itself would create complications.

Thus it is virtually impossible to build a flat kite from wood and cloth that will lift 5000 pounds. This is a classic example of a scale factor problem like those discussed in Chapter 3. In this case there is a change of about three orders of magnitude from a toy paper kite to a pyramid kite.

It is also seen that the fundamental problem is in keeping the kite stiff. The wooden cross members are the primary source of the weight. This is why air-foil kites are used by Clemmons. Her 30-foot kite is an air-foil kite and has no wooden members. But in order to create such a kite complex aerodynamic forces must be properly examined. This requires considerable mathematical analysis, which is usually performed with the aid of a computer. This clearly would have been beyond the capabilities of the ancient Egyptians.

The other way of making a kite rigid is to eliminate the cross pieces and use a solid material instead of cloth. This approach leads to an aircraft wing. Making a functional wing requires considerable mathematical effort as well as a good understanding of fluid dynamics. It seems certain that this approach was also well beyond the capabilities of the Egyptians of the time.

There is also an important practical problem with this idea. The lift varies with the square of the wind velocity. Any small change in the wind speed creates a huge change in the lift. One can only imagine the operational difficulties that arise when moving a 5,000-pound block with random support. The block could easily become a wildly swinging menace. A large number of workers would be needed to properly maintain control of a block. In this case it is their weight, rather than their strength, that would be most useful in keeping the moving block in check. A substantial fraction of the weight of the block must be employed. This corresponds to about 20 workers (3000 pounds) or more. Using 20 workers to stabilize a block does not really result in any time or manpower savings.

THE STANDARD THEORIES: LEHNER

Dr. Mark Lehner is an academic archaeologist with a strong interest in how the pyramids were constructed. As mentioned previously, he actually built a small pyramid in Egypt in a project that was televised by NOVA on February 4, 1997. It consisted of 186 blocks and was about 20 feet high. This simple experiment has provided important measurements of worker performance that have been used here. However, Lehner is not an engineer and apparently has had little actual experience in the manipulation of heavy objects. There are additional points to be noted as well (Lehner, 208). The whole experiment was limited to a total of 6 weeks for filming. This was broken down into 3 weeks for quarrying and three weeks for building. A motorized front-end loader was used to move and set the base course of blocks. Iron and steel tools were used for nearly all operations. However, Lehner did test copper tools and found that they would work the local limestone well.

The initial problem with the quarry volume (see Chapter 7) is noted by Lehner (p. 206). However, it is glossed over rather than addressed. In one sentence he states flatly: "The calculated amount of stone removed is c. 2,760,000 cu. m. (97.5 million cu. ft)...." He then uses exactly two sentences dismissing this legitimate on-site observation and measurement.

He also states (p. 206) that "30 to 50 percent of the stone was wasted" because of the channeling method of quarrying. But Lehner's own efforts indicate that this estimate is grossly low. A 30% waste factor corresponds to only 4 inches of kerf on a standard block (see Chapter 7). Lehner provides a picture of a worker standing halfway up to his thigh in the channel between two blocks (p. 207). It is clear from the photograph that there is an open space between the channel sides and both sides of the man's leg. This is obviously not 4 inches. Smith, who based much of his work on Lehner's, states that the channel is about "two hands wide" (p. 146) and also "wide enough for a man to stand in sideways," 145). Smith's estimate matches the photograph much better. The estimate used in Chapter 7, that a channel is 10 inches wide, is based on Lehner's photograph and Smith's descriptions and is believed to the best numerical value based on this visual and verbal documentation. A 10-inch channel results in 75% waste.

On page 209 Lehner states that "a 2-ton stone on a sledge can be pulled by 20 men or fewer." On page 203 he provides a photograph of workers pulling a block and the caption states that twenty men were used. This photograph does not show the full complement of pullers. On page 224 there is a better picture that shows all or most of the men involved in pulling and pushing a block. At least 18 men are shown and they appear to be expending considerable effort. However, on page 224 he refers back to page 208 (*sic*) and states that "10-12 men could eas-ily pull a 2-ton block mounted on a sledge up an inclined roadway."

One might view this as simply an editorial oversight except that he goes fur-ther to reduce the required number of men from 10 per ton to 3 per ton. This is partially based on a famous ancient relief (Lehner, 203) that shows 172 men pull-ing a statue that is estimated to be 58 tons and some other experiments using a "fairly friction-free surface." He then uses this new estimate to determine the workforce needed for the whole pyramid. Quite simply, Lehner blatantly dis-misses his own experimental results. He chooses to use a value that is 1/3 of what he measured in the field using the same techniques that he says were employed by the ancient Egyptians.

Lehner (p. 224) indirectly suggests that the distance the block must move is 1038 feet (19 minutes at 54.7 feet per minute). However, the maps on pages 205 and 230 shows a quarry with about the same footprint as the Great Pyramid about the length of a pyramid side between them. On page 206 he says that the distance from the quarry to the pyramid is "300 m (985 ft)." The average distance a block must travel is from the middle of the quarry to the middle of the pyramid. Since a side of the Great Pyramid is about 750 feet long the average distance is roughly 1500 feet (as defined in chapter 2). Again, Lehner is ignoring his own work and choosing to use a value that considerably favors the standard methods that he champions.

Lehner (p. 224) further proposes that the stone haulers could move at a rate of "1 km (0.62 miles) per hour." However he provides no support for this assump-tion at all. This is a rate of 54.7 feet per minute or about one foot per second. As we saw earlier, an average walking speed is about 4 feet per second (Appendix 3, TranSafety 1997). It is very difficult to accept that the workers could move as fast as a quarter of the normal walking speed while dragging a multi-ton weight. Even Smith (p. 172), a strong supporter of Lehner, provides a speed estimate of only "4 meters per minute" for the smallest blocks or only 13 feet per minute. Lehner's estimate is about a factor of four too fast.

Using these extremely favorable values Lehner (p. 225) estimates that 1360 workers were needed to move the stones (over a 23-year period). However, as noted above, he reduced number of workers by a factor of three, shortened the distance by 30 percent and increased the speed by a factor of four. If one uses Lehner's own original values from the NOVA experiment for the number of haul-ers and Lehner's own quarry-to-pyramid map-distance along with Smith's esti-mate of pulling speed, the number of workers skyrockets to 21,216.

Quarrying 2.5 million blocks at a rate of 1.4 blocks per man-day (Lehner, 206) requires 3.5 million man-days. Over a period of 23 years this effort calls for about 415 additional workers.

Lehner (p. 225) goes on to provide an estimate for "stone setters" but provides little support for his estimates. For the purposes of this discussion these stone setters will be ignored. The result is that Lehner provides experimental evidence that about 21,631 workers were needed to build the Great Pyramid. This does not include numerous tasks like loading and unloading sledges. Nor does it include the major task of building and removing a large ramp which requires an additional effort of at least 50%. In short, Lehner's NOVA experiment supports the generally accepted academic notion that about 30,000 workers worked every single day for the full 23-year reign of Khufu (Lehner, 224) in order to build the Great Pyramid, using the standard methods. This is actually not all that surprising since others have examined the requirements as well. As noted in Chapter 3, there is a certain minimum energy required for any project. If the methods are the same then the energy efficiency of the assembly is the same and since the materials are the same, the overall efficiency of the system is also the same. Thus any reasonable analysis using the techniques assumed by the standard theories will result in a manpower requirement that is similar to any other analysis using the same standard techniques.

However, Lehner (p. 225) states that: "Our calculations suggest that Khufu's pyramid could have been built by two crews of 2000." These calculations are based on the extremely favorable values discussed above. They have been shown to be inordinately biased towards a small workforce. They have been shown to ignore the existing evidence and are inconsistent with Lehner's own research. The apparent reason for these illogical and unscientific "calculations" is to counter the inherently unpalatable and unconvincing concept that tens of thousands of Egyptians labored without relief for decades to build the Great Pyramid. These "calculations" are a subtle yet profound indication that Lehner himself cannot accept that concept either.

THE STANDARD THEORIES: SMITH

In 2004 Dr. Craig Smith published a book, *How the Great Pyramid was Built*. Smith is an accomplished civil engineer by training and profession with an interest in the Egyptian pyramids. His book relies heavily on the work of Lehner and Hawass (Smith, 10). It is important to note that Smith is more of an engineering manager than a hands-on engineer. This is apparent in his introduction (pp 16–27) where he discusses his work in terms of "program management" and "work breakdown structure." He also discusses directing major civil engineering projects. On the surface, it would appear that Smith would be the ideal candidate to examine the Great Pyramid and determine how it was built.

However, it seems evident that the pyramids were evolutionary in their design. The methods and procedures that the Egyptians employed were developed over hundreds of years. They were fundamentally copies of existing structures that, other than size, varied only slightly over 3000 years. Pyramids are not really complex structures when compared to modern civil engineering projects. They are basically just a pile of blocks. And, while it is necessary to manage the workers properly, everyone on the pyramid job site could perform everyone else's job (with a few exceptions). Compare this to a modern building construction site where there are: design engineers, heavy equipment operators, concrete workers, welders, crane operators, iron workers, electricians, plumbers, masons, woodworkers, glaziers, painters, laborers, and on and on. There is a much greater need for the proper labor management of a modern structure than there was for the pyramids.

The point is that trying to force-fit modern top-down management techniques into the ancient Egyptian construction style may not shed much light on how the Egyptians accomplished their fantastic feats of engineering. This top-down approach does provide a basis for a numerical analysis of the required tasks. And this is useful as a tool for measuring the effort involved for the various chores. But this analysis is based upon the standard techniques. The result is that his program management analysis of the building of the Great Pyramid does not really provide anything new. Rather it numerically clarifies the existing suppositions.

Because Smith is an engineer, much more attention will be focused on engineering details and their implications than was the case with Lehner. Obviously, if both Smith and Lehner incorporate a questionable engineering practice it is Smith that must be challenged. Smith is the engineer and should have a much better grasp of engineering principles. Lehner can be excused for making inappropriate engineering suggestions because he may simply be ignorant of concepts that lie outside of his area of expertise. Although, theoretically, he should not make such suggestions, in practice everyone speculates on how the Great Pyramid was built. Naturally, an archaeologist would have strong opinions on the subject and it would be absurd to seriously propose that he should refrain from voicing them.

The first challenge to Smith (p. 111) is his determination of the quarry size. He states that it has an "area of 600 cubits to 700 cubits by 800 cubits." (In the glossary he defines a cubit as being 54.4 centimeters which corresponds to 20.6

inches.) No references are supplied for this estimate. He says: "Furthermore, the survey would have showed...." This is a curious phrase that suggests that a survey was performed while at the same time indicating that it is actually conjectural. It is also clear that his values are "accurate" to 100 cubits. Thus those values only have one significant digit (refer to Chapter 2 for a discussion on significant digits). In the trade this is called a "WAG," a "Wild-Ass Guess."

Conspicuous by its absence is Lehner's value (p. 206) of the quarry volume, which is: "c. 2,760,000 cu. m (97.5 million cu. ft)." This measurement is accurate to three significant digits and makes it two orders of magnitude more precise than the WAG above. Any proper engineer will always embrace a measurement with three significant digits over a WAG. Nor is it plausible to suggest that Smith was ignorant of Lehner's published value. Lehner and Hawass encouraged Smith (p. 13) and reviewed his efforts (Smith, 24). These three are colleagues in the study of pyramid construction. Smith references Lehner's *The Complete Pyramids* (Smith, 281) where this quarry volume is specified. It is impossible to believe that Smith did not read this section on pyramid construction where this value is clearly noted.

Also on page 111 Smith provides a value of "30 to 40 percent for trimming and waste" for quarrying the blocks using the channeling technique. This value is simply wrong. As noted above, 30% waste requires the channels to be only 4 inches wide. Smith (p. 145) says that the channel was "wide enough for a man to stand in sideways." On page 146 he states that the channel was "about two hands wide." And there is Lehner's photograph (p. 207) that shows a workman standing in a channel. (Lehner's statement that "30 to 50 percent" was wasted is even larger than Smith's.) Smith clearly did not take the time to perform this fundamental calculation.

This illustrates a common situation where high-level program managers fail to verify important engineering details. Normally this is not something they need to be concerned with because they rely on the lower-level engineers to be accurate. However, is it always dangerous to accept values from an unfamiliar or non-engineering source without verifying them. In this case, a few minutes with a calculator would have shown Smith that the wastage must be about 75% or double what he estimates on page 111.

Smith (p. 111) concludes that, "Clearly, limestone was present in sufficient quantity...." But it is not clear at all. Using cubits does not clarify the subject. Using a WAG instead of a true measurement does not clarify the subject. Failing to calculate the waste properly does not clarify the subject. The true result of his conclusions is not clarity but confusion and inaccuracy.

Smith's essential examination of the quarry is critically flawed. He is unable to show that there were sufficient building materials available to the Egyptians for the Great Pyramid using the methods that he proposes. Nor does he discuss the additional and significant ramp requirements (29% of the volume of the Great Pyramid) (Smith, 171) in relation the quarry volume. This omission is crucial.

The examination of the available worker population in Chapter 9 showed that his basic assumptions were incorrect. There is neither the eligible population he proposes nor is it likely that any additional people would be available during the flooding season. On page 206 he states; "The literature indicates...a workforce variously stated as 100,000 to 400,000." However he provides no references for this statement, which directly contradicts Lehner's remark on page 224: "a figure in the range of 20,000 to 30,000 is generally accepted."

Smith provides estimates for the four first-order tasks on page 206. "In all, 8021 workers are required to perform these four tasks working continuously over twenty years." Yet on page 230, he states, "the total labor expended on the project is 33.7 million labor-days." These numbers do not agree. Converting: 33.7 million labor days equals 92,329 labor years. Over twenty years this adds up to an average of 4616 men. This is a difference of nearly a factor of two.

Smith pointedly ignores Lehner's experimental results and proposes physical characteristics for his workers that border on the supernatural. Lehner's NOVA pyramid-building experiment provided hard empirical evidence that about 10 men per ton were needed to pull a sledge under typical conditions up a 4 degree ramp (7.14% slope). Smith (p. 172) specifies 5 men per ton while pulling a block up a 10 degree ramp (16.7% slope) as defined on page 164. He rationalizes this choice of figures by referring to studies of optimal and momentary sledge pulling over well-lubricated surfaces. Of course, such work in the field is neither optimal nor momentary. A brief intense task (like pushing a car a few feet) cannot possibly be repeated continuously for 10 hours a day, day after day, for twenty years. It is simply wrong for any engineer to base worker performance standards upon such ideal measures.

He expects the workers to carry 45 kilograms (100 pounds) "working continuously throughout the day" (Craig Smith, 205) with a two-handled basket (photograph Craig Smith, 141), which is certainly not very ergonomic. This is two-thirds of the body weight of a person weighing 150 pounds. Compare this to the ergonomic backpack load of 45 pounds for the difficult military "ruck marches" (Stew Smith, 2006) which are certainly not daily events. Experienced backpackers on the Appalachian and Pacific Crest trails carry a maximum of about 35 to 40 pounds (Les Smith, 2004).

Ergonomics is a critical factor in Energy Management but it is not well applied by Smith. On page 224 he shows a sledge hauling apparatus that consists of ropes and wood that allows many workers to pull as a unit. This is shown in operation on page 189. The men (four abreast) walk forward and push wooden members that are roped together and tied to the sledge. There are two very significant problems with this approach.

The first is that in addition to hauling the stone the men must carry the wood and rope. The wood must be large enough not to break under the stress of two men pushing with a rope in the middle. Experience shows that a two-by-four is insufficient (two inches by four inches nominal cross section). A four-by-four seems more than adequate. A cross-section halfway between these two is 3.5 inches and will be assumed. Each man carries the equivalent of one meter (3.28 feet) of this member. At 45 pounds per cubic foot for wood (Chapter 6), this corresponds to about 12.5 pounds per man. Smith expects his workers to carry about a third of the hiker's backpack weight (above) while simultaneously pushing a pyramid block.

Secondly, pushing a heavy weight is much harder than pulling. This is fundamental. Children instinctively know to pull backwards on the rope in a tug of war. This is because the knees can be bent when pulling backwards which allows the largest muscles in the body to be fully applied. It also lets the heels dig into the ground for better traction. Pushing up a very steep incline of 10 degrees greatly exacerbates this problem. It is doubtful that any significant power could be developed in this manner.

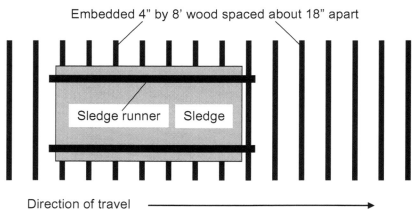

Figure 10-1: The positional relationship between the sledge and embedded wood employed by Lehner and proposed by Smith. About 16 pieces of wood are used per 25 feet.

Smith (p. 189) does incorporate a ramp surface with embedded timbers that is similar to the approach Lehner used (photograph p. 203) for the NOVA experiment. The wood appears to be about 4 inches wide and about eight feet long spaced about 18 inches apart (center to center). The wood is oriented perpendicular to the direction of travel (see Figure 10-1) and requires about 5.3 pieces per 8 feet of linear travel. This is extremely wasteful of expensive materials and it seems very unlikely that the Egyptians would use this method. Additionally, repeated passes of the sledge would wear grooves into the wood. These depressions would tend to keep the sledges moving over the same parts of the wood, causing more and more wear. Eventually the wear would require the replacement of the wood or refinishing of the roadbed. Neither is desirable. It is much more logical to orient the boards end to end as shown in Figure 10-2 and modify the sledges appropriately. (Many different sledge designs are possible.)

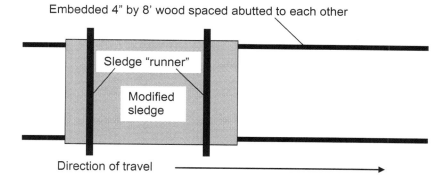

Embedded 4" by 8' wood spaced abutted to each other

Sledge "runner"

Modified sledge

Direction of travel

Figure 10-2: Changing the geometry provides many benefits. Most significantly only 6 pieces of wood are needed per 25 feet.

This has the following advantages: 1) It reduces wood usage by 63%, 2) It provides a much greater wood surface to slide on which reduces wear, 3) The wear is even over the whole piece, 4) The moving sledge has little contact with the ground which significantly reduces dirt contamination of the sliding surfaces. In effect it puts the runners on the ground (like railroad rails) instead of on the sledge. The sledges would be built differently with the "runners" at right angles to the direction of travel. In this case, wear on these "runners" would be beneficial because it would help keep the sledge properly aligned on the rails and reduce wander. In some ways this is similar to the "slide-plates" described in Chapter 5.

The last problem with the standard methods to be discussed is the question of moving the block on the pyramid proper. (This was briefly noted in Chapters 4 and 5.) This is a gotcha. In order to place a block in a particular position, it must be moved there over that course of the pyramid itself. This is self evident. The problem is that the surface of the pyramid course is rough-cut limestone. Hauling a sledge loaded with a 5000-pound block over this surface would result in enormous friction. It seems certain that the friction would be increased by at least an order of magnitude over the low-friction lubricated sledge/wood interface. Additionally, the sledge runners would be ruined very quickly. The relatively sharp points of newly quarried rock would tear into and embed themselves in the much softer wood. Trying to move a sledge over this surface does not appear feasible. The surface must be prepared to accept the sledges.

This means that a roadbed (or equivalent) must be constructed on every course for the blocks. Worse, each and every block location on every course must be serviced by the roads because every block must be moved by a sledge to its proper position and a sledge can't move over bare rock. In short, every course must be fully covered by a "road" in order for the sledges to place their load properly. This is a lot of additional work.

An estimate of this can be determined by applying the information created in appendix 2. Here it was found that 2.55 million blocks were needed for the Great Pyramid. Each block was defined as 4 feet by 4 feet (by 2.3 feet tall). The total course area is defined as 2.55 million blocks times the block area (16 square feet per block). This becomes 40.8 million square feet of area to cover with a "road." For comparison the road/ramp from the quarry edge to the base of the pyramid is about 1/5 of a mile. A road 20 feet wide that comprises 40.8 million square feet would be 386 miles long, or nearly 2000 times the that length. This is a massive task that is not included in any of the standard method estimates found.

But wait, there's more! Every "road" must be removed before the next course can be placed. There is no evidence that any blocks were placed on pyramid "roads"; the blocks are clearly placed stone upon stone with no intervening layer of anything between them. Nor would the builders want to place heavy blocks on a material that would shift and settle over time. To do so would endanger the stability of the whole structure. The example of Maidum is not easily forgotten.

DISCUSSION

There were two basic reasons to include this chapter. The first is to show that there are very significant problems with all of these proposed theories. (And many additional points could have been addressed, as well.) Some of the problems are obvious from the start and some of the problems require a basic understanding of the underlying science before the difficulties become apparent. But all the previously proposed theories are seriously flawed. They ignore evidence found at the Giza site, require superhuman abilities and impossible materials or presume a society that conflicts with human nature.

The second reason for this chapter is to illustrate the similarity between the conventional archaeologists/engineers (Lehner, Smith and Hawass) and the unconventional scientists (Davidovits and Clemmons). They are all smart, well-educated people with doctoral degrees. But the scientific discussion appears to be more like a political debate. Facts are ignored and data is "spun" so as to provide the best support for a particular idea. Therefore, it is not surprising that the arguments become personal.

In 1999, Hawass was quoted as saying, "Egyptologists call people with these kinds of ideas 'pyramidiots'." (Cray, 1999). Lehner publicly belittled Davidovits in the NOVA video, *This Old Pyramid*. That may have been a response to a statement made by Davidovits in his book: "This issue, however, is a matter for hard science, which must be confirmed or disputed by qualified scientists. It is not ultimately for Egyptologists, who are specialized historians, to approve or reject" (Davidovits, 1988, p. 239). Naturally this conflict does little to clarify the puzzle of the pyramids. It simply results in the entrenchment of all sides.

Science is supposed to be the impersonal and unbiased examination of nature. It is seen that this is not always the case. This is especially true when unconventional interlopers try to answer a problem that conventional science cannot. And that is really the fundamental problem. The conventional ideas don't work. They are simply not credible. As a result, other people are providing alternative explanations. The archaeologists respond with ways to make the standard methods more palatable, and in the process tend to rely more and more on speculation and supposition rather than on observation and measurement. There is nothing mysterious about this exchange. It's just human nature. Scientists, engineers, archaeologists and Egyptians are all human and all succumb to human nature.

The Egyptians still have a lot to teach us. But in order to learn, we must be willing to listen to them. They speak to us today through their artifacts, monuments, artistry and humanity. It seems that a proper understanding will require a perspective that matches their enlightenment and resourcefulness. This can be achieved but it requires a willingness to examine the evidence in an unbiased light and without preconceived ideas or personal agendas.

Conclusion

The fundamental problem with the standard methods proposed for building the Great Pyramid is that the use of ramps and sledges creates an implausible scenario. It is extremely hard to believe that 25,000 men would willingly give up 23 years of their lives to live in isolation and work at an inhuman pace. This situation is intuitively perceived as improbable, although this may not be something that can readily articulated. Instead there is a feeling — not of wonder, but of suspicion. A suspicion that something is missing, that something is not quite right. In order to answer this uneasy feeling, some people propose alternative methods of building the Great Pyramid. Unfortunately, these ideas are usually poorly thought out and ignore the evidence.

These imaginative ideas often generate considerable publicity because of the ubiquitous curiosity about the pyramids and subtle dissatisfaction that is associated with the standard methods. Naturally, the archaeologists who have spent much of their lifetimes studying the evidence find these interlopers and their wild ideas disagreeable. The result is quite predictable: hostility and entrenchment.

Instead of a scientific debate about the issues, there is argument and polarization. The exchanges have become much more like politics than science. And there has been a subtle but significant change in the position of the archaeologists. Instead of suggesting that the Egyptians could have built the Great Pyramid with ramps and sledges, they now insist that the Egyptians did use ramps and sledges. This bias makes it difficult for them to consider or accept anything different.

All sides fail to acknowledge evidence found at Giza, refuse to accept experimental results, ignore proper measurements and twist the facts to suit their needs. Very little critical thinking has been observed.

Human nature is the signal cause of this predicament. The standard methods are not credible. Thus people propose other ideas. This causes the academics to react. Yet it would seem that the real solution to understanding the ancient Egyptians requires that we look at their nature. They have sent clues to us from the past. It is for us to analyze these clues rather than to overlook them. Perhaps we can better learn the nature of their abilities by examining our own humanity.

CHAPTER 11. CONCLUSION

THE APPROACH

The approach taken here is rather different from the standard academic research. Typically, if a conscientious researcher cannot conduct research firsthand from primary resources, he gathers and studies as many previously published books and articles as possible. Then, after careful consideration of these works, he sets forth an idea that seems the most logical and apparent based on the available data. Such is not the case here.

Instead this inquiry was treated as more of a forensic investigation; a mystery to be solved. The facts of the scene were examined, clues were found and the suspect's means, motive and opportunity were probed. With this type of analysis, studying other people's conclusions does not contribute to the understanding of the situation. Instead, as seen in mystery novels, these different ideas often conflict with the evidence and confuse the issue at hand. Thus ignoring the conclusions of earlier researchers allowed an unbiased and independent analysis. The research was not directed. The researcher had no agenda. The inquiry followed where the clues led.

The major sources of clues were Lepre and Lehner. They are well known in the academic archaeological community. Lepre provides an excellent overview of the pyramids and is precise, with great attention to detail. His drawings and data on the pyramids have been an extremely useful source. Lehner, and the NOVA experiment, provide actual field data. For an engineer, nothing is better than actual measurements under actual working conditions with actual people. Simulations and controlled experiments are important and useful, but a real life demonstration is the best predictor of real life performance. And, while neither of these scientists is an engineer, they have provided an excellent foundation on which to build a case.

The ideas presented here as new are original with the author. However, it is certainly possible that some of these ideas have been previously suggested. There is a huge body of work concerning the pyramids that is beyond managing. If a previous article has described any of these ideas and it has not been referenced, it is simply because it did not come to the author's attention. Every attempt has been made to provide appropriate sources. As noted above, an extensive literature search was deliberately not performed.

THE ARCHAEOLOGICAL EVIDENCE

This work is different from other works in a number of important aspects. The first is that it is based entirely upon archaeological evidence, standard engineering principles, common sense and creativity. It accepts that the Egyptians were smart people and that they would use the best available technology and methods available to them. These people were building very large block structures for hundreds of years before they attempted the incredible Great Pyramid. It cannot be believed that they learned nothing about moving large stones in large quantities during that time. They built their masterpieces on the Giza plateau because they had the means and experience to do so with a reasonable amount of effort. And if one looks for the evidence of this, it can be found.

The quarter circles are a scintillating solution to an extremely difficult problem of block transportation. Their simple and subtle shape completely eliminates the loss of lifting energy, thereby making it ridiculously easy to move a block. This by itself is an incredible boon to pyramid construction but the additional benefits are staggering. The quarter-circle road can be moved from place to place, as desired, at a rate of one linear mile per man-day. It can operate on ramps as well as on the pyramid proper. These peculiarly shaped tools also keep the block elevated so that ropes can be easily passed underneath them for lifting. With the large base area of the quarter circles, the enormous weight of the block is distributed over a large area, which reduces road wear. Nor are these devices something created by the writer. These quarter circles have been found at various pyramid sites. The genius of the idea belongs entirely with the ancient Egyptian engineers.

The raised fulcrum lever is such a fundamental mechanism that it would be astonishing if the Egyptians didn't know about it. A clear and unmistakable example of such a lever is found in the ancient illustrations of the Egyptian Book of the Dead (plate 3) (Faulkner 1994). Here the lever functions as a balance-beam scale. A vertical post is shown, held in position by a stand that rests on the floor. There is a horizontal member centered on this post. At each end of this member are weighing pans suspended with string. There is no doubt that this is a scale because the illustration and translated text discusses the embalmer weighing the heart of the deceased. Additionally a hieroglyph is shown that is nearly an exact duplicate of this illustration. There can be no doubt that the Egyptians were cognizant of the raised fulcrum lever.

The cantilevered design is a natural improvement that would suggest itself to anyone actually using a raised fulcrum lever. It is readily apparent that if the supports are in the way, they can be moved. Once that is accomplished, it would be seen that the long set of legs would have to be anchored in some manner. The cantilevered concept is neither subtle nor difficult to understand.

Nor does it require exceptional intelligence to design a two-step procedure to lift a block one course. It only takes experience and reasonable amount of applied engineering. Clear evidence of this is found with the "Proto-pulley" or Lehner's "Mystery Tool." This tool is not mysterious at all. Once it is examined with close attention to detail, its purpose becomes obvious. This tool is unmistakably a lift-lever rope guide. Once its purpose is revealed, the lever design becomes evident.

The archaeological evidence of quarter circles and rope guides is not disputed. These artifacts exist. Moreover each is precisely designed and fabricated for one, and only one, very specific purpose. These tools cannot have been designed by accident. Nor has anyone proposed any other possible function (that is realistic). Applying only these two tools provides an improvement in efficiency by over two orders of magnitude when compared to sledges and large ramps. This evidence also proves, without any doubt and contrary to the opinions of many other researchers, that the ancient Egyptians were brilliant, resourceful and imaginative.

There is also a very noteworthy discovery that is not often mentioned. The Red Pyramid (aka the North Pyramid) at Dashur has dates inscribed on at least two of its blocks. This pyramid was built by Pharaoh Sneferu, who was the father of Khufu (The Great Pyramid) and who was the pharaoh who initiated the successful building of all the very large pyramids. The Red Pyramid is the third largest pyramid built, containing about 60% of the volume of the Great Pyramid. The dates are inscribed in red ink and are believed to identify when the blocks were placed. "One of these blocks bears a date which has been read as the twenty-first year of the reign of Seneferu and, being situated in the north-east corner, it should indicate the year in which the work of construction begun; the other block, seen by Richard Lepsius half-way up the face of the pyramid, was dated in the following year" (Edwards, 283).

If the normal connotation of "half-way up the face" is used, it means that the point was half the linear distance along the face (rather than meaning half of the volume of the pyramid). This point corresponds to a height where 87.5% of the volume of the pyramid had already been placed (see Appendix 2), which equals about 51% of the Great Pyramid's volume. A direct ratio incorporating this production rate indicates that the Great Pyramid could have been built in two years. However, since the higher blocks take longer to set in place, an inflated schedule of three to four years would be realistic. This is also a reasonable match to the original estimate of four to six years.

CIRCUMSTANTIAL EVIDENCE

Additional evidence for the procedures described here, as it relates to quarrying and casing stone finishing, is somewhat circumstantial. In these instances the existing evidence contradicts the conventional theories. It is seen that the "channeling" method for quarrying blocks is extremely wasteful of stone. This would require a quarry about twice as big as the one actually used. By applying a simple engineering approach, a quarrying tool is suggested that is clearly within the capability of the Egyptians to conceive, fabricate and apply. This "spear-chisel" has the advantage of enabling a worker to create deep narrow channels about an inch wide. It also uses the whole upper body of the worker, which results in a significant amount of energy applied to the point; this speeds up stone removal. Curiously, when this tool is used to compare the available stone in the quarry with the stone used in the Great Pyramid, it is found to be in perfect agreement. While it is true that these spear chisels have not been found or identified as such, it is also true that the Egyptians had a great many different types of chisels.

The huge problem with the casing stones is the vast quantities necessary to sheath the Great Pyramid. At least 80,000 to 100,000 of these precision-cut blocks were needed. They were made from high-quality Tura limestone. This stone was not local and required a fair amount of effort to bring to Giza. It was not a resource to be wasted. The conventional thought is that each and every one of these stones was hand-crafted by incredibly skilled stone masons. However, it is not reasonable to believe this. The height, squareness and face angle were perfectly matched to the four adjacent blocks in the pyramid to fractions of a degree and hundredths of an inch. If there was the smallest error, it would have been painfully obvious.

Instead it has been proposed that simple machining fixtures were used to allow anyone to fabricate the stones to the required precision. It has been shown that these basic fixtures were certainly within the technical capabilities and intellectual aptitude of the people of the time. The fundamental concepts of machining, guiding the cutting tool (or the working material), are still used today. An example of this is the fence on a modern table saw. The fence permits anyone to make repeatable and identical cuts with great precision. If one assumes that the Egyptians had the capacity to learn from hundreds of years of pyramid building experience, it seems abundantly clear that this fundamental idea of tool control would have been implemented.

These latter two proposed techniques do not save as much time as the quarter circles and lift levers do. However, they address two significant problems with the standard theories of channel quarrying and casing stone finishing. There may be other methods that answer these difficulties. But the use of spear chisels and simple machining concepts seem to be the most direct and easiest to implement. They also appear to be the most likely approach.

OTHER IDEAS

It has been seen that many well-educated writers who purport to know how the Great Pyramid was built propose ideas that are inconsistent and ignore important details. They do not address contradictory evidence or problems with their approach. They choose data that supports their position and abandon experimental results and observations that do not. This is true for the unconventional theories as well as for the approaches championed by Lehner, Smith and Hawass, which are considered the "standard" theories. In fact, the important and valid experimental benchmarks that Lehner produced in the NOVA experiment are not used by either Lehner or Smith. It is unacceptable from a scientific or an engineering standpoint to overlook this data.

However the most unsettling notion that these other researchers seem to share is an assumption that the Egyptians were primitive, stupid, and lived under an oppressive pharaoh. But common sense and the plateau of Giza trumpet a different truth. These mind-boggling creations were not built by weak minds and strong backs. They were built by outstanding intelligence and unbounded creativity. Oppressive regimes do not tolerate these characteristics. Nor do oppressive governments last 3000 years, or create exquisite works of art, or care for the well being of all their people. Every indication is that the ancient Egyptian society was one of enlightenment and reasonable prosperity.

GOALS AND OBJECTIVES

The primary goal of this research was to show that the Great Pyramid could be built in much less time than is currently accepted. Naturally, it is believed that this goal has been satisfied with the evidence presented. Using very conservative measurements it was found that about 4000 workers could have built the Great Pyramid in about four to six years, working at a leisurely pace. These methods are eminently feasible and attainable with the technology known to exist at the time. Additionally, important artifacts that previously went unexplained, such as the quarter circles and stone rope guides, are shown to have precise functions when used as described.

This work is the first complete engineering investigation of the Great Pyramid that provides a reasonable man-power estimate that is in accordance with the archaeological evidence. It has been seen that there is no need to attribute superhuman powers to the Egyptians. Nor is there any need to presume that their society was anything other than sophisticated and sensible. The idea that 25,000 men worked for over 20 years under unyielding exertion, every day, for 12 hours a day is simply not credible. And it is important to recognize that suggesting that something is technically possible does not mean that it was actually accomplished in that manner.

The building of the pyramids strengthened the social fabric rather than straining it and creating a social burden. It is important to consider these projects as part of the social gestalt. Nor is it a coincidence that the longest living human society should also be the society that produced a hundred pyramids and as yet uncounted numbers of other huge public works. The suggestion of an all-volunteer force of young and energetic adults to work directly for the pharaoh on the pyramids and other projects satisfies many aspects of human nature. It fosters pride, teamwork, social values and direction to young men at an age when they benefit most from such training. Perhaps this is the real masterstroke of the pharaonic empire: a truly integrated government.

Another goal of this work was to put a human handprint on the Great Pyramid. No superhuman efforts are needed. In fact, the work schedule generated in these pages is extremely conservative when compared to typical estimates. Many authors expect the 25,000 workers to toil for 12 hours a day for 365 days a year for 23 years to complete the task at the maximum output possible. If those same standards of effort were applied with the techniques described here, then

25,000 workers could (in theory) complete the Great Pyramid in just over 90 days. Instead, it is proposed that 4000 workers took about four to six years. Projects of that scale are fairly common today. And it must be remembered that the people of ancient Egypt were the same as people of today. The human race has not changed in any measurable way in the last 5,000 years.

Numbers and Engineering

In engineering and science, numbers and calculations are the means to determine whether things are possible, practical and useful. They are the measure of the utility of the idea. Unfortunately, many people find working with numbers daunting. It is for that reason that all the calculations here have been presented in a step-wise manner to simplify the analysis. Unfortunately, this leads to the inclusion of additional numbers and mathematical steps. However, these individual steps are easier to follow.

It is critically important that these computations be made and presented. And, hopefully, they are presented in a manner that is clear and understandable. These numbers define how well the concepts match real life. If these values are incomplete or confusing, then the strength of the arguments is diminished. Considerable effort has been made to explain the calculations and how they are developed. In order to judge the efficacy of the approach, the reader — as well as the writer — must be sure the reasoning and analysis make sense. "Even for the physicist, the description in plain language will be the criterion of the degree of understanding that has been reached" (Heisenberg 1958).

Engineering is considered by many to be an advanced field of study. The truth is that the vast majority of engineering effort is nothing more than common sense with attention to detail. However, the details are critically important to get right. The Space Shuttle *Challenger* was launched in cold weather despite the detail that the O-rings could fail. The Tacoma Narrows Bridge fell because its wind resistance wasn't analyzed. The Three Mile Island nuclear plant melted down because a valve stayed open while the indicator said it was closed. The list is endless. That is why the numeric details are presented to support the theories proposed in these pages. They are absolutely necessary for the proper evaluation of the methods presented. Every effort has been made to uncover any hidden aspects, unforeseen problems or other significant ramifications.

Conclusion

For the first time a complete and detailed set of instructions is presented that allow the building of the Great Pyramid with a believable number of workers in a rational amount of time. For the first time these proposed methods are based upon archaeological evidence. For the first time the Great Pyramid is seen as only a small part of a much larger and systematic pharaonic plan to strengthen the Egyptian society. And, for the first time the ancient Egyptians are given credit for being creative, imaginative, intelligent and resourceful.

The Egyptian pyramids in general and the Great Pyramid in particular are human accomplishments on such a grand scale that they are nearly unimaginable. But they are human constructions. And because we are human, they belong to our heritage. We should share with pride the thought that fellow humans were able to raise from the earth these magnificent monuments. They clearly demonstrate that the potential of the human mind is boundless. They express a joy and love of life that has never been equaled. And probably never will be equaled. It is for us to celebrate the legacy that these brilliant souls have bequeathed to us. The wonder and awe is not found in the pyramids but rather in the people who built them. People just like us.

APPENDIX 1. TABLE OF 100 EGYPTIAN PYRAMIDS

(Summarized from Lepre)

Num (1)	Location	Date (2)	Size in feet (L, W, H)	Volume (3)	Volume Rel. (4)	Comments
1	Athribis	2887	unknown			brick
2	Abu Roash	2887	75,75,55	0.103	0.001	brick
89	Seila	2887	71,71,53 est.	0.089	0.0009	
93	Zawaiyet el-Amwat	2887	60,60,??			
95	Abydos	2887	unknown			brick
96	Ombos	2887	unknown			brick
97	Nagada	2887	60,60,??			
98	El Kola	2887	61,61,28	0.035	0.0004	
99	Edfu	2887	unknown			brick
100	Elephantine	2887	unknown			brick
40	N. Sakkara	2868	411,358,204	10.005	0.106	the "Step Pyramid"
38	N. Sakkara	2849	400,400,210	11.200	0.119	step pyramid type
17	Zawaiyet el-Aryan	2844	275,275,145	3.655	0.039	"layer" pyramid
16	Zawaiyet el-Aryan	2843	590,650,330	42.185	0.448	never completed

Num (1)	Location	Date (2)	Size in feet (L, W, H)	Volume (3)	Volume Rel. (4)	Comments
87	Maidum	2837	472,472,301	22.352	0.237	collapsed, associated with Huni & Sneferu
88	Maidum	2837	130,130,80	0.450	0.005	brick
66	Dashur (Sneferu)	2813	720,720,320	55.296	0.588	the "Red Pyramid"
71	Dashur (Sneferu)	2813	620,620,335	42.924	0.456	the "Bent Pyramid"
72	Dashur (Sneferu)	2813	181,181,107	1.168	0.012	
5	Giza (Khufu-main)	2789	763,763,485	94.117	1.0000	the "Great Pyramid"
6	Giza (Khufu)	2789	140,140,90	0.588	0.006	
7	Giza (Khufu)	2789	145,145,95	0.666	0.007	
8	Giza (Khufu)	2789	143,143,93	0.634	0.007	
3	Abu Roash	2766	300,300,200 est.	6.000	0.064	
4	Abu Roash	2766	unknown			
9	Giza (Khafre-main)	2758	704,704,471	77.812	0.827	
10	Giza (Khafre)	2758	65,65,40	0.056	0.0006	
12	Giza (Menkara)	2739	356,356,218	9.209	0.098	
13	Giza	2739	110,110,65 est.	0.262	0.003	
14	Giza	2739	110,110,65 est.	0.262	0.004	
15	Giza	2739	117,117,75 est.	0.342	0.004	
60	S. Sakkara	2721	330,235,60	4.653	0.049	mastaba, not pyramid
11	Giza	2717	150,70,40	0.420	0.004	mastaba, not pyramid

Num (1)	Location	Date (2)	Size in feet (L, W, H)	Volume (3)	Volume Rel. (4)	Comments
24	Abu Sir	2717	unknown			queen Khentkawes
35	N. Sakkara	2715	231,231,145	2.579	0.027	
36	N. Sakkara	2715	50,50,??			
37	N. Sakkara	2715	55,55,??			
19	Abu Sir	2708	257,257,156	3.434	0.036	
20	Abu Sir	2708	40,40,??			
25	Abu Sir	2696	195,195,125 est.	1.584	0.017	
26	Abu Sir	2696	unknown			
27	Abu Sir	2696	unknown			
28	Abu Sir	2696	unknown			
18	Abu Sir	2692	unknown			
45	S. Sakkara	2692	180,180,115	1.242	0.013	
23	Abu Sir	2685	360,360,227	9.806	0.104	
21	Abu Sir	2664	274,274,165	4.129	0.044	
22	Abu Sir	2664	50,50,34	0.028	0.0003	
67	Dashur	2653	unknown			
47	S. Sakkara	2645	125,125,??			
48	S. Sakkara	2645	265,265,165	3.862	0.041	
51	S. Sakkara	2640	79,79,60	0.125	0.001	
52	S. Sakkara	2640	35,35,??			
53	S. Sakkara	2640	70,70,50	0.082	0.0008	
54	S. Sakkara	2640	unknown			
55	S. Sakkara	2640	255,255,170	3.685	0.039	
56	S. Sakkara	2640	unknown			
57	S. Sakkara	2640	50,50,??			
58	S. Sakkara	2640	75,75,??			
59	S. Sakkara	2640	unknown			
41	N. Sakkara	2617	220,220,143	2.307	0.024	
42	N. Sakkara	2617	unknown			
29	N. Sakkara	2587	50,50,??			
30	N. Sakkara	2587	50,50,??			
33	N. Sakkara	2587	210,210,130	1.911	0.020	

Num (1)	Location	Date (2)	Size in feet (L, W, H)	Volume (3)	Volume Rel. (4)	Comments
34	N. Sakkara	2587	50,50,??			
44	S. Sakkara	2579	unknown			
46	S. Sakkara	2573	250,250,160	3.333	0.035	
49	S. Sakkara	2553	310,310,200	6.407	0.068	
94	Dara	2458	420,420,250 est.	14.700	0.156	brick-rubble pile 15 feet high
31	N. Sakkara	2459	245,245,160	3.201	0.034	
32	N. Sakkara	2455	unknown			
43	N. Sakkara	2452	unknown			
50	S. Sakkara	2389	75,75,103	0.193	0.002	
39	N. Sakkara	2227	325,325,200 est.	7.042	0.075	
75	Lisht	2111	275,275,180	4.538	0.048	
91	Lahun	2100	85,85,55	0.132	0.001	brick
76	Lisht	2082	350,350,190	7.758	0.082	
77	Lisht	2082	50,50,30	0.025	0.0002	
78	Lisht	2082	50,50,30	0.025	0.0002	
79	Lisht	2082	60,60,35	0.021	0.0002	
80	Lisht	2082	55,55,32	0.032	0.0003	
81	Lisht	2082	50,50,30	0.025	0.0002	
82	Lisht	2082	55,55,32	0.032	0.0003	
83	Lisht	2082	55,55,32	0.032	0.0003	
84	Lisht	2082	55,55,52	0.032	0.0003	
85	Lisht	2082	50,50,30	0.025	0.0002	
86	Lisht	2082	70,70,40	0.065	0.0007	
68	Dashur	2046	265,265,155 est.	3.628	0.039	
69	Dashur	2046	unknown			
92	Lahun	2011	350,350,150	6.125	0.065	brick core
65	Dashur	1998	350,350,255	10.413	0.111	brick core
70	Dashur	1959	342,342,250	6.043	0.064	brick core
90	Hawara	1959	335,335,180	6.734	0.072	brick core
74	Mazghuna	1910	180,180,115	1.242	0.013	brick core
73	Mazghuna	1901	200,200,120 est.	1.600	0.017	

Appendix 1. Table of 100 Egyptian Pyramids

Num (1)	Location	Date (2)	Size in feet (L, W, H)	Volume (3)	Volume Rel. (4)	Comments
64	S. Sakkara	1885	165,165,105	0.953	0.010	
63	S. Sakkara	1820	310,310,200	6.407	0.068	brick rubble pile 10 feet high
61	S. Sakkara	1750	80,80,50	0.107	0.001	brick core
62	S. Sakkara	1750	170,170,120	1.156	0.012	brick core

Notes:

1) Number is Lepre's identifying number.

2) Date is the beginning year of pharaoh's reign

3) Volume is measured in millions of cubic feet.

4) Relative volume is a fraction of the Great Pyramid (or Khufu's Pyramid), Lepre's number 5.

Summarized from: *The Egyptian Pyramids, A Comprehensive Illustrated Reference by J. P. Lepre*, 1990, Macfarland and Company, North Carolina

APPENDIX 2. COURSE BY COURSE LAYOUT OF AN IDEAL GREAT PYRAMID BUILT WITH IDENTICAL BLOCKS

Course	Blocks per Side	Height in Feet	Side Length in Feet	Blocks per Course	Sum of Blocks	Fraction of Total
1	191	0.0000	764.000	36481	36481	0.0142962
2	190	2.3124	760.362	36100	72581	0.0284431
3	189	4.6248	756.724	35721	108302	0.0424415
4	188	6.9371	753.086	35344	143646	0.0562921
5	187	9.2495	749.448	34969	178615	0.0699958
6	186	11.5619	745.809	34596	213211	0.0835533
7	185	13.8743	742.171	34225	247436	0.0969654
8	184	16.1867	738.533	33856	281292	0.1102329
9	183	18.4990	734.895	33489	314781	0.1233566
10	182	20.8114	731.257	33124	347905	0.1363373
11	181	23.1238	727.619	32761	380666	0.1491757
12	180	25.4362	723.981	32400	413066	0.1618727
13	180	27.7486	720.343	32400	445466	0.1745696
14	179	30.0610	716.704	32041	477507	0.1871258
15	178	32.3733	713.066	31684	509191	0.1995422
16	177	34.6857	709.428	31329	540520	0.2118194
17	176	36.9981	705.790	30976	571496	0.2239583
18	175	39.3105	702.152	30625	602121	0.2359597
19	174	41.6229	698.514	30276	632397	0.2478243
20	173	43.9352	694.876	29929	662326	0.2595529
21	172	46.2476	691.238	29584	691910	0.2711463
22	171	48.5600	687.599	29241	721151	0.2826053

Course	Blocks per Side	Height in Feet	Side Length in Feet	Blocks per Course	Sum of Blocks	Fraction of Total
23	170	50.8724	683.961	28900	750051	0.2939306
24	170	53.1848	680.323	28900	778951	0.3052560
25	169	55.4971	676.685	28561	807512	0.3164485
26	168	57.8095	673.047	28224	835736	0.3275089
27	167	60.1219	669.409	27889	863625	0.3384381
28	166	62.4343	665.771	27556	891181	0.3492368
29	165	64.7467	662.133	27225	918406	0.3599057
30	164	67.0591	658.494	26896	945302	0.3704458
31	163	69.3714	654.856	26569	971871	0.3808576
32	162	71.6838	651.218	26244	998115	0.3911422
33	161	73.9962	647.580	25921	1024036	0.4013001
34	160	76.3086	643.942	25600	1049636	0.4113322
35	160	78.6210	640.304	25600	1075236	0.4213644
36	159	80.9333	636.666	25281	1100517	0.4312716
37	158	83.2457	633.028	24964	1125481	0.4410545
38	157	85.5581	629.389	24649	1150130	0.4507139
39	156	87.8705	625.751	24336	1174466	0.4602507
40	155	90.1829	622.113	24025	1198491	0.4696657
41	154	92.4952	618.475	23716	1222207	0.4789595
42	153	94.8076	614.837	23409	1245616	0.4881331
43	152	97.1200	611.199	23104	1268720	0.4971871
44	151	99.4324	607.561	22801	1291521	0.5061224
92	108	210.4267	432.932	11664	2099206	0.8226386
93	107	212.7391	429.293	11449	2110655	0.8271253
94	106	215.0514	425.655	11236	2121891	0.8315285
95	105	217.3638	422.017	11025	2132916	0.8358489
96	104	219.6762	418.379	10816	2143732	0.8400875
97	103	221.9886	414.741	10609	2154341	0.8442450
98	102	224.3010	411.103	10404	2164745	0.8483221
99	101	226.6133	407.465	10201	2174946	0.8523197
100	100	228.9257	403.827	10000	2184946	0.8562385
101	100	231.2381	400.189	10000	2194946	0.8601573
102	99	233.5505	396.551	9801	2204747	0.8639981
103	98	235.8629	392.913	9604	2214351	0.8677618
104	97	238.1752	389.274	9409	2223760	0.8714490
105	96	240.4876	385.636	9216	2232976	0.8750606
106	95	242.8000	381.998	9025	2242001	0.8785973
107	94	245.1124	378.360	8836	2250837	0.8820599
108	93	247.4248	374.722	8649	2259486	0.8854493
109	92	249.7372	371.084	8464	2267950	0.8887662

Course	Blocks per Side	Height in Feet	Side Length in Feet	Blocks per Course	Sum of Blocks	Fraction of Total
110	91	252.0495	367.446	8281	2276231	0.8920113
111	90	254.3619	363.808	8100	2284331	0.8951856
112	90	256.6743	360.170	8100	2292431	0.8983598
113	89	258.9867	356.532	7921	2300352	0.9014639
114	88	261.2990	352.893	7744	2308096	0.9044986
115	87	263.6115	349.255	7569	2315665	0.9074648
116	86	265.9238	345.617	7396	2323061	0.9103631
117	85	268.2362	341.979	7225	2330286	0.9131945
118	84	270.5486	338.341	7056	2337342	0.9159596
119	83	272.8610	334.703	6889	2344231	0.9186593
120	82	275.1733	331.065	6724	2350955	0.9212943
121	81	277.4857	327.427	6561	2357516	0.9238654
122	80	279.7981	323.789	6400	2363916	0.9263734
123	80	282.1105	320.151	6400	2370316	0.9288815
124	79	284.4229	316.513	6241	2376557	0.9313272
125	78	286.7353	312.874	6084	2382641	0.9337114
126	77	289.0476	309.236	5929	2388570	0.9360349
127	76	291.3600	305.598	5776	2394346	0.9382983
128	75	293.6724	301.960	5625	2399971	0.9405027
129	74	295.9848	298.322	5476	2405447	0.9426486
130	73	298.2971	294.684	5329	2410776	0.9447370
131	72	300.6095	291.046	5184	2415960	0.9467685
132	71	302.9219	287.408	5041	2421001	0.9487439
133	70	305.2343	283.770	4900	2425901	0.9506642
134	70	307.5467	280.132	4900	2430801	0.9525844
135	69	309.8591	276.494	4761	2435562	0.9544501
136	68	312.1714	272.855	4624	2440186	0.9562622
137	67	314.4838	269.217	4489	2444675	0.9580213
138	66	316.7962	265.579	4356	2449031	0.9597284
139	65	319.1086	261.941	4225	2453256	0.9613841
140	64	321.4210	258.303	4096	2457352	0.9629892
141	63	323.7333	254.665	3969	2461321	0.9645446
142	62	326.0457	251.027	3844	2465165	0.9660510
143	61	328.3581	247.389	3721	2468886	0.9675092
144	60	330.6705	243.751	3600	2472486	0.9689199
145	60	332.9829	240.113	3600	2476086	0.9703307
146	59	335.2953	236.475	3481	2479567	0.9716948
147	58	337.6076	232.836	3364	2482931	0.9730131
148	57	339.9200	229.198	3249	2486180	0.9742863
149	56	342.2324	225.560	3136	2489316	0.9755153

Course	Blocks per Side	Height in Feet	Side Length in Feet	Blocks per Course	Sum of Blocks	Fraction of Total
150	55	344.5448	221.922	3025	2492341	0.9767007
151	54	346.8571	218.284	2916	2495257	0.9778435
152	53	349.1695	214.646	2809	2498066	0.9789442
153	52	351.4819	211.008	2704	2500770	0.9800039
154	51	353.7943	207.370	2601	2503371	0.9810232
155	50	356.1067	203.732	2500	2505871	0.9820029
156	50	358.4191	200.094	2500	2508371	0.9829826
157	49	360.7314	196.456	2401	2510772	0.9839235
158	48	363.0438	192.817	2304	2513076	0.9848264
159	47	365.3562	189.179	2209	2515285	0.9856920
160	46	367.6686	185.541	2116	2517401	0.9865212
161	45	369.9810	181.903	2025	2519426	0.9873148
162	44	372.2933	178.265	1936	2521362	0.9880735
163	43	374.6057	174.627	1849	2523211	0.9887981
164	42	376.9181	170.989	1764	2524975	0.9894894
165	41	379.2305	167.351	1681	2526656	0.9901481
166	40	381.5429	163.713	1600	2528256	0.9907751
167	40	383.8553	160.075	1600	2529856	0.9914021
168	39	386.1676	156.437	1521	2531377	0.9919982
169	38	388.4800	152.798	1444	2532821	0.9925641
170	37	390.7924	149.160	1369	2534190	0.9931005
171	36	393.1048	145.522	1296	2535486	0.9936084
172	35	395.4171	141.884	1225	2536711	0.9940885
173	34	397.7295	138.246	1156	2537867	0.9945415
174	33	400.0419	134.608	1089	2538956	0.9949682
175	32	402.3543	130.970	1024	2539980	0.9953696
176	31	404.6667	127.332	961	2540941	0.9957461
177	30	406.9791	123.694	900	2541841	0.9960988
178	30	409.2914	120.056	900	2542741	0.9964515
179	29	411.6038	116.418	841	2543582	0.9967811
180	28	413.9162	112.779	784	2544366	0.9970883
181	27	416.2286	109.141	729	2545095	0.9973740
182	26	418.5410	105.503	676	2545771	0.9976389
183	25	420.8533	101.865	625	2546396	0.9978839
184	24	423.1657	98.227	576	2546972	0.9981096
185	23	425.4781	94.589	529	2547501	0.9983169
186	22	427.7905	90.951	484	2547985	0.9985065
187	21	430.1029	87.313	441	2548426	0.9986793
188	20	432.4153	83.675	400	2548826	0.9988361
189	20	434.7276	80.037	400	2549226	0.9989929

Course	Blocks per Side	Height in Feet	Side Length in Feet	Blocks per Course	Sum of Blocks	Fraction of Total
190	19	437.0400	76.398	361	2549587	0.9991344
191	18	439.3524	72.760	324	2549911	0.9992613
192	17	441.6648	69.122	289	2550200	0.9993746
193	16	443.9772	65.484	256	2550456	0.9994749
194	15	446.2896	61.846	225	2550681	0.9995630
195	14	448.6019	58.208	196	2550877	0.9996399
196	13	450.9143	54.570	169	2551046	0.9997061
197	12	453.2267	50.932	144	2551190	0.9997625
198	11	455.5391	47.294	121	2551311	0.9998099
199	10	457.8514	43.656	100	2551411	0.9998491
200	10	460.1638	40.018	100	2551511	0.9998883
201	9	462.4762	36.379	81	2551592	0.9999201
202	8	464.7886	32.741	64	2551656	0.9999452
203	7	467.1010	29.103	49	2551705	0.9999644
204	6	469.4134	25.465	36	2551741	0.9999784
205	5	471.7257	21.827	25	2551766	0.9999883
206	4	474.0381	18.189	16	2551782	0.9999945
207	3	476.3505	14.551	9	2551791	0.9999980
208	2	478.6629	10.913	4	2551795	0.9999996
209	1	480.9753	7.275	1	2551796	1.0000000
210 (3)	0	483.2876	3.637	0	2551796	1.0000000

Notes:

1. The size of a block is 2.3124 feet high and 4.000 feet square (making the course height 2.3124 feet). The block height is calculated by dividing the height (485.6 feet) by the number of courses (210).

2. Several successive courses have the same number of blocks. This is expected. The lower course will have slightly larger spacing between the blocks so that the difference is spread out over the whole course length.

3. The last "course" (210) consists only of a capstone or pyramidion, which has smaller dimensions than a full block.

4. A value of 80,184 casing stones is calculated by summing the blocks per side and multiplying by 4 (for 4 sides).

Appendix 3: Time/Motion Analysis for Lifting a Block

Introduction

Time/motion analysis is a simple procedure to help determine how long it takes to perform some task. The procedure is to break down the task into simple steps and measure or estimate how much time each step requires. Then the time required for the whole task is simply the sum of the small tasks. It is usually easier to measure or estimate small tasks than complex ones.

The benchmark measures are the time it takes to climb a flight of stairs and the time to walk 25 feet (7.6 m). The measures were made with a 50-year-old male subject in good physical condition.

Benchmark measures	Normal	Slow	Value used
Climb 8.5 feet of stairs (height)	7 sec	12 sec	15 sec
Walk 25 feet	6 sec	10 sec	10 sec

In both cases the value used in the calculations is nearly double the typical value. This is done for two basic reasons. The first is that it is not reasonable to expect that a "normal" pace can be maintained over a prolonged period of time. This is especially true for climbing stairs. (Although it is presumed that the pyramid workers were significantly younger than the subject performing these tests.) The second reason is to be conservative. Distances not equal to the benchmark values are proportionally estimated.

Note: the operations often take just a few seconds. This may sound too fast. However, a few seconds is a fairly long time to perform simple operations. For example, tying a shoe usually takes less than 5 seconds.

Note also that the measured normal walking time is 4.167 feet per second. This agrees very closely to the published value of 4 feet per second (TranSafety 1997).

3-PERSON, 2-STROKE LEVER ANALYSIS

In this case, a 12:1 lever about 18 feet long will be used. This requires 3 people to "stand" on the end to counterbalance a 5,000 lb. block (each person is 150 lbs). Adding in the weight of the lever provides a 10% margin for losses. There will be two strokes, lifting the block 1.25 feet each time, with the block supported between strokes. The person-end of the lever will move about 15 feet up/down per stroke. The people are identified as A, B and C.

The analysis starts with a block already rolled into position and person A at the lever end on the lower course, ready to attach the block to the lever. Persons B and C have climbed to the top and raised the lever, and are waiting to transfer to it.

STEP 1   10 seconds

Attach the block to the lever. It is presumed that two simple rope slings will be used. They only need to be slipped around the block ends. Since the block is on quarter circles, the block ends are off the ground. Additionally, the slings could be designed for easy on/off operations. In reality, this can probably be done in just 5 seconds.

STEP 2   7.5 seconds

Person A walks to the person-end of the lever to start climbing up. During this same time the other two people start to transfer onto the lever.

STEP 3   25 seconds

Person A climbs 15 feet. During this time the other two finish transferring to the lever.

STEP 4   10 seconds

Person A transfers to the lever and it drops. The block is lifted 1.25 feet. This presumes that it takes 5 seconds to transfer and 5 seconds to drop.

STEP 5   5 seconds

Secure the lever to the ground. A simple rope loop is all that is needed. This is required because as person A moves to support the block, his weight is removed and the lever would rise.

STEP 6   7. 5 seconds

Person A walks to the block-end of the lever. The other two people start the 25-second climb to the top.

STEP 7   5 seconds

Person A places a support under the block.

STEP 8   7. 5 seconds

Person A walks back to the person-end of the lever.

STEP 9   5 seconds

Persons B and C reach the top of the climb. Person A releases the lever hold-down.

STEP 10   15 seconds

Persons B and C pull the lever into the up position (with ropes) and use a simple rope loop to hold it in place. This puts slack into the lever/block ropes. Person A starts the 25-second climb.

STEP 11   5 seconds

Person B moves the "ratchet" to prepare the lever for the second lift. Note: the "ratchet" can be a simple hook to which the lift rope is moved in order to take up the slack. It is 1.25 feet from the original position. Basically, person B takes the rope loop off of one hook and places it on the second hook.

STEP 12   5 seconds

Person A finishes climb and person C transfers to the lever.

STEP 13   5 seconds

Person B transfers to the lever.

STEP 14   10 seconds

Person A transfers to the lever and the lever drops.

STEP 15   5 seconds

The lever is secured to the ground.

STEP 16   7. 5 seconds

Person A walks to the block end of the lever. Persons B and C starts climbing.

STEP 17   5 seconds

Person A removes the block support.

Step 18   5 seconds

Person A places higher block support (with quarter circles and even with new course).

STEP 19   7. 5 seconds

Person A walks back to the person-end of the lever and removes the lever hold-down. Persons B and C finish climb.

STEP 20	10 seconds

Block is transferred to new course. Note: other people and time are allocated for this as part of moving the block. Person A walks to the block-end of the lever during this time. Person B changes "ratchet" position.

STEP 21	5 seconds

Person A removes block support. Persons B and C start to lift lever.

STEP 22	10 seconds

New block rolled into place. Again, other people are allocated for this. Persons B and C finish lifting lever.

This brings the analysis back to the initial starting conditions. Person A is ready to attach the block, the lever is in the up position and "ratchet" is in the proper location. Persons B and C have climbed back up and are ready to transfer their weight. The total time required for these steps is 177.5 seconds. This is slightly less than 3 minutes (180 seconds).

2-PERSON CONSIDERATIONS (REFER TO CHAPTER 6 FOR ERGONOMIC DISCUSSION)

In order for a 2-person team to be as efficient as a 3-person team, they would have to perform the same actions in 4.5 minutes or less (9 man-minutes total). This does not appear likely.

If two people were used instead of three, the beam would have to be lengthened by 50%. This would increase the beam weight to over 200 pounds with the lift weight being 100 pounds. This is too much weight for a single person to lift from above (over half of the body weight). With two people sharing the load, the weight is 50 pounds and is marginally acceptable because it is a third of the body weight. Additionally, the walk length and climb height are increased by 50% as well, which proportionately increases the time for these tasks.

There is also a problem because in the three-man analysis person A was performing other tasks while the other two people were climbing up and lifting the lever. Since both people are required to lift the lever, there is no one to perform these tasks. These tasks will have to be done in a serial manner rather than in parallel. This will also require additional time. In short, using a 2-man team will take more man-hours than a 3-man team. The 3-man team appears optimal for lifting the blocks.

CONCLUSION

Three minutes is a reasonable and conservative value for three men to lift a block a full course. This corresponds to 9 man-minutes per block per course of 2.5 feet. To lift an average block the average height of 100 feet, 360 man-minutes or 6.0 hours is required.

References

Bush, J. "Building Pyramids", *Science Digest*, March 1978, pp. 61-63

Cray, Dan, 1999, "How do you Build a Pyramid? Go Fly a Kite", Time.com, http://www.time.com/time/magazine/article/0,9171,35072,00.html

Davidovits, Joseph, *The Pyramids: An Enigma Solved*, 1988, Hippocrene Books, New York, New York

Decamp, L., *The Ancient Engineers*, 1979, Ballantine Books, New York, New York

Dollinger, Andre, 2006, "The People of Ancient Egypt", http://www.reshafim.org.il/ad/egypt/people/lifespan of Egyptians

Dollinger, Andre, 2006, "Cities and Citizens", http://www.reshafim.org.il/ad/egypt/people/citizens.htm

Doyle, Rodger, "Not So Revolutionary", *Scientific American*, December 2006 pp. 42

Edwards, I. E. S., *The Pyramids of Egypt*, 1979, Penguin Books, New York, New York (note: later editions may not have the passage about the dates marked on the Red Pyramid)

The Egyptian Book of the Dead, Translated by Raymond Faulkner, 1998, Chronicle Books, San Francisco, California

Evans, Humphrey, *The Mystery of the Pyramids*, 1979, Thomas Y. Crowell, New York, New York

Fernandes, Dennis, May 2005, Florida Department of Transportation, personal communication

Fonte, Gerard, C. A., *Building the Great Pyramid: An Energy Management Approach*, 2000, (unpublished). The PAK Engineers, East Amherst, New York

Fonte, Gerard, C. A., "Building the Great Pyramid in About 385 Days: A Case Study in Energy Management," 2005, Proceedings of the Construction Research Congress

Heisenberg, Werner, *Physics and Philosophy*, 1958, p. 168, Harper and Row, New York, New York

Herodotus, *The Histories*, translated by G. C. Macaulay, 2004, Barnes and Noble Books, New York, New York

Lehner, Mark, *The Complete Pyramids*, 1997, Thames and Hudson, New York, New York

Lepre, J. P., *The Egyptian Pyramids: A Comprehensive Illustrated Reference*, 1990, McFarland and Company, Inc., North Carolina

NIOSH, *Prevention Guidelines: Topic, ergonomics applications manual for the revised NIOSH lifting equation*, 1994, pg 6, 10, National Institute for Occupational Safety and Health, US Department of Commerce, National Technical Information Servide

NOVA, *This Old Pyramid*, 1992, WGBH Educational Foundation, Boston, Massachusetts

Portland Cement Association, 2006, "Frequently Asked Questions", http://www.cement.org/tech/faq_unit_weights.asp

Robison, G. B., 1960, "Rockers and Rollers", Mathematics Magazine, Vol. 33, pg 139-144

Smith, Craig S., *How the Great Pyramid was Built*, 2004, Smithsonian Books, Washington, DC

Smith, Les 2004, "Hiking/backpacking/Camping, Subject: Weight of a Full Backpack" http://experts.about.com/q/Hiking-Backpacking-Camping-331/Weight-full-backpack.htm

Smith, Stew, 2006, "Training for Ruck Marches", http://www.military.com/opinion/0,15202,83481,00.html

Snook and Cirillo, 1991, "The Design of Manual Handling Tasks: Revised Tables of Maximum Weights and Forces", Ergonomics, vol. 34, no 9, pg 1197-1213

Tindol, Robert, 2001, "Researchers Lift Obelisk with Kite to test Theory on Ancient Pyramids" NationalGeographic.com, http://news.nationalgeographic.com/news/2001/06/0628_caltechobelisk.html

Tompkins, Peter, *Secrets of the Great Pyramid*, 1971, Harper and Row, New York, New York

Transafety 1997, "Study Compares Older and Younger Pedestrian Walking Speeds", Road Engineering Journal, http://www.usroads.com/journals/p/rej/9710/re971001.htm

USATODAY.com, 2001, "Mammoth Kite Used to Raise 6,900 pound Obelisk" http://www.usatoday.com/news/science/2001-06-23-obelisk.htm

Wagon, Stan, 1970 "An amusing Property of the Catenary", UBC Mathematics Department, http://www.sunsite.ubc.ca/LivingMathematics/V001N01/UBCExamples/Animation/catenary.html

Weisstein, Eric W., 2005, "Hyperbolic Cosine", from Mathworld, A Wolfram Web Resource, http://mathworld.wolfram.com/HyperbolicCosine.html

Note: All internet references as per late December 2006

INDEX

7419203R0

Made in the USA
Lexington, KY
19 November 2010